BORN-AGAIN SKEPTIC
&
OTHER
VALEDICTIONS

"I was driving around and realized, I'm still alive. Now what am I gonna do?"
—*Steven Wright*

"I'm home for two or three months, and then I run out of hotel shampoos."
—*George Steinmetz*

FIRST EDITION, 2011

Born Again Skeptic & Other Valedictions
© 2011 Robert Murray Davis

ISBN 978-0-9833052-4-8

Except for fair use in reviews and/or scholarly considerations, no part of this book may be reproduced, performed, recorded, or otherwise transmitted without the written consent of the author and the permission of the publisher.

Cover Design by Mongrel Empire Press

**MONGREL EMPIRE PRESS
NORMAN, OK**

ONLINE CATALOGUE: WWW.MONGRELEMPIRE.ORG

This publisher is a proud member of

[clmp]

COUNCIL OF LITERARY MAGAZINES & PRESSES
w w w . c l m p . o r g

Book Design: Mongrel Empire Press using iWork Pages

For Brendan, Matthew, Lucas, and Mia
　　　　　　　　　　when they learn to read.

Acknowledgments

The following essays have been previously published:

"Borders." *Southwestern American Literature* 36:2 (Spring 2011) 47-52.

A version of "Centennial" was originally published in the author's home town paper, the *Boonville Daily News*, as "A Father's Legacy: Bob Davis' Reflections," May 9, 2008.

"When Was Postmodernism?" *World Literature Today*, 75:2 (Spring 2001), 295-298. As "Cind a existat postmodernismul?" Studii culturale, no. 61 (April 24-30 2001), 16-17.

"Books: An Addiction." *New Works Review*, 3:1 (January-March 2000). http://www.new-works.org/3-1/Davis3-1.html. (This was an early version expanded for this book.)

"Loosening Up." *Commonweal*, 127:5 (10 March 2000), 26-27. (Editor's title of "Get Off My Rocks.")

Material about Fred Hoffman in "Model and Mentor" is adapted from "Two Grumpy Mentors and the Making of a Scholar." *North Dakota Quarterly*, 63, no. 2 (Spring 1996), 184-188.

BORN-AGAIN SKEPTIC
&
OTHER
VALEDICTIONS

by

Robert Murray Davis

2011

Contents

Is This an Autobiography? — 1
Preparing Faces — 4

Roots

Hearth & Home — 11
Intersections — 15
Centennial — 22
Cousins — 26
Pottage — 32
Close Enough — 38

Routes

Fork It — 54
By-Ways — 60
Breathing the Air — 69
Borders — 73

Recoveries

St. Francis's Cleaning Bills — 83
Born Again Skeptic — 91
Dry & High — 104
Doing Times — 110

Ladies' Man?	119
Books: An Addiction	125
Leftovers	137

Discoveries

Research & Recovery	147
"Stuff a Wife Can Understand"	154
Museums	164
Get Off My Rocks	176
Going Nowhere in an Orderly Fashion	182
If You Don't Like My Peaches. . .	189
When Was Post Modernism?	197

Valedictions

Faithful Sam Marx	207
Model & Mentor	216
Conventions	226
Old Sons-of-Bitches	232
Twentieth-Century Man	245
Erasures	252
What the Distant Say	260
Author Bio	264

IS THIS AN AUTOBIOGRAPHY?

My friend and intellectual sparring partner Frank Chin wrote an essay titled "This Is Not an Autobiography" in which he maintained that the genre is saturated in the Christian need to confess and that no self-respecting Chinaman (his term) would use it. Years later he refused to write a blurb for my book about my experience in a Jesuit college in the first half of the 1950s.

I didn't resent that because Frank and I have enough history to get past disagreements and because when he complains too much, I sing "I need someone to love me" from Hoagy Carmichael's "Hong Kong Blues," if not to shut him up, at least to slow him down. Even more annoying is my contention that much of his writing is autobiographical, even if he has never written an autobiography.

I won't send him this book because he is nothing if not consistent, and I already know what he'd say. It's certainly autobiographical, and as several of the pieces demonstrate, I have apparently ineradicable connections to Catholic theology and culture.

The book even has, in a fragmented, Cubist way, the general pattern of an autobiography, perhaps even of the *Künstlerroman* or artist's story. Beginning with accounts of my origins, it shifts to geographical wanderings, personal struggles, passages through various aesthetic creeds, and—unlike the *Künstlerroman*, awareness of decline and impending mortality—though in no particular order and with no major epiphanies or road-to-Damascus revelations.

There are elements of the apologia, though I doubt that Cardinal Newman, author of *Apologia Pro Vita Sua*, who seems on the verge of beatification by the Church, would approve. What it doesn't have is a teleology, thesis, or moral—unless the epigraph from Steven Wright's stand-up routine can be stretched to provide one.

I was drawn to Wright's line because, in my mid-seventies, the question I find most alarming is any variation on "What did you used to do?" Writing from retirement—an ancient mode, come to think of it—is a way to keep doing whatever it is I do. And I take consolation in Cacambo's remark in *Candide*: " Let us go forward. If we do not find something pleasant, we may at least find something new."

In previous books, especially *Mid-Lands: A Family Album* and *A Lower-Middle Class Education*, I obviously drew upon my experience, but I was more interested in portraying a specific time and place, first a small Midwestern town in the years after World War II, in the second the culture of a small Catholic college in the Eisenhower years. *Midlife Mojo: A Guide for the Newly Single Male* was more procedural than confessional. I didn't know that *The Ornamental Hermit: People and Places of the New West* was a "road book" until my publisher told me that this was the only label they could use to market it.

Responses to the first book were (almost) universally generous, even warm. My surviving English professor said, with some surprise, that it was a good-natured book. Some of my college contemporaries enjoyed the second book, although one reviewer of the manuscript thought it the work of an intellectual snob and the English professor said that it showed that I wasn't one of the sterling products of the college. I didn't resent the view of the first, since it gave me the great phrase "irony deficiency." And to the professor I replied that none of the good boys had written about their experience. My children were relieved that the third wasn't more explicit about my post-divorce adventures. The reviewers of *Hermit* decided that I was on a quest for an identity.

Perhaps the last response led to some of the pieces in this book, since I have always had less anxiety about who I was than about what I was going to do. At any rate, *Born-Again Skeptic and Other Valedictions* is less about the times I've lived through—fairly happily on the whole—than about my opinions, my personality or persona, and my character—or, some might think, my lack of it. To those I would say, I'm sorry you can't take a joke.

PREPARING FACES

A graduate student in English who was also in the Marine Reserves described a conversation with a Master Sergeant over a few beers. The conversation turned to women, and someone asked the sergeant if he'd ever been married.

"Yeah, I was married."

"What happened?"

"Got divorced."

"How come?"

Slamming his fist on the table, he said, "Because she was a God damned civilian, that's why!"

That story reminded me of a conversation at a former graduate school roommate's house with him and another professor. His wife overheard us discussing the intellectual standings and shortcomings of colleagues and former professors and exclaimed, "You people are warped! Graduate school warped you people."

Years later, a woman I was dating said that I shouldn't be so critical. "Well," I said, "I'm a critic." And a reader and a writer. Past seventy and still active, that's not what I do. It's who I am.

Or a large part. While I was in my first full-time teaching job, my then brother-in-law and his family came to visit, and he and his wife wanted to come to one of my classes. Afterward, he said, "You didn't sound a bit like Megan's daddy!" Megan was barely a toddler, and in the classroom I had my game face on, one that my children saw more and more as they grew older, not, as far as I can tell, to their disadvantage. Or perhaps they have come to regard me as normal.

Apparently the disciplines of military service and academic life can indoctrinate lifers in both kinds of disciplines so deeply that they have difficulty thinking outside the confines of their worlds or to understand the motivation of people who voluntarily leave them. I've heard the term "good soldier," and the highest praise that one of my most successful graduate school contemporaries could render was "good academic."

Although I've never been on a parade ground, like my siblings I apparently have a parade ground voice, slightly modulated for my professor voice. A friend says that, when she asks me a question in public, I reply as if I were addressing a class—and not just a seminar. Once a young man made the mistake of asking me about Shakespeare—not even my field—and, as my friend said later, "Bob talked for fifty minutes!" She said that to another retired professor, who said, matter of factly, "Well, that's what you do."

Retirement from official duties, military or academic, doesn't seem to make much difference in attitudes, at least to those who are really committed. I am a little shocked at my ex-wife's post-retirement lifestyle, for instead of writing the book she's eminently qualified to do, she's taken up quilting and walking her dogs. When I told her about this book, she said "I can't believe you're still doing that." I replied that I can't believe everyone else isn't. But another former colleague has an active career as poet, translator, and essayist, and I've edited two books and published four others and a chapbook of original work since my move to the lotus-land of an over-55 community on the fringe of the Phoenix area, what Ezra Pound might have called in his phrase from *Hugh Selwyn Mauberley* a "haven from sophistications and contentions," though my companion, unlike the stylist's "placid and uneducated mistress," is not without education and is anything but placid. But the largely Republican business-industrial population is far from uncontentious. Still, my friend's education and experience are not the same as mine, and the conservatives here cannot be called sophisticated—at least about things that interest me—and in any case they seem to have left behind their former professions. In the ordinary course of life, I don't think much about these things as I retreat into my study to read and write, correspond with writers and professors around the world—thank God for e-mail!—and like Pound's stylist exercise my talents and generally get to keep doing all the pleasant parts of the academic job while shucking unpleasant ones like grading papers, going to meetings, and dealing with the idiocies of departmental and university politics.

But occasionally I leave my little enclave to go to a conference, to give a reading or lecture, and to encounter the kind of people among whom I spent most my adult life. And the farther away I go—Bucharest the longest trip, Hungary, Slovenia, and Spain the most frequent—and the more time I spend in literary and scholarly atmospheres, the harder it is to come back to this haven where no one really speaks my language.

Not because my Penelope is, even initially, distant or unwelcoming like Odysseus's wife. It's I who have to readjust, ease back into the routine of comfort and intimacy, and act what passes here for normal, or as normal as I can seem. I regret that my uneasiness, however temporary, causes distress, but it seems nearly impossible to conceal. It's like talking to my brother, who stayed in our home town—I revert to the accent and vocabulary of my youth. Back in what I have come to consider the normal world of letters, I absorb its atmosphere and ways of thinking and talking.

After Odysseus returned to Ithaca from ten years of battle at Troy and another ten of wandering, his wife welcomes him and, not unnaturally, wants to know if he has any excuse for leaving again.

He replies that the prophet Tiresias has said that to achieve final peace, he would have to walk inland, carrying an oar, to a place where the people use no salt, until someone asks him why he's carrying a winnowing fan. Then he can go home.

Most readers regard this as a reprieve from travel, as I did in my early twenties. Now that I am what the AARP calls "mature," I suspect that Odysseus might look sternly at anyone who looks as if he is about to ask a question, tell him to shut the hell up, and go on with his travels. But perhaps that's because I haven't adjusted well enough to civilian life. But except in Tennyson's poem "Ulysses," which, though I agree that "How dull it is to pause, to make and end, / To rust unburnished, not to shine in use" can stir the spirit, like Homer's hero I always plant my metaphorical oar and head to the comfort and support as Megan's and her siblings' father and their children's grandfather.

Roots

Hearth & Home

The first and only house my parents owned, which they bought in 1947, goes back as far as the late 1850s, but the kitchen was a third or fourth addition to the original building, originally a farmhouse. Before that, the summer kitchen, and perhaps the winter one, was in a dirt-floored basement. As soon as we moved in, the kitchen became the center of family life.

It did so for a very practical reason. When we moved in, the only heat in the house came from large gas stoves in the dining room and one of the downstairs bedrooms and the large iron cook stove in the kitchen. That threw off more heat than the gas stoves combined, and it was a magnet in winter, since none of the upstairs bedrooms, where my siblings and I slept, had any heat at all until my father rented the house to the Missouri Training School for Boys and a furnace was installed for the comfort of the youthful felons.

The cook stove stayed until my parents had the time and money to begin to remodel the house. First they, and I as the oldest child, began to remove wallpaper. We went through eight or ten layers until we got to the brick that had been the outer wall of the original house. Then Mom got built-in cabinets with a new sink and a gas stove which I best remember her using to light cigarettes, her hair pulled back over her cheek. She kept the drip coffee pot long after someone had burned away the wooden handle, so that we had to use a hot pad to grab a screw and pour the coffee precariously.

As in many farmhouses, the kitchen was and still is the main point of entry from the large back yard that serves as a parking lot, and it was and is the location of all but the most ceremonial meals.

Our family's normal meals were anything but ceremonial. They were probably more decorous than in my father's family home, since he once hit his older brother in the face with a plate of butter and headed down the road to take refuge in the tallest tree. We were too busy eating to waste food, especially butter that I was in charge of churning, or the many vegetables that we laboriously tended in the large garden.

We were voracious eaters. Friends comment on how fast I eat, and I say that they've not seen my siblings at table. One friend did. At the rehearsal dinner for my daughter's wedding, a tray of pizza was set before me and my siblings. I preferred other toppings but took two pieces of what was offered. I had begun chewing on the first when another tray appeared, and my sister said, "You aren't going to eat that, are you." It was not a question, for she grabbed the slice from my plate. The defense rests.

Meals in the kitchen tended to be hurried affairs. Our father was a trader, buying and selling anything moveable and some things that weren't, and he didn't have a schedule like the fathers of my friends. After the youngest child got old enough to leave with sitters, my mother, who was not at all domestic, went back to work. At one point she hired a very nice woman named Nell as cook and housekeeper. She was a much better cook than Mom, especially of gingerbread, and had the sense to leave us alone until things got out of hand.

When Mom died in 1966, we made funeral arrangements while sitting around the kitchen table. After the period when the young felons occupied the house, Dad moved back in. Among his many talents was cooking, and when I visited him he would fix dinner. Once I offered to do the dishes—something I'd done, at his insistence, all the time I lived in that house. "No," he said, "I'll do them." As he stood at the sink, I said, "You know, Dad, you ought to get a dishwasher." His back was to me, but he shuffled in a way that showed he was embarrassed. "Aw," he said, "I don't want to get married again."

With that attitude, I don't know that he could have, even to a woman of that age and region.

By the time that Dad died in 1988, when again we gathered around the kitchen table to discuss what to do next, my sister and her husband were living in the house. Later the negotiations about their buying out my brother's and my shares took place at the same table.

Since then, they have remodeled the house extensively and imaginatively, but although the kitchen is at least in its third revision, it remains the point of entry and often the final destination for family and visitors. The new table is the oldest one we've had in the kitchen, since my sister is an avid antique hunter, but it still serves as first mail drop and a favorite place to gather. Nobody uses the gas stove to light cigarettes, and the crocks and churns in my sister's collection are strictly for show, but the raw brick remains as a decorative feature.

The kitchen, like the rest of the house, has a legacy for all of us. Memories of the iron stove came in handy when I stayed for a week in a cottage in the Orava Mountains of Slovakia and did the cooking for my host on a smaller version. When my brother accompanied me to New Brunswick, I made a point of taking him to an inn on the Saint John River to have some gingerbread in memory of Nell. And the house gave my family, who had only been in Missouri for eight years and were still regarded as outlanders when we moved in, a base and an instant history.

Now my family has been in the house more than half a century. When we gather for our semi-annual reunions, as many of us, going on three dozen, as can fit into the kitchen gather there, and not just the oldest of the three generations.

I don't know who will inherit the house from my sister and her husband. My sister would like to gather her children around her. But her son-in-law's career is going so well that a move back from the west coast seems unlikely. She has succeeded in moving her son and his family back from Ohio to the house across the back yard that our grandfather converted from an equipment shed, and they've begun to burrow into the community. Since this is the only family home that my sister can remember, she will do her best to see that it stays in the family.

It looks as though she won't have to work too hard. Her daughter-in-law, at least as energetic and opinionated as she is, has a taste for farming that skipped the generation after my father's. She has acquired heritage species of horses, sheep, and chickens to stock the barnyard and fields and as a result of livestock attrition is starting to modify her live-and-let-live attitude toward coyotes. If her younger son's fascination with animals persists and develops, both the acreage and the house will continue to fill their original function and the kitchen will continue to be the heart of the house and the family.

INTERSECTIONS

On the way back from a consulting job in Dumas, Texas (a whole 'nother story, as they say in Oklahoma) on a misty February morning, I headed up US 87 towards Dalhart and realized that the only time I'd been there was in 1952 when my mother and I were returning from a visit to my father's sister in Albuquerque. We stopped for coffee at a café on the right side of US 54, and knowing Mom's need for caffeine, it must have been the first one we had seen since Tucumcari.

At mid-morning, the only patrons were a few Mexicans, as they were then called, in undershirts drinking beer. Mom didn't seem concerned, perhaps because she may have hung out in tougher joints with Dad during their days in Prohibition-era Kansas City before I was born. So I tried to act as cool as a six-foot 160-pound seventeen-year-old could. The coffee, thick and sweet, was the best I'd tasted before or since. Over the years, that coffee was my sharpest and most frequent memory of the trip.

Coming at Dalhart from another angle more than half a century later, I dug a little deeper into memory. If I was seventeen, how old was Mom? The answer was startling—43, then the age of my oldest child, Megan, who's thirty years younger than I.

Beyond simple arithmetic lay the realm of emotional calculus, where trajectories and end-points have no numbers. I can remember, not always pleasantly, what I was like, and I have some sense, though probably not as clear as I sometimes think, of what Megan is like. But what was Mom like—then or ever—not as my mother but as an independent individual? It is impossible to know, of course, but what could I infer by triangulating from Megan's and my experience at 43? From memories of the rest of the trip? From my knowledge of Mom over the years until her early, painful death from stomach cancer in 1966?

The trip itself. We'd driven a 1952 Plymouth four-door sedan off Dad's used car lot, first to Wichita where his brother lived with his large and expanding brood, then hitting Route 66 west of El Reno, Oklahoma. We stopped on the dark roadside to nap and drove on in time to see the sunrise illuminate the Sandia Mountains that lie just east of our destination.

In Albuquerque, Aunt Cary was a tireless and knowledgeable guide. She seemed to know every Anglo and many of the Hispanics in the region, and she clearly thought that Mom was a major addition to the Davis family. But I was too self-absorbed to pay much attention to the adults.

On the way back, we left Dalhart in increasingly oppressive heat. In those days, I don't know that any cars had air conditioning—the Plymouth certainly didn't—and the wind from the open windows and the hood vent offered no relief. After several stops for cold drinks, Mom had an idea, as she almost always did. At a hardware store in a small Kansas town—Liberal? Pratt?—she bought a white enameled wash basin, then found an ice-house and got a large block of ice. The breeze from the vent passed over the ice and cooled us just a little.

In Wichita, after another brief visit with my uncle's family, we rented a trailer and loaded some pieces of family furniture that Dad's half-sister had stored. Mom was a supremely confident driver, but she told me to back the trailer to the loading dock. I don't know if she was, reluctantly, recognizing her limitations or was trying to show me mine. I'd never backed a trailer before, but I did it fairly handily and discovered that, like using chopsticks, it's a lot easier if you don't think about it.

Mom took the wheel and we continued on US 54 to El Dorado, where some teenagers whistled at Mom. From the passenger seat, I yelled, "Hey, that's my mother!" She shushed me, pleased with the tribute even though it came from a three-quarter rear view. I realized that she had some vanity about her looks as well as her brains and that she didn't like getting older. That came up when I mentioned that Dick Metz, with whom she'd gone to high school, was called a veteran golfer.

What else did I learn about Mom from this trip? It was the longest I took with her, and the longest she ever took. Over the years, I came to realize that she would go anywhere at a moment's notice—to Texas in a large truck carrying a prize bull; to Lawrence, Kansas, to type a seminar paper for me; to Chicago, first a rare trip with Dad as a way of dealing with my sister's entry into the convent, then with my sister on her return to secular life—just about anywhere for any or no reason. As her mother said when Mom's funeral procession pulled away from the church, she always liked to go for a drive.

What Mom really craved, I now realize, was adventure. As a girl, her favorite movie star was Pearl White, called Hollywood's "Stunt Queen," who appeared in *The Perils of Pauline* and dozens of other films. Like Pearl, Mom suffered injuries from her exploits, mostly from riding horses regarded as wild—or riding them wildly. As her composure in the Dalhart café showed, she was confident, even fearless, except in the presence of mice or black cats, an odd parlay when I think of it.

She was ingenious, in a way adventurous, in dealing with daily life. She had an independence of usual ways of thinking and acting. She once complained that I didn't suffer fools gladly. I replied that I didn't suffer them at all if I could help it. I should have said, looking pointedly at her, that I must have picked it up somewhere.

The ability to think in unusual ways and to regard a difficulty as a challenge rather than a problem showed in the impromptu air cooler. No matter what the situation—academic, psychological, financial—she had a solution. My ex-wife once said that I'd have made a good pioneer, and that attitude, if not the abilities, comes from her, her father, and her husband. My ability to figure and finagle may have been cultivated by my Jesuit teachers, but they worked on ground that she had helped to prepare.

That independence and ingenuity made her seem unusual for a woman of her time and place because she was aware of a larger world. If she couldn't explore it physically as much as she wanted, she could and did read widely, and like her father, she believed that books were an essential part of a house's furnishings. She enjoyed words in other ways: crossword puzzles, stories, jokes, any source of information for its own sake.

Even people who knew her probably didn't know how unusual she was, and those who depended on stereotypes from pre-*Feminine Mystique* days obviously couldn't. When I told a spiritual advisor of my engagement to another graduate student, he said that was a bad idea because she would stack the dishes in the sink and read a book instead. That didn't daunt me, first because Dad insisted that the children do dishes; second because I regarded, as he should have, reading books as more important. Aside from the dishes, Mom's approach to domestic science was casual if not cavalier.

Mom could cook, though nowhere near as well as her mother, a first-generation American-Polish-German who embodied the Kinder-Küche-Kirke ethos of the nineteenth century and later. Mom and baking had an especially uneasy relationship. She would not even attempt to bake cakes, and my sister remembers a batch of cookies so hard that, even soaked in water and then milk, the dog refused them. Housework was not a high priority: non-toxic was good enough. Once I brought a college girlfriend to the house, warning her in advance that the house would be a mess. She thought that was just a pro forma disclaimer, but a long time later she said that she had for years been delighted and consoled to discover that it was a mess.

The poet Wordsworth called duty "stern daughter of the voice of God," regretting that in youth he had "deferr'd the task, in smoother walks to stray." Mom followed the second course. One of her favorite expressions was "You owe it to yourself," a pleasant contrast to Dad's "While you're resting, get up and do" something sweaty and unpleasant. Mom had too much energy to rest very much, and if she were playing basketball today would have had the ideal attitude for a point guard. But instead of domestic tasks she preferred being with a variety of people and doing what she clearly thought of as a real job.

She was, from the point of view of my friends and mostly of me, an ideal mother because she knew how to enjoy life and was tolerant of minor lapses in behavior and judgment and was, mostly, content to let me learn from small mistakes that Dad focused on while being surprisingly tolerant of big ones. She seemed to assume that we would want to succeed, to learn, and to be independent—whether or not we wanted to. She wasn't a Fifties TV mother. As she lay dying, one of my classmates said "She never had a bad word to say about anyone." I replied, "Clearly you didn't know her very well."

The question was, did I? The next two generations of her descendants have led very different lives. For example, at 43, I had a full professorship, three early teen-aged children who didn't remember their grandmother, and a wife with a Ph.D. who had just resumed her academic career and whom Mom didn't care for, perhaps out of envy at her opportunities. I'd been to both coasts and to Canada and it looked like I was settling into a secure academic marriage and a predictable career. (Two years later the marriage fell apart, and I traveled farther and for different reasons than I could ever have anticipated.) Megan at 43 had a four-year-old son, a successful practice as a family therapist, and an interest in commercial real estate. Her brother, now 43, has an advanced degree in international business, is a financial advisor in the Northwest with a wife, two sons, and a house full of antiques overlooking a lake. At some point, he hopes to travel with me to Budapest. I hope that I guide him as efficiently as Mom did me and that perhaps he might learn something about his father.

What did Mom have? A clerical job, for which she was undoubtedly over-qualified, which she used to finance her children's higher education. More brains, better looks, and far more curiosity, as far as I could see, than the mothers of my contemporaries. Very limited opportunities for travel. Born thirty years later, she could have been an executive, a teacher, a writer. Or she could have done, as her daughter now does in a large company, whatever they couldn't stop her from doing.

In fact, her life, at least the last ten years or so, could have been happier, and all of it could, in terms I learned to consider, might have been more fulfilling. Of course, my regrets about Mom's lack of scope for her talents may be misplaced or at least exaggerated. Unlike many mothers, she got to work outside the home and clearly enjoyed that. Like her older son and her daughter, she had the considerable satisfaction of knowing, or thinking she knew, more than anyone around her. I do have some regrets, especially for not knowing more about Mom's qualities, appreciating them, and letting her know I appreciated them.

Looked at the other way, I wonder what, in William Butler Yeats' terms, as a grown woman she would have thought her child

> With sixty or more winters on its head,
> A compensation for the pang of his birth,
> Or the uncertainty of his setting forth?

I think that she was disappointed in my marriage, but it's just as well that she didn't live to see the divorce or my subsequent defection from the Catholic Church. She was disappointed that I never learned to play the piano and that I ignored her recommendation that I read David Copperfield—then or in forty-five subsequent years as a college professor.

But in other ways I seem to have assimilated some of her lessons. I left home to make words a source of pleasure and profit. I've moved with surprising ease in places where I couldn't read the alphabet, let alone speak the language—adventures she would have enjoyed. I came to believe, as a matter of course, that intelligent and independent women are worth knowing. I'm probably more independent-minded than she would have liked, but the apple hasn't fallen far from the tree. Her desire for knowledge has persisted. A high school contemporary told me recently that he admired me back then because I liked to know things.

There are other seemingly trivial legacies. Mom was superstitious, and while I won't go miles out of the way to avoid crossing the path of a black cat—my sister said that she finally pushed herself to do so, but said a Hail Mary just in case—I still think before I do. I still put on my right shoe first without thinking about it, and when I spill salt, I toss a pinch over my left shoulder. On a more commonplace level, while I still won't wear anything yellow or flowered, I still have a drawer full of underwear, larger but clearly the same as the kind she bought me at J. C. Penney.

So Mom's influence persists below the surface. And very obviously on the surface, for she left her children and grandchildren the gift of self-confidence. When Megan was about five, her Sunday School did a lesson on failure. Asked how she felt about that, she said, "I don't know. I never failed at anything." That didn't persist, but later a psychologist said that our family had two rules: take care of yourself and succeed. Those aren't bad standards to have. They come in part from other family members, but Mom was central to their formation and transmission.

CENTENNIAL

May 1, 2008, was the centennial of the birth of my father Mathew Cary Davis, known in Boonville first as M.C. and then as Matt. I've written about him in *Mid-Lands: A Family Album*—in fact, when I looked back at the book, I realized that it is really about him. But that was indirect.

His birth date is ironic on at least three levels. It's the major Communist/Labor holiday, originally commemorating the workers killed in the Haymarket Massacre in Chicago in the late 19th century. Dad was so far to the right that he could have passed for an anarchist. Later, the Catholic Church appropriated the day as the feast of St. Joseph the Worker to get in on the act. Dad seemed to be one of the least religious people I've known—except for his father-in-law, R. J. Murray.

Before either of these celebrations, May Day was a major pagan holiday for Celts and Scandinavians and, for the Germans, *Walpurgis* (Witches Night), celebrating the beginning of summer. I don't think that anyone could realistically imagine Dad dancing around a Maypole (though Mom said that they had their first date at a dance), and though he'd take a drink, he didn't seem to do so in the Bacchanalian spirit associated with paganism. But for him it may have been a sign of life. When he was in his 70s, he rolled a tractor on himself. My brother arrived, distraught, and found him unconscious. Then Dad opened his eyes and said, "Anybody got a drink?" Everyone decided he was ok.

One word I thought might describe him is "saturnine," but that means "sluggish in temperament; gloomy; taciturn." Dad was anything but sluggish. Nor was he exactly gloomy, although "exuberant" won't fit either. "Taciturn" means "temperamentally disinclined to talk," but Dad could talk when he needed to. "Laconic" fits better, since he was as careful with words as he was with money.

Although he was a terrific salesman of cars, trucks, and anything else that moved or stood still, and perhaps an ever better trader, he didn't fit the stereotype of the voluble salesman. He believed in getting to the point: "Tell you what. I'll give you $200 cash (or whatever he'd calculated the thing was worth, down to the penny) for that right now." In a more expansive mood, when negotiations had stalled, he'd say, "Tell you what. I'll flip you for the difference."

He wasn't averse to a gamble, though I tell people that if he stayed sober and stuck to poker, it wasn't really gambling. The most valuable advice he ever gave me was not in words but by example: he showed me that I was far from the best card player alive. Saved me a lot of money and trouble.

In his youth he was a handsome man and apparently popular. His sister sent him the copy of his high school yearbook which included the inscription to "a real hunk of man." But it disappeared not long after he saw it. And when, in college, I visited his older brother's family in Wichita, I told my uncle that I was sorry I bothered him to pick me up at the station because some girls from KU had offered to give me a ride. "Just like your old man," he snorted.

Dad tried to teach me the things he liked, such as fishing and hunting, but I was too young to keep up in the fields. He took me to MU basketball and football games and Cardinals baseball games. He tried to teach me how to throw a punch in case of playground fights—I was outweighed by at least two classes—but though everyone in the family knew that he had a violent temper, I saw him even come close to losing it only once. Perhaps he looked tough enough that he didn't have to, but that may be a small boy's perspective.

No one now living seems to know much about his life before he came to Boonville in 1939 to open or take over a pool hall. We have brief glimpses, like scattered still photos, of what he did: working for a dry cleaner/bootlegger in Arkansas City, Kansas; dropping out of high school to work in the oil fields with his future brother-in-law and encountering his older brother in a gritty camp in west Texas; selling insurance door to door in Lyons, Kansas, during the dust bowl; living on a hardscrabble Morgan County farm in the mid-1930s; leaving there to get a job selling lessons (about what?) door to door in Coffeyville, Kansas, because "your mother got to chewing on me."

That story came from one of the rare times he talked about himself, sitting in the dark under the walnut trees on the place he and Mom had bought after World War II. He told other stories about rural Missouri in the 1930s, but I can't remember all of them and if I'd had a tape recorder, he wouldn't have said as much as he did.

What we did know about him was that once he came to Boonville at the age of thirty, he seemed to be able to succeed at whatever he tried. When the US entered World War II, he went to work on the Katy Railroad, although he'd never done anything like that. When the war ended, he took a job as sales manager at the Schlotzhauer Buick and International agency. How he talked his way into that job no one knows, but it began his career as salesman and later cattle trader for which he was best known.

He wasn't as solitary as he sometimes seemed to me. He had a series of partners: Gene Darby, an older man who may have been a kind of mentor; Sam Jewett, a stereotypical salesman; Ham Horst, who seemed at least as laconic as Dad. And he had a number of friends, decreasing with the years. The only one I knew well was Bill Robinson, a local barber, who was his longest surviving and perhaps his best friend. They'd sit and complain about whatever level of government caught their attention.

Given this attitude, it seems odd that Dad had intermittent political ambitions. Once he thought of running for sheriff as a

Democrat (Dixiecrat would be a better term), but Mom threatened to leave him if he filed. He was tough, but he wasn't that tough. Later he won a term on the Boonville City Council and was known as "Maverick Matt" by the *Daily News*. (His son John seems to have followed in his footsteps.) And though he detested government programs, he filed for Social Security at the earliest opportunity.

After I married in 1958 and stopped returning to Boonville during summer vacations, I saw less of him until Mom's final illness, when he showed a side I'd never seen, solicitous, almost tender, in spite of the stoicism that was his external response to every form of disaster, including his own illness and approaching death.

Cousins

And so do his sisters and his cousins and his aunts.
—*H.M.S. Pinafore*

Friends who are only children of only children, others who don't have an extended family, and still others who have lost touch with whatever extended family they might have, express their envy when I mention my various and far-flung cousins. For a long time this seemed odd to me. It wasn't merely that I was used to having cousins scattered over the west. Where I grew up, most people did: my sister-in-law had fifty-one in a ten-mile radius. More immediately important, however, was the fact that my father's mother and her daughters were enthusiastic genealogists, and Southerners on top of that, and they, especially my Aunt Cary, worked hard at transmitting information about all discoverable branches of the family, living and dead, and when necessary, commanded attendance at funerals and exceptional family gatherings, whatever quarrels and coolnesses might have arisen.

Since Cary died, at the age of 102, I'm the oldest member of the extended family on either side. In fact, except for my siblings and me and our children, on my mother's side of the family there don't seem to be any Murray descendants, though there are some distant Litschgis in Evansville, Indiana. On my father's side, however, I have nine surviving first cousins and about as many offspring of Cary's children, whatever they are. Second cousins? First cousins once removed? Cary would have known, and my sister Beth, who has taken over the genealogical records, might be able to figure it out—or give an answer that at least sounded definitive.

The job of keeping the living members of the family in contact seems to have fallen to me. I move around a lot more than my siblings and first cousins. I've always been less averse than the rest of my family to making long distance calls, and I probably spend more time on e-mail than the rest of my family put together. Besides, I learned from Cary that this is what one does, without question or even much thought.

But I must get something out of the activity. Or, as my father would have put it, it must be good for something. And as I've gotten older and become, technically, what used to be called the head of the family, I have begun to think about family, especially about my peers, the cousins.

It took me a long time to get to this point, partly because of my birth order in the generation. Cary's two children were enough older that when I met them, a couple of months before my fifth birthday in 1939, I saw them as nearly grown up. Thirteen years later, I was a college student and they were settled into their own family lives, and by 1965, when I stopped in Albuquerque on my way to a job in California, one cousin had died and another had a wasting and terminal disease.

My uncle Gough's children were six and more years younger and lived what then seemed a long way away. But the real reason I didn't see them often was that our fathers couldn't stand each other. My uncle's children thought that it had something to do with a car wreck on the way to visit Cary, and I do have a dim memory of my father on the floor of our house moving my toy cars around and talking about court appearances and testimony. But stories my mother told indicated that the animosity went much further back, and when Cary's granddaughter gave me some family correspondence, it was clear that the conflict began in childhood.

My uncle's children and I didn't know much about the quarrel, and we didn't care, but I didn't see them often enough to form a real bond. My brother's daughters are always bucketing half-way across the country or all the way across the

Atlantic to attend weddings and baby showers and christenings and other ceremonies dear to the mid-Missouri female heart because they more or less grew up with their many cousins in varying degrees of distance. I couldn't, without some effort, even remember the names of all of mine, let alone their children.

Yet over the years I knew that they existed, and I maintained a low-level curiosity about them and when I saw them managed to learn some things. At first it was more about my family than about theirs.

Most obvious was the fact that the Missouri Davises looked different and lived a different kind of life. The New Mexico cousins were blond and destined to be professional class. My female cousin was not only the first architect I ever met, she may have been the first of that profession I ever heard of. They lived in Albuquerque, a few blocks from the University of New Mexico, in what seemed an exotic landscape of desert and mountains. Aunt Cary collected rainwater in barrels, which seemed odd to someone from damp Missouri, and gardened ferociously, ignoring climate and soil conditions as far as possible. But she grew flowers and shrubs, not vegetables for the table and cellar as we did in a much larger plot at the edge of a small town.

The Wichita cousins had features like ours, especially the deep-set eyes, but our body-types followed those of our fathers. They were, and are, shorter and stouter. They too lived in a city, in a house that seemed very large and elegant, though Wichita was far less exotic than Albuquerque, and their father had cultural and social pretensions that ours ignored. Theirs listened to opera, sitting in an easy chair; ours listened to whatever was on the radio, and he sat down only when he was tired. The only similarity I could observe was their voices, which had the same timbre if not the same vocabulary. (That's true of my brother and me. We once tested a friend's tape recorder by speaking alternately, and in playback had trouble telling which of us was speaking.)

I learned from visiting them that people could live different kinds of lives. This might not seem startling, but to a child and even a teenager it can be a revelation. Going into the houses of friends was different, partly because they existed in the same milieu, partly because, however welcoming, they were not family. Aunts and uncles looked at you differently, as extensions of themselves and as possible alternatives to, as well as peers of, their own children. From the youthful viewpoint, the similarities were both familiar and unsettling, producing the uneasy recognition that here were people enough like you so that, with a slight genetic shift, you could be them or they you.

It is also possible to learn that one's family situation is not unique or as necessarily fortunate or oppressive as one had thought. For example, my daughter, not older than eight, returned from a visit to her aunt, uncle, and cousins and observed, "In every family, there's always one parent that yells." While this may have been a hasty generalization, she was learning something about family dynamics, if only Davis family dynamics.

That kind of perspective is a useful, perhaps essential, part of growing up. So is the process of learning that one's parents were not always the fully formed, seemingly all-powerful beings that one sometimes thinks them. Even if family stories don't get told, and in my family they always do, the way that siblings and other family members react to them can show children that their parents exist in previously unsuspected temporal and social frameworks.

As we get older, we can see other patterns emerge in choices of profession and life-style. In my extended family, people seem to gravitate towards teaching and the helping professions, perhaps because it gives us the opportunity to order people around. My two oldest Wichita cousins teach or have taught, and one each of their children is teaching or preparing to do so.

My daughter is a therapist. Some of the next generation New Mexico family are in medical professions; another teaches. Others have inherited the family interest in music from my music teaching grandmother and are more or less accomplished and dedicated performers. Some seem to have inherited the wild gene that turned my uncle to oil speculation and my father to the modern version of horse trading and follow, or at least talk about, various schemes that range from dot.com companies to raising leeches commercially.

I'm not sure where the restlessness comes from. As a young single woman, Cary left Kansas in the late teens of the last century to work for the Santa Fe Railroad in (what was then East) Las Vegas, New Mexico. I've traveled extensively. As I was writing the first draft of this essay my son was spending two months in South America before moving to Seattle and finding a job and a wife; a niece taught in Japan, Switzerland, Norway, and Sri Lanka, worked as a nanny in Australia, and seems now to be settled back in Switzerland, and another niece left for three months in Europe, then went to Alaska by way of Seattle, and returned to Seattle to marry a college boyfriend and settle down.

There's also a class if not a family resemblance. When Cary turned ninety, my brother and sister and I visited her, and she commanded a gathering of her grandchildren, some of whom apparently didn't speak to each other except at her order. We turned out to dress and talk and react pretty much in the same way—fairly downscale in dress, very direct in speech, and unsurprised at anything that might be said. None of this may be genetic, for my adopted children exhibit all of these family traits. They may come from the fact that our families allowed and even encouraged us to speak our minds, more by example than direct precept and sometimes in contradiction to what they told us.

The real point of cousins and other extended family members is that they are like you, but they aren't you. They suggest patterns of behavior, but they don't determine them. They help to create a context and to establish sanctions—what in fancy terms is called an ethos that is more personal and specific to you than that of the official communities that surround us.

And they give perspective. Maybe that's what my cousin Mike, who is fourteen years younger than I and whom I hadn't seen in almost fourteen years, meant when he said at the end of a three-hour conversation that it was great to talk to someone who knew where he was coming from. He may have meant it in the Sixties sense, but he was also talking about the family viewpoint and, in a very different sense from rightwing campaigners, family values.

I don't know what it's like to be without this kind of perspective, but it seems to me that people who don't have it must look at others as if they were figures in a Byzantine painting, two-dimensional and impenetrable. People with families see the world as if it were a painting from the high Renaissance. Some may regard their families as figures in an Andrea del Sarto painting, smooth and unwrinkled. My family looks more and more to me, and seems to look to the rest of us, like a series of Rembrandt self-portraits—shadows, warts, and all—that change and grow more interesting.

POTTAGE

[The Bible] provides a stage where we can find ourselves.
—*Andrew Brown*

While I was making very preliminary preparations to go to my family's biennial reunion in Boonville, Missouri, where my parents settled sixty-five years ago, I mentioned to a friend that I would be making a rare visit to my brother and sister, John and Beth, who have lived there or near there all their lives.

"You must be very different from them," she said. I could see why she would think so. Since I left to enter a doctoral program in 1957, I've spent more time in Hungary or the Canadian Maritime provinces than I have in Boonville and was the first member of the family to be in Europe since Herman Litschgi came from Baden Baden in the 1870s. I taught at various universities for forty-five years, published a number of books, and have a modest international reputation as a scholar.

My brother John, five years younger than I, has done a number of things: run a country store on the outskirts of Boonville that would have made a 7-11 seem like a specialized boutique; owned a muffler shop; been a county commissioner Then, like our father, he became a maverick city councilman, a corrections officer for the Missouri prison system, and now, beginning in his mid-sixties, owner of a funeral home. Like Dad, whom he resembles from the neck up, he knows almost everybody in the county. I have the impression that Dad was more respected as a sharp trader than he was liked, but most people seem to like Johnny because he is affable, funny, and a marvelous teller of stories which he sometimes acts out. I tease him about going into politics because it finally gave him the chance to talk that, as middle child, he'd never had in the family. A lot of other people tease him to see what he will say. And he always has something to say. Once, before he was in his teens, Mom took him to the library. Some clueless woman said, "Oh, are you the smart one?" "No," he replied, "I'm the good-looking one.

Our sister Beth, five years younger still, supposedly looks like our mother, though I can't see it. But in quickness of mind and sharpness of tongue and general fearlessness, they are a lot alike. Born thirty-five years later, Beth has been able to be more openly assertive. She travels widely throughout the Midwest as trouble-shooter for a large chain of electrical supply stores. Although she is not unpleasant, unless she needs to be, she meets problems head-on, a lot like Dad but much noisier. For a while, she was a nun. Years after she left the convent, she went back for a reunion of her class. When they visited an elderly nun, almost deaf, who had been their supervisor, each woman would lean down and give both her secular and religious name. The old nun would say, feebly, "Well, I should remember, but I'm sorry; I don't." Until Beth leaned in and said "Sister, I was Mary Beth Davis, Sister Mary St. Matthew." The old woman sat up and said, loudly, "Mary Beth!" I once said that I could see why she entered the convent—conflict with Mom—but I couldn't understand why the Sisters of St. Joseph had taken her. Why not? Well, a little thing like the vow of obedience. Indignantly, she said, "I promised to obey anything I thought was reasonable!" Another angle on her character: a friend who had met Beth and her husband Bert asked how tall he was. About 6'3", I said. "Really," she said, "I thought Beth was taller." As they say in the NBA, she plays bigger. Or at least louder.

After Dad died, it took the three of us a while to sort out who would get what and for how much. Beth and her husband bought John's and my shares of the house that our parents had bought after World War II—the only one they had ever owned —and they have poured money and a lot of sweat into the structure that dates back before the Civil War and evolved over the years before we owned it, was made habitable by modern standards under our parents' care, and has been turned, grounds as well as house, into something like a work of art by Beth and Bert. It's now on the Register of Historic Places, including the expensively and lovingly restored smoke house, the family equivalent of a folly on an English estate, except that it's used for storing junk.

Johnny bought out Beth's and my share of the land that Dad had developed on the opposite edge of town, sold some, rented some, and on the rest remodeled a large metal-sided building for the funeral home he's wanted to build for at least fifteen years. (I can't account for his impulse, but he grew up across from a cemetery, got into part-time supervision and maintenance of two cemeteries, and apparently got hooked.) Asked who the architect was, he said that he drew the plans on a piece of graph paper because 8½ x 11 was close enough to the floor plan's 80 x 100. And made it work. Better judgment, maybe even his, dissuaded him from getting a phone number with the final figures spelling 2DI4, though with the local sense of humor that might not have been a deterrent to business. More obvious is his sense of compassion and his genuine desire to help. Beth and I like to be helpful, but we are more inclined to batter a problem into submission.

What did I get? Money, of course. Freedom from dealing with all that grass and those leaves and a whole set of buildings that need constant maintenance. Freedom from having to find something to do in a small town. But objectively speaking, I must seem rather like Esau, who sold his birthright to his younger twin Jacob for a mess of pottage.

I hadn't read the book of Genesis at all in fifty years, and then not carefully, and the mess of pottage was all that I remembered of the Esau-Jacob story. Going back to the King James Version—the nuns who taught me would be horrified—I keep for reference, I was fascinated by the story. For those whose memories need refreshing, as in much of Genesis, the story is about family, inheritance, creation of a tradition and a people increasingly aware that they are chosen. Unlike the New Testament, in the Old a lot of begetting goes on, often leading to violence against family members and strangers alike.

Basically, Rebekah, wife of Isaac (who had his own paternal issues), has twin sons, Esau, born first, and Jacob, who emerges clinging to his brother's heel. Rebekah, the prototype of the Jewish stage mother, has a convenient vision that the older will serve the younger, clearly her favorite. She conspires with him to masquerade as Esau to receive his father's blessing and ultimately become not Jacob but Israel, and then advises Jacob to flee his brother's wrath when Esau discovers the trick. The only consolation that Isaac can offer to Esau—apparently a blessing is irrevocable—is that he will finally prosper and shall "break his yoke from off thy neck."

A whole lot of other stuff happens to Jacob, but, tricky as ever, he survives, flees his father-in-law, and returns to his homeland, very nervous about meeting his brother, whom he hopes to placate by gifts. Surprisingly, Esau refuses, saying "I have enough, my brother; keep that thou hast unto thyself."

Perhaps I'm extrapolating from my feelings, but it seems to me that Esau subconsciously didn't want the blessing. (That's if an Old Testament character could have a subconscious, though Jehovah does seem to alternate between Superego and Id.) He's described as "a cunning hunter, a man of the field," while Jacob is "a plain man, dwelling in tents" and clearly more suitable at this point to settling down and begetting. After all, Esau "despised his birthright" and sold it. Despite his later anger at being supplanted, he gets over it, begets a whole line of dukes of Edom, and disappears from the story.

I don't know that I despised my birthright, but in a sense I did sell the outward and visible signs of my parents' legacy. Metaphorically speaking, I'm a man of the field in that I've done a lot of traveling, feel at home, or not, as much one place as another. Instead of a sword, I have a laptop. Unlike the Prodigal Son, I haven't blown my portion on riotous living or wound up living with swine (I raised hogs as a teenager, and though I liked them better than any other farm animals, that was enough), but when I go back, my sister-in-law cooks very good brisket.

But I didn't leave without a birthright or a blessing. Like Esau, I inherited the ability to survive and even thrive. Mom's machinations, hard work, and financial support got me into college and beyond. From her and her father I got the love of words and of travel. From the whole family I got an appreciation for hard work, thrift, and intelligence, especially intelligence in women, an inheritance that is more fungible than sheep and cattle. Or buildings. Or a position in the society and politics of my home town, which, though I wouldn't want to live there, is a great place to visit.

When I do, I can say, with Esau, "I have enough." Outsiders may think I have more than enough, since one asked if my brother weren't envious of what I've done and where I've been. Not as far as I could tell, I said. Neither of us could do what the other does; each seems to respect and support the other's accomplishments. (The same person had met Beth and never suspected for a moment that she could envy anyone.) The wife of a high school friend of my brother's saw us together and said, amazed, "You like each other!"

Possibly, as my sister once said, that's because, though we're close, we're not in each other's faces. On another occasion, she told someone who asked if she had any siblings that she had a brother in Oklahoma she saw once a year and a brother in Boonville she saw twice a year. That's an exaggeration, but so much of our communication takes place at a distance that when Beth told Bert that her brother had called with the news that his mother's garage was on fire, he asked, "How did Bob know?"

My siblings and I keep each other posted on the doings of the next two generations, so the connection remains strong. As

I said to the friend who thought I must be very different from my siblings, "You'd think so, until you see us together." We're all fairly large, noisy, opinionated, skeptical, and laugh a lot. This is the kind of inheritance we share, and we think it a blessing that doesn't have to be divided, though people who have married into the family may disagree. My daughter says they stand in corners at family reunions and say to each other, "Can you believe this?" The youngest generation so far—there's been a fair bit of begetting—seems to enjoy us, though not as much as we enjoy each other.

Close Enough

A displaced and disgruntled New York writer once said, in a parting shot, "You know exactly who you are!" I still can't decide whether she was envious, angry, contemptuous, or—least likely—perceptive. She liked to startle people, and on many occasions she had tried, and failed, with me, since I would respond to her most outrageous statements as if they were perfectly normal conversation. This unsettled her and may have given her an exaggerated sense of my composure and self-awareness.

At the time, I didn't think much about the overt content of her remark because I had been a tenured full professor for years and was too busy living my life to wonder, even inexactly, who I was or to care what she thought I was. Now, in my mid-seventies, I still don't wonder a lot, since I'm one of the least other-directed people I know, except for my forebears and siblings, but she's not the only person who has tried to encapsulate my character, and naturally I'm curious about my public persona.

Over the years, I've collected some odd and surprising observations. A former lover said that I was "the blackest white man I've ever known." A Chinese-American, surveying a crowd, remarked that "you and I are the only colored people here." An American Indian writer decided that "you're not like the ordinary white dude." Another Indian looked in the back seat of my station wagon said, "This is an Indian car!" (Actually, it was the car of a person raised in a rural area, where everything but the driver's seat is devoted to miscellaneous storage. My brother's pickup looks the same.) A Hungarian woman thought that I was "a very colored character," though I think she meant colorful. On another occasion, a prototypical New York academic insisted that when she first met me that I was wearing snakeskin boots and a Stetson, neither of which I've ever owned. But a woman from Texas said that I was the most complicated person she'd ever met. And the writer's husband, just to bring me back to earth, thought that I seemed at first like just "a good ol' Missouri boy."

He should have known, since he came from an immigrant family who had settled in Montana. I don't know if Montana has good ol' boys. They do have cowboys but no one ever took him for one because over the years he had become indistinguishable from the New York writers with whom he associated for decades. Still, each of us was, in his way, a walking illustration of James McMurtry's remark that a good ol' boy could become an intellectual, but an intellectual could never become a good ol' boy.

In the academic and broader cultural worlds where I spent most of my life, where anyone with a provincial background looked indistinguishable from anyone else, perhaps I did look like a good ol' Missouri boy. The son of a famous New York literary critic delivered himself of what obviously seemed to him a complicated idea, and when I said, "Yes, of course," he said, "I'd have to explain myself to most people." "Well," I said, "just because I talk funny doesn't mean I'm stupid." Another man, deeply immersed in Hollywood, said, "It's amazing what you've accomplished considering where you come from." I answered that one of the places I came from was some very smart people—all of whom had Midwestern roots. From them I acquired a curiosity about a wide variety of things and an ability, indeed an eagerness, to adapt to places and circumstances that means that I've never been homesick. And from my classmates in a small town school, parochial in at least two senses, the ability to deadpan responses that disconcerted the New Yorker with a variety of what a fellow townsman and writer called "red assing." He and many of my contemporaries have their own stories about being labeled and transcending labels, and several have spoken of the value of experience in a very small school where almost everyone suited up for sports, acted in school plays, sang in the chorus, and worked on the yearbook—a variety that students in larger schools do not have. So even within seemingly tight limits, it was possible to cross borders.

I didn't begin to put the comments of these sophisticates into a larger context until I read Neil Campbell's *The Rhizomatic West*. (As Dave Cormier says in his blog, "A rhizomatic plant has no center and no defined boundary; rather, it is made up of a number of semi-independent nodes, each of which is capable of growing and spreading on its own....")

Neil is a Brit, or maybe a Scot, and he presents an outsider's view of the West, and like many other revisionists, he rejects Frederick Jackson Turner's view that the frontier ended in 1890 and argues instead for continuous encounters with and breaching of physical borders, "a reorientation of culture both as roots and routes, both dwelling and traveling...."

When I ran into Neil at a conference, he wondered why I had been sent the book (easy—I requested it) because everyone knows what I think about theory. Relax, I told him. As soon as I understood his thesis, about page two, I said "Of course" because his book describes not only me but a large number of Americans, and I'm pragmatic enough to use anything that works for my often idiosyncratic purposes.

Neil cites a number of theorists, not all of whom write impenetrable academic prose. Drawing on diaspora theory, he rejects fixed notions of identity to embrace "change...as dynamic and productive, with identity 'traveling' and encountering [something—the object is not clear] along its complex 'routes' of diasporization...." He also draws upon Gloria Anzaldúa's contention that "identity is a 'kind of stacking or layering of selves, horizontal and vertical layers, the geography of selves made up of the different communities you inhabit....'"

One kind of "community" can be found in so-called "minority" languages spoken by those outside the dominant culture. This doesn't just apply to Spanish or Hmong or dozens of other languages spoken at home or among contemporaries.

Perhaps, I realized, the various comments on my chameleon-like character are the result of layers or various dialects I have added over the years. Or the various borders I have crossed.

My former colleague wasn't entirely wrong about characterizing me as "a good ol' Missouri boy," since I was raised in the middle of the state in the middle class. But that's not quite accurate, since my parents had migrated northeast from Kansas before I turned five, and for a long time we were regarded as outsiders. For much of that period we lived, and my sister and her husband still do, on the border between town and country, so that I grew up milking cows and slopping hogs, occasionally bucking hay bales, and doing various kinds of manual labor from which I was eager to escape.

Even then, I seemed to be more aware of borders than my contemporaries. For one thing, I traveled, sometimes alone, far more than they did. Not quite five, I was put on a train to Kansas to visit an aunt who then took me to New Mexico, an entirely different landscape. Five years later, I caught, alone, a bus for Indiana to visit my maternal grandparents. Later, partly out of loyalty to my birthplace but more, probably, out of perversity, I was a fan of University of Kansas teams instead of the University of Missouri, twenty-five miles away, and, because I had measles during the 1941 World Series, of the Brooklyn Dodgers rather than the St. Louis Cardinals, whose broadcasts were ubiquitous. When the Dodgers called up Jackie Robinson in 1947, I had to deal with expressions of the locals' by no means latent racism until I reached my present size.

A year or so after Robinson unsettled major league baseball and racial attitudes in general, I discovered the broadcasts of the New Orleans Jazz Club on WWL "from high atop the

Roosevelt Hotel" in New Orleans. Not all of the musicians featured were black, but I was able to expand my knowledge of and taste for a music so unfamiliar to my home town that, when I wanted to buy my first LP record (Louis Armstrong and His All-Stars), it had to be special ordered. About the same time, a contemporary had somehow discovered modern jazz, including Bebop, and that was another border to cross. (To realize how significant this was, you would have to know something about the vapid popular music of the late 1940s and early 1950s.)

So I was trying to become more sophisticated, though at the time I couldn't have used the term. I thought I was doing pretty well, having gotten a little and very useful training as a journalist and having read most of the Kansas City *Star* every day. Then I went to college in Kansas City and learned from my more urban if not more sophisticated classmates that I had an accent. I tried to shed that as fast as I could and was encouraged when a man from Kansas City (a sort of Irish-American Speedy Gonzales) said that I seemed pretty sharp for someone who wasn't raised there. I found a role as gadfly and campus character, a wit personality if not a wit, and tried to set myself apart from my contemporaries by educating them about jazz and books, of which I had a little knowledge, and about women, of which I had none. I also learned from my professors, sometimes reluctantly, about a still larger intellectual realm, so the orientation clichés about "education" coming etymologically from the Latin "leading out" or "drawing forth"—crossing borders—were justified in ways that the speakers wouldn't have recognized.

After a summer as a small-town reporter, a job I dimly realized I was over-qualifited for, I started graduate school at the University of Kansas, dropped into a group that was mostly older, some of them combat veterans of World War II or Korea, and far more attuned to the customs of the academic world. Years later, one man said that I and my best friend from college were regarded as golden boys, bright and athletic. That was even odder than being regarded as a cowboy, since I felt that I had to become earnest and hard-working for the first time in my life, using my father's example in ways he'd never imagined. This was another and in some ways a narrower world in which, as is often said, one learns more and more about less and less.

When I moved into the larger and more competitive graduate program at the University of Wisconsin, I was still so locked into the earnest mode that a woman I dated characterized my affect as that of "a very proper butler." I was trying to survive among people smarter and better educated—often more interesting than some of the big-name professors from whom I took courses. Again, more and more about less and less, with new definitions of conduct and success. On one occasion, though, I was seen as exotic by an East-Coast colleague, obviously gay even in those closeted times, who was so High Anglican that on feasts of Blessed Virgin, when no services were held at his church, he went to the Italian-American Roman Catholic parish, where the niches for statues were outlined by small light bulbs—in order to mortify his senses, he said. When he learned that I had actually done manual labor and worked up a sweat, he looked at me in wonder.

By this time, I had become bi-dialectal, if not bi-lingual, using the academic vocabulary and accent in the winter and the down-home version during summer vacation—what Neil Campbell might accept as a "minority language." Rarely did I trip up, but once, running a recreation program in a Madison, Wisconsin, suburb the first summer I spent out of Boonville, I switched accents—and discovered that the kids couldn't understand what I was saying.

All the while, I had the occasional uneasy, partly unconscious fear that someone would find out that I was a provincial rube who didn't really know anything. Years later, I discovered that many people feel that way, but I doubt that the knowledge would have consoled me then.

Toward the end of my doctoral program, I had some success, unexpected by anyone including me, and when I moved to my first full-time job at a larger version of my undergraduate school, I realized that my new colleagues had not crossed any number of borders. Most were from the Chicago area, with degrees from Chicago-area schools. With a few exceptions, they were not as bright and challenging as my contemporaries at Wisconsin. On one social occasion, I shocked some people by saying that I wanted to write as well as well-known critics like Edmund Wilson, Dwight Macdonald, and George Orwell.

But not until I moved to a branch of the University of California did I begin to realize that the earlier layers of my experience might be an advantage. One of my first students—who remained a friend for more than forty years—said that he respected me because I would explain something in a book not, as his other professors did, by referring to another book, but by my experience. Since I wasn't then aware that I had any, this seemed odd.

But over the years it's become clearer that I did have experience, at least of a kind rare in the academic world. Dealing with students at the University of Oklahoma who blamed their academic and social confusion in this new environment on the smallness of the high school they attended, I could say, truthfully, that my graduating class had seventeen people in it. My divorce drove me across a number of cultural as well as physical borders, and I acquired a whole new set of experiences in a delayed version of adolescence, free to explore emotionally as well as geographically. Challenged on political and social issues by students in Budapest, still nominally Communist in 1981, I said that I was far more of a worker than any of them. And like my Oklahoma-raised son, who discovered that, in Canada at least, he was exotic, I came to see that my past could be used to advantage, as when the students were struck by a professor in jeans who refused to be disconcerted by standard challenges.

At the end of my first stay in Europe, I was asked to lecture on Henry James's *The Bostonians* at the University of Paris—as strongly marked a border as I could imagine. In that novel, a Southern intellectual comes into conflict with a Northern bluestocking, and in discussing James's treatment of regional and gender differences, I remarked that the book was in a way the story of my life. Some members of the audience were astonished that a professor would draw upon his experience, but I seemed to get away with it, and after that decided that I had come to a place where I would never again have to apologize for or defend my background.

In fact, I had begun the process of understanding that moving between communities and languages, to go back to Neil Campbell's terms, can have shock value. Once, at my father's general store, a bulldozer operator said something snarky about my profession. I looked at him and said, "I could learn to do what you do in six weeks. You couldn't learn to do what I do in a hundred years." (When you call me that, smile.) Moving the other way, at a revue tracing the career of Bob Wills and the Texas Playboys, I startled a native Oklahoman from a small town by intoning "Ah-haah!" at the right point in a song. Another time, when a woman with a fake English accent said, on learning my profession, "Oh, no, I made a grammatical error in front of an English teacher," I replied "No shit?" Her shock and confusion cheered me a lot, and later I used the story to loosen up a group of gymnasium students in Slovenia whose headmistress had said that their grammar wasn't very good. During the early 1970s, a radical student pointed down the hall to the custodian sweeping it and said, "Don't despise that man!" Why would I, I answered. I used to do that kind of work. Two of my neighbors, skilled craftsmen, referred to me affectionately as "the hillbilly professor."

And the cowboy image recurred. The New York academic insisted that I dressed like a cowboy because, when we first met in the Philadelphia airport to catch a flight to Atlanta, she challenged my directions to the gate. "Well," I said, "you can do what you want, but if you want to get to Atlanta, you'd better follow me." Perhaps she thought I was Gary Cooper, though I prefer Paul Newman's line in *Hombre* answering a snooty Eastern woman's question of why she should pay attention to a man who is culturally Indian: "Because I can cut it, lady." Later, a visiting Canadian urged me to by a leather poncho at a garage sale and add a flat-brimmed hat and maybe a cigar. "Hell," I said, "my colleagues are already afraid that I'll challenge them to a shoot-out." A former graduate student said that her classmates were terrified of my taking over as director of the program because they felt that a new marshal had come to town. Well, I did start enforcing regulations, and a few students were delighted to know that there was some coherence and that they would get the same answers every time they raised the same question. And some appreciated my ability to face down academic bureaucrats.

Of course, I wasn't a cowboy or hillbilly, exactly, but I could use that perception to sand-bag people who thought so. Once, lunching at the Musso & Frank grill in Hollywood with a well-known biographer and a long-time Hollywood figure with whom I was working on a project, the biographer mentioned an interview he had done with Christopher Isherwood in *London Magazine* and wondered, rather condescendingly, if I'd heard of that journal. "I've published in it," I said. Pause. "*That's* where I've seen your name!" After that, he was very polite. In my more familiar academic world, I had become successful enough that many people didn't know that I had breathed any other kind of air. One colleague, from New York and a far more sophisticated background, used to come to me for information, leading with "Davis, you know stuff." One incoming colleague with whom I'd corresponded thought that, from my style, I must be an Englishman. (Well, some three hundred years removed.)

After I had written several drafts of this piece, I ran across an article about Sidney Weinberg, the architect of Goldman

Sachs' greatest success who ended his education after his public school days in Brooklyn. In the old days, Malcolm Gladwell says in "The Uses of Adversity" (*New Yorker*, November 10, 2008, p. 39), the path from rags to riches was possible, but in the late twentieth century, it was riches to riches. Why did Weinberg succeed? Because, Gladwell asserts, "there are...times and places where minorities benefit by asserting and even exaggerating their otherness." I'm not Jewish, and I never spoke Yiddish, but my provincial dialect has similarities to Yiddish as "the language of people who are interested, in [Yuri] Slezkine's words, in 'the maintenance of difference, the conscious preservation of the self and thus of strangeness.'"

In other words, I didn't invent this strategy, nor did I borrow it. But I can use it now because I was both lucky and attentive. The worst department chair I encountered once tried to reprimand me for questioning a decision not arrived at openly and when I was clearly not chastised, said rather plaintively, "I don't know why you have to pay attention to little things. You do such marvelous work." My reply—"I do marvelous work because I pay attention to everything"—ended the conversation. Because I can cut it, lady.

By this time it was clear to the chair as well as to most other people that I didn't care what labels were applied to me and that I could say what I wanted. I often heard the response, as I did when I told the Musso & Frank story, "You didn't say that, did you?" The man who thought I was "a good ol' Missouri boy" went on to tell his interviewer that I have "a reputation for frankness." That's kind enough.

Sometimes frankness works well. Several years after I told a temporary instructor that, contrary to what she was led to believe, there was no chance of her being hired permanently, she ran into my daughter and, on discovering who her father was, said that she was grateful because I was the only person who would tell her the truth.

Credit for that has to go to my mother. I thought that she taught me always to tell the truth. Later, after some unfortunate repercussions of telling truth to power, I realized that she had probably told me never to lie—a distinction that makes a real difference.

My candor may explain some of the comments I quoted at the beginning. Why am I black? Partly, perhaps, because I know something about black music and culture—a good deal, apparently, by most white standards, due to my memory for rhythms in music and language. Why am I colored or not like other white dudes? Perhaps because I am find other cultures interesting and because, coming from a kind of cultural periphery, I can sympathize with and to some degree understand their border crossings. Why, as another former student puts it, do I have the Europeans eating out of my hand? Perhaps it was, she thought, because I'm not stuffy. Perhaps it's because some of the good ol' boy layer emerges enough to surprise very different kinds of people and put them at ease. Perhaps interviewing techniques I learned in my abortive journalism career taught me how to ask a question and listen to the answer—and to seem to understand and be interested in it. Perhaps it's because I pay, or try to pay, attention to everything. Perhaps it's because, as a Bangladeshi writer said, "You're the least politically correct person I ever met!" As I told the American Indian writer about a colleague I described as being in her "holy Indian" mode, "I'm equal opportunity. I believe that a member of a minority has the right to be as full of shit as anybody else." That's a right I also reserve for myself. And that seems, sometimes, to be both refreshing and reassuring.

At least to some people, enough to make my life interesting, who share my particular attitude toward life and experience. My Chinese-American friend and I share a taste for what, in the 1960s, was called Black Humor. His son's mother says that the boy has decided that his father, Ishmael Reed, and I are the same person who shows up in different colors: We're big, noisy, and know a lot. A gay Mvskoke writer and I were the only ones to laugh and frown in the right places at a Sherman Alexie reading while everyone else was listening in politically correct attitudes, and later he was grateful that I understood what his novel was doing when the gay press was dismissing it. Several people recognized the affinity between a Slovenian writer and me, the kind I've experienced with writers from Slovakia and Hungary, including one who, a few minutes into an interview, tore up his prepared résumé because he realized that we could talk as human beings. Or the Slovenian gymnasium student who asked a provocative question, got a counter-thrust he hadn't expected, and came up to acknowledge a kindred spirit. To adapt Kipling, "there is neither East nor West, Border, nor Breed, nor Birth, When two smartasses stand face to face, tho' they come from the ends of the earth!" Thus, when a textbook representative told me that the department chair of a small school had said, "That Davis is a smart son of a bitch. But he is smart," I decided that it would make a good epitaph. A friend said that no one would put that on a tombstone, but I have a nephew, a very subtle smartass, who sells tombstones and can hardly wait to do the inscription.

My reaction is easier to understand by way of Mikhail Bakhtin's view that crossing borders, or looking at something from more than one point of view—dialogically—can develop the sense of humor that "demolishes fear and piety before an object, before a world, making of it an object of familiar contact...." That's a good description of what one of my former professors called my lack of a sense of reverence. Like a joke, you either get it or you don't.

Finding people who get it, wherever they may be, is one of the things that keeps me going, and these people form a mostly virtual community which I cherish and try to foster. As a Hungarian friend said in a letter of recommendation, I seem to think that everyone I know ought to know everyone else I know as if attempting to create a new community.

Perhaps my friends have some idea of who I am and where, psychologically, I live. I hate to disagree with Neil Campbell, who, before I read his stimulating book, had reviewed my *The Ornamental Hermit: People and Places of the New West* in very kind terms. He thought that it was "about identity and belonging, about the desire to find a 'home' in a world of homelessness...." I think that he was more correct when, in his book, he quoted Marc Augé: "people are always, and never, at home...[and] the frontier zones...no longer open on to totally foreign worlds." In those terms, I belong everywhere and nowhere, but I don't feel the need of an identity because I seem to be making it up as I go along. In a sense, to use characters from Evelyn Waugh's novels, I began as Paul Pennyfeather, the innocent ingénue who ends where he began, safe in his Oxford womb, and ended (at least in the view of some of my less mobile acquaintances) as the peripatetic Basil Seal, of whom it's said "No one minds him being rude, but he's so teaching."

There have been a lot of routes, and I hope to follow more. But I always come back to roots. My colleague was kind enough to testify to my "very solid core of integrity and intellectual honesty." I've discovered that this isn't necessarily an advantage in the academic world or anywhere else, but I hope that's true. If it is, it comes less from years of academic training than from my family's values, expressed far more by example than in words, an example that continues to be reinforced by my siblings. Along with that came the confidence expressed, as an in-law put it in exasperation, "The trouble with you Davises is that you think you can do stuff better than anybody else!" Or to adapt the Hollywood remark about sincerity, confidence is the most important thing. And if you don't have it, fake it.

Looking at identity issues more generally, I remember the Slovak writer Pavel Velikovsky's contention that someone can be Central European without ever having been in Central Europe; conversely, people born there cannot, in spirit, be Central European. A similar distinction might be applied to being American. I don't want to label less flexible people as not being "real Americans," but those like the woman whose remark I quoted at the beginning seem to be Americans by the letter rather than the spirit, no matter how many physical borders they have crossed.

Routes

Fork It

When you get to a fork in the road, take it.
—*Yogi Berra*

Years ago, at a backyard wedding of a young colleague, a graduate student assembled an impromptu combo and allowed me to sing a couple of blues numbers, a performance that he called "screaming in C." After I left the microphone to dance and mingle, an attractive woman asked, "Aren't you sorry you didn't do that?" Instead, I gathered, of becoming a college professor. I was flattered by her attention and appreciation; only later did I begin to think about various paths I could have taken to have had a very different kind of life—or lives.

Some paths were chosen for me—not just genetically but consciously. When my parents were asked about double promoting me from first to third grade, they could have refused. Had they done so, I would have stayed with my age group and might have been socially less awkward, physically less accessible to playground bullies, and slightly more successful as a high school athlete. But no matter how hard I worked, I was never going to be recruited by even the smallest college; a sudden growth spurt at fourteen or so lifted me above my classmates and made me a dangerous target; and when I got to college the age difference was no longer a factor. More important was the fact that I was able to finish a year of college before I turned eighteen and had to register for the draft. That meant that I did not have to take the test then required of those seeking student deferments. The U.S. was still fighting the Korean War, and had I been forced to take the math test, I might now be eligible to join the Veterans of Foreign Wars.

Another choice I didn't get to make was what instrument to play in the school band. I don't know how instruments were assigned, but my father got a good deal on a used trombone. I really wanted a saxophone because even in the jazz-deprived local environment, I could hear that the sax could swing and the trombone, even as played by Tommy Dorsey, couldn't. (If you doubt me, listen to his attempt on "The Lady is a Tramp" versus the lyric solo in "Song of India.") As soon as my parents allowed me to, I stopped taking lessons and then eased out of band onto the basketball team, which everyone agreed was much more important. As it turned out, athletics never led anywhere profitable, but had I been able to play music I liked with an instrument I liked, I might have stuck with it rather than merely envying Coleman Hawkins and Charlie Parker. (Sun Ra and Pharaoh Sanders, not so much.)

College offered another road not taken. My mother seemed always to assume that I would be the first person in my direct family to go to college—Dad regarded it as her area—and since I wanted to be a newspaper man (I'd never heard the term "journalist"), I assumed that I would go to the oldest journalism school in the country, twenty-five miles up the road at the University of Missouri. I'd gone to a workshop for high school students the summer after my junior year, and the following summer I was approached about joining a couple of fraternities. My immediate future path seemed clear.

At what seemed like and probably was the last minute, Mom discovered that Rockhurst College—now called "a liberal arts college in the Jesuit tradition" because they've run short of Jesuits—offered a partial scholarship for valedictorians from Catholic high schools. So off I went, to a much more structured dormitory experience (good from my parents' perspective and, at this distance, from mine), a liberal rather than vocational education, and at least a start towards becoming a rootless bohemian intellectual rather than a roving reporter. And in Kansas City, Missouri, much larger and farther from home than

Columbia, I was free to explore a real city without guides or (mostly bad) peer influences.

Still, when I graduated I applied for jobs as a reporter in a couple of small Kansas towns and got one in Great Bend. Forty years later, back in Kansas City to promote my book on my Rockhurst years on local television, I stood with my surviving English professor and the newspaper moderator on the balcony of Union Station looking north towards the Kansas City *Star* building. I said, "I wonder what would have happened if, instead of going to Great Bend, I'd applied for a job there? I could have been a good journalist."

He agreed, but he didn't know the real reason I'd left Kansas City. If I'd stayed, I would probably have married my only serious college girlfriend, and I somehow knew that this would close off any number of roads.

The Great Bend job was so boring that it was easy to choose the next road that led to graduate school at the University of Kansas and forty-five years as an English teacher. One minor fork showed up there—a colleague from Great Bend called to invite me to apply for a job as sports editor at a southwestern Missouri town. I was flattered that he thought me competent, but in the first place I was beginning to find my feet as a graduate student and in the second it was my ex-girlfriend's home town.

After two years at Kansas, I had to decide whether to go on for a Ph.D., and where. Fortunately, a branch of the University of Tennessee didn't offer me a teaching job, so I went on the University of Wisconsin. That was perhaps more a jog rather than a fork in the road, but it was like moving from AAA baseball to the major leagues. For one thing, as the narrator of Mark Harris's novel *The Southpaw* learns, when you get to the big leagues, you got to learn to get eat out in a big league way. Everything came at me faster and trickier, but it made me more alert if not stronger, and I learned as much—probably more—from my peers as I did from all but one of my professors, who like the manager in Harris's novel, might have been very human in the off-season, or anyway in the very remotest part.

One was so human that, not far into the semester, he had a breakdown and his seminar had to be cancelled. The students were asked to put down the name of an author they'd like to study in order to be given independent study courses by various faculty members. I wrote the name of Evelyn Waugh, and though that's another and complicated story, the decision has affected my life for more than half a century.

When I went on the market for my first full time job, I had several offers, fairly common in those fat days of the academic marketplace. Some came from schools that were too small; some from schools too remote for someone still working on a dissertation married to a woman with even better academic credentials who also needed a job. That meant the Loyola University of Chicago for me and the adjoining Catholic girls' school for her at more money than a contemporary got from Yale. The ethos and atmosphere seemed reassuringly like Rockhurst's; the new colleagues were friendly and encouraging and, on closer acquaintance, less and less intimidating and therefore less challenging.

After two years, a completed dissertation, and my wife's sudden unemployment, I was ready to move to a department that would allow me more time for research and more interesting colleagues. Again, I had a choice, and the University of California-Santa Barbara offered me more money and a better place to raise children than the University of Southern California. I took the job expecting to make two moves, but the second came more quickly for me and for most of my cadre than we expected. I could have stayed at least for a while, but I didn't want to walk around shaking a bell and mumbling, "Unclean! Unclean!" So I went on the market—still good enough for me to get a serious offer at a larger salary at the University of Oklahoma, where I stayed for thirty-three years. It wasn't a dead end, though I occasionally tried to find a road out—some good stories about that—to find that the market had crashed.

Once established at OU—not difficult in those days—I had to make choices among scholarly projects. A solicited offer to compile a bibliography of the modern English novel was at first tempting, but a cost-benefit analysis made it easy to turn down. So was the offer to become executive secretary of a minor professional organization (a job occupied successively by two Wisconsin contemporaries). Other choices turned out to be professionally fruitful and personally satisfying.

From that, most of my important choices were personal rather than professional. Most important was the decision to defer—essentially to refuse—to go to marriage counseling. Thirty years later, I stand by the choice. Counseling would have bought some time, but the relationship was in a death spiral, and both of us have clearly been better off apart.

After the divorce, I realized, as Graham Greene wrote to his estranged wife, that I was "profoundly antagonistic to ordinary domestic life" or, as someone warned a woman I was dating, "He's not domesticated." Freed from the burden of home ownership—I hoped never to own or even to touch another lawn mower—I spent twenty years as a nomad, my departmental office increasingly used as a mail drop and book repository. A colleague looked around it and said, "Clearly this is the office of a single man," with comfortable chair and decent sound equipment. Given the choice of fostering a relationship or leaving the country, I left. The most promising and most frequently revived one ended, at least on my end, when, at two a.m. in Bratislava, I realized that I could not survive a move to her city, on her turf, immersed in the complicated and repetitive details of her family's life.

After I took the road out of Oklahoma for the last time—a choice made without a pang, since I'd long wanted to live in the Southwest—I finally bought a house (minimal maintenance, no yard, easy to lock up and leave) near my oldest child and began to construct a new life out of the viable parts of the old. My first emotional entanglement ended abruptly because, as she complained, "You have the strongest barriers of anyone I've known." In other words, I wouldn't choose her road.

Looking back at most of the roads I've chosen, I can see that I picked them because they seemed to offer possibility rather than finality. I've accepted, even embraced, some limitations—grandfathering in ways I never anticipated, entering a partnership loose enough to give both of us freedom as well as intimacy. And, having outlasted the Biblical life expectancy, I realize that choices will diminish even further, that all forks lead to a dead end. Still, I see no need, as long as there's a choice, to put my head into a cul-de-sac.

And though I wonder how my life might have turned out had I chosen different roads, I have no serious regrets and no complaints at all because I would probably have lived as comfortably as most Americans of my time and class, which is quite comfortably indeed. As it is, I've done pretty well and could well have done worse. When the attractive woman apologized for asking why I didn't regret not becoming a singer, the answer came easily: "Given what I know of my character, I'd have been dead a time long ago." Perhaps I have never known enough of myself to satisfy the ancient Greeks, but, as Dirty Harry advises, I do have some sense of my limitations.

By-Ways

Over the past few decades, I've driven back and forth across the US and parts of Canada—not all at once—so many times that 500 miles often got me to afternoon coffee break. Whatever sentiment I attached to roads, particularly to overhyped ones like Route 66, long ago dissipated.

On the other hand, I'm not wedded to Interstates or blue highways or the ones identified by more than two numbers. To get to destinations I have traveled to so frequently that, as my mother used to say, "The telephone poles wave at me," I've used any route that MapQuest could imagine and some, like farm to market roads at right angles to each other in west Texas, that would drive the nagging road-Nazi voice in my new GPS to chant "Recalculating."

This kind of travel has the advantage of reminding me that, whatever the demographics, I live in a country that remains rural and, by European standards, relatively empty. In some ways, it's getting emptier, as one can see in the farmhouses abandoned because mechanized agriculture doesn't need as many workers or because, with improved roads, farmers can commute from town.

I've decided that it's not possible for me to "read the landscape," as some people put it, because I suspect that many people lack the vocabulary to give precise description of the topography, and everything subsumed by that term, as well as the economic, social, even cultural factors involved. When I'm driving, I respond to landscape as I do to music, technically uninformed, responding to the rhythms as the terrain rises and falls or changes from cropland to grazing land to desert and back, noting almost unconsciously the disappearance of saguaro cactus as I would the muting of strings or percussion and the swelling of bravura passages in canyon walls or twenty-mile vistas. Rarely do I stop to admire a view, just as I don't pause a CD track to repeat a passage.

Perhaps because I'm a townsman, it's easier to respond in more specific ways to more populous areas, even the ones that aren't all that populous. And, I realize, the responses vary, partly due to size and location. And on whether I have or can make up a story about it.

Even on the interstates, I've become familiar with towns that have, over various trips, come to be seen as oases. On my first road trip east, I pulled off I-70, weary from the battering of the wind from the open windows—no air-conditioning—at Richmond, Indiana, near the Indiana-Ohio border. I chose it partly for convenience, partly because it had a back-story for me: the jazz musician Bix Beiderbecke had recorded there in the 1920s. The town has a number of motels and restaurants just off I-70, and in the 1980s even had a movie theater in a strip mall near where I stayed, and a pleasant enough main street leading into the center of town, though I missed the rose festival advertised between the interstate district and downtown. But I don't stop there anymore because once I had a car with a/c, I could blow through it as far as the Cleveland suburbs. But I still feel affection for it.

The same for Burley, Idaho, the first town of reasonable size north of the Utah border. I've stayed there for some of the same reasons I like Richmond—and I remember it because, on a ferry to Victoria, British Columbia, a man admired my cargo pants and asked where I got them. "On sale at the K-Mart in Burley, Idaho," I said. Now the K-Mart is gone, and the pants don't fit anymore, but I have a fond memory of Burley even if I never stay there again. Just over the Idaho border on I-84, Ontario, Oregon, has been a pleasant stop I've recommended to friends, but I don't have any stories about it and won't stay there again unless I get a late start from Seattle.

I probably will keep stopping in Panguitch, Utah, which I discovered years ago, partly because it's a decent day's drive from Phoenix and partly because it has an odd kind of charm that Kanab, to the south, lacks, at least for me. Kanab passed a "natural family" resolution widely seen as homophobic, and a counter person in the Dairy Queen put his thumb in my milkshake cup and couldn't see anything wrong with that. But a young Mormon woman in Panguitch made a pot of coffee for me even though she had no reasonable prospects of selling more than one cup. There are charming late nineteenth century brick houses and a restaurant with really good barbecue and the start of a lovely drive up Highway 89 along a river valley. Of course, Panguitch has some of these amenities because it lies near three spectacular national parks, but it succeeds in not really looking like a tourist town.

Sometimes a town can be memorable because I really needed it, like Artesia, New Mexico, which loomed out of the night at the end of a long, icy highway. I'm fonder of that place than I am of Van Horn, Texas, about two hours east of El Paso. Until I got a late start headed out from Fort Worth to Phoenix on a grey winter day, I had never heard of it. Nothing about Midland or Odessa inclined me to stop there, and a shabby gas station in Big Spring didn't make me want to stop any longer than I had to. Pecos wouldn't put me far enough to make the next day's drive reasonable, and nothing in the bleak landscape tempted me to slow down, so Van Horn seemed the obvious choice. The motel I chose was cheap enough, and it was too dark to see much of the town even if I hadn't been too tired to explore. Later, on a trip east, I got there before sunset and had time to drive around. The best food I could find was at a truck stop, and the town, putting it as kindly as possible, did not seem at all attractive. Now, I find that just over half of the inhabitants have a high school education. (That's according to city-data.com, which also notes that 0.7% of all households are lesbian couples and 0.4% are gay males, which must be lonesome for them). Basically, it's a hell of a long way from anywhere else, but that makes it more like a real oasis than any of the towns I find more attractive. So I'm glad it's there.

Other towns have tempted me to leave the interstate to explore them, even when I haven't needed to spend the night. One of these is Baker City, Oregon, the first green spot north of the Snake River Valley, and the first place that may have made the pioneers on the Oregon Trail think that the trip might have been worth it. When I finally stopped there, I discovered that it has a Grand Hotel, formerly the best between Salt Lake City and Seattle—it serves a good lunch in pleasant surroundings—and some interesting nineteenth century and a couple of official-looking art deco buildings. Still, the panoramic view of the town sticks more in my imagination than the close-ups. (Pendleton, up the interstate, in a wider view looks dry and unattractive.)

Sometimes, my motive for exiting is curiosity. That's the case with Thoreau, New Mexico, just east of the Continental Divide and the exit that tries to be a tourist trap with souvenirs and one dilapidated gas station. Mostly it's the name that attracted me—pronounced with the accent on the last syllable, like kangaroo—and the contrast in landscape and vegetation with Henry David's Walden so glaring that Henry might have to think his reaction to nature as, Aldous Huxley argued in "Wordsworth in the Tropics," William would have if plunked down in a tropical jungle. The town, refreshingly non-tourist and largely Navajo, has no facilities just off the highway. A little way in, you can find basic services—food, mail, churches, health services. But on my one visit, I couldn't see any place to buy clothes or shoes. It does have suburbs, after a fashion, with Indian kids riding bikes, one with training wheels, followed by a dog. To those tired of franchised kitsch, it's an interesting place to drive around in, but probably one visit is enough.

The same is true of Grants, New Mexico, although it's more Hispanic than Indian without any clear cultural markers.

I usually stop there for gas either off the interstate or after joining it from the route through the Zuni Pueblo. I've driven through it once on old Route 66 in an attempt to see where they keep the 8800 people promised by the census. Couldn't see any obvious answer, but a clerk at a truck stop said that most of them are in prison. Even that turns out not to be true: prison accounts for about 300 people.

But at least Grants has had a minor population increase in recent years, partly due to the revival of uranium mining, though nowhere near the boom days of the Cold War, and partly due to the fact that I-40 runs right by it. Towns, especially smaller ones, off the interstate grid have not fared so well. Floydada, Texas, a town I've passed through many times, has lost over 11% of its population in recent years. My only reasons for remembering it are that I surprised my son-in-law by being able to spell the name, which he'd run across in a James McMurtry CD, and for the story about twenty Pentecostals who believed that the Devil was going to destroy the town, packed themselves tightly into a car and fled towards Louisiana, at which point they decided that the Devil had cursed their clothes, which they removed before piling back into the car, then crashing into a tree and being taken into custody. (Chris Stuart wrote a song, "Twenty Naked Pentecostals in a Pontiac"; see *http://www.skeptictank.org/nakedps.htm*.)

Otherwise, towns of that size don't interest me much, probably because I come from one a little larger and find them not different enough to strike my imagination. That's true of many places where Main Street is the highway—too many to mention. The exceptions strike me because they represent the least common denominator of urbanity. Guthrie, Texas, seat of King County, has fewer than 300 people, too small to support a Dairy Queen—almost unprecedented in Texas—but it does have a library and a courthouse and, the last time I passed through, a couple of gas stations. One has a restaurant and carries snacks and supplies—but not, at least in summer, Hershey bars because they would melt in a room without air conditioning. But you can see real cowboys, since Guthrie is the headquarters of the 6666 Ranch. For some reason, the minimalism appeals to me.

Matador, Texas, to the northwest, is larger but semi-minimalist because the town square has never filled in on one side. It used to have a movie theater, but it's closed. Signs of decay like this or the front of the burnt-out school in Oklahoma—Faxon? Olustee?—have a poignancy unmatched even by empty storefronts or rows of antique shops in fading towns bypassed or never on newer transportation modes. Still, Matador is doing better than Goldfield, Nevada, which, though it is the seat of Esmeralda County (total population about 1200), has so far declined from its peak population of 20,000 or so during the early twentieth century gold boom that it is unincorporated—a condition which, along with its designation as a living ghost town, makes it unusual if not unique.

Some towns add layers as times and modes of transportation change. The oldest part of Las Vegas, New Mexico, much of it adobe or territorial architecture, centered on the Santa Fe Trail. Then the Santa Fe Railroad came through and gave rise to a Victorian-era boom in brick commercial buildings and elaborate frame residences for the growing Anglo population. Now I-25 passes east of the town, and the last time I was there, it was so difficult to access gas stations and convenience stores that I can't imagine any but travelers desperately needing pit stops bothering to exit.

That's easier to do in Tucumcari, New Mexico, and most travelers may not realize that the businesses just off I-40 are the outer ring of development. A few, seeing restaurants or cheaper old motels, may drive down what was once Route 66 and view the decaying buildings that once served the tourist trade. But I didn't realize until I'd stopped there more than a dozen times that there's an inner ring along the railroad, still further decayed or providing services that only residents use or even know about.

Some bypassed towns try to reinvent themselves as destinations. My home town, Boonville, Missouri, where Main Street used to be US 40, is now several miles from I-70. To compensate, it seems to have some kind of festival every month, if not week, and may be reduced to having a "Festival Festival" to attract visitors. It's a great place to raise kids, most of whom leave as soon as they can. But one could argue that the city fathers and mothers must be doing something right, since the population has increased 35% since I left in the 1950s, partly by becoming a bedroom town for Columbia, twenty-five miles away, and partly by sucking banks and other businesses from smaller towns in the county.

Other towns have had mixed luck. Branson, Missouri, has had so much success—motto: "You thought our entertainers were dead"—that most native Missourians won't go near the place because of traffic and bee-hive hairdo congestion. Some towns, lacking space and other resources, are more user-friendly. Jerome, Arizona, is a good example: a decayed mining town, it has restaurants, craftspeople, and specialty shops along its one major street winding down the mountainside. Rumor has it that the marshal refused to arrest a nude woman bicycle-rider for being offensive because he wasn't offended. I don't know how that would play in Sedona, home of New Agers, intergalactic vortices, and gucchied merchandise—sort of like Santa Fe without the culture and history. One has the feeling that real, if sometimes unconventional, people live in Jerome, or perhaps I have a preference for funk.

Like Moab, Utah, and Blackwater, Missouri, which I've written about elsewhere, and Gagetown, New Brunswick, which lost its importance when traffic on the Saint John River ended, Jerome has succeeded in re-inventing itself. All of these towns interest me far more than towns that are wholly or partially invented, like Green Valley and Sedona in Arizona, results of developers' very disparate visions.

In fact, I distrust places that have had too much publicity. I've always preferred Albuquerque to Santa Fe because it seems more real to me, partly because the architecture is messier and more various, not strait-jacketed into conformity to an artificial vision of what Santa Fe was supposed to have looked like. If I can help it, I won't go to Las Vegas, Nevada, or ever again to Leavenworth, Washington, a cuckoo-clock inspired monument to German kitsch.

Perhaps over the years I anticipated photographer Andrew Cross's his "anti-travel programme" which foregrounds "the relationship between the objects of travel and the experience of travel," presenting shots of motel signs, overpasses, and intersections in his book to show "other kinds of landscapes which are otherwise considered irrelevant." (See *http://www.andrewcross.co.uk/website/book_along_some.html* for examples from his book *Along Some American Highways*.) As I have indicated throughout this essay, I share his interest in the process rather than the destination, though I prefer "anti-tourist" to "anti-traveler."

But even more important to me, in a way, are the places I don't go. Driving along US 54 in Kansas last summer, I passed a number of towns whose main streets lie at angles to the highway. Over and over, as I have been at other times on other roads, I was tempted to turn down the Main Street to see what the town looked like.

Why was I attracted? Perhaps it was because, as a boy, I spent time with an uncle and aunt in Otterville, Missouri, a village with sidewalks only in front of a two-block commercial district, and at least at my relatives' house, no indoor plumbing. It was a kind of refuge from pressures on a sometimes confused and lonely boy. Later, traveling with my father's driver to help deliver produce to grocery stories, I was in and out of villages all over my county and into some adjoining ones. All seemed miniature versions of my home town, a relative metropolis, simpler and more manageable by my limited experience and imagination.

Focused on reaching the end of that stage of a 10,000-mile journey, I didn't turn down any of these by-ways, not even the one to Haviland, Kansas, which promised home-made bakery goods and fresh coffee. Nor, years earlier, did I turn down the street to Eldorado, Oklahoma, even when my bi-coastal passenger said that the most elegant woman he'd ever met came from there.

What would I have seen in any of these towns? Perhaps, in the best cases, a place free from erosion caused by demographic and economic shifts, tidy, with modest prosperity. In others, like some of the villages in my home county, perhaps an unmistakable bank building, no doubt converted to other uses or boarded up. Some brick two-story buildings occupied, if at all, on the first floor by a general store or an antique store. At most two gas stations, one whose pumps have been removed to scrap yards or museums chronicling how it used to be. Other store buildings, like my uncle's successive feed store and lumber yard, homes to spiders and dust or like my grandfather's general store in Florence, Missouri, full of stored materials that no one will ever use.

Would the sights down these main streets have pleased or depressed me at signs of a youth I had left behind? Better to sustain the illusion. Better still not to Google the town's name and find precipitate population decline or very modest growth. Better not to have too much information, like that about Barclay College in Haviland, a Friends Bible school with fewer than 200 students who probably find the bakery a refuge from the earnestness demanded by the catalogue.

Best, perhaps, to sustain the illusion and to take comfort in the fact that, unlike the Hotel California in the Eagles song, you can always leave.

BREATHING THE AIR

A large part of the charm of unfamiliar small towns is that it's easy to enter and leave without getting out of the car to feel, as the demented priest says in Scott Fitzgerald's "Absolution," "the heat and the sweat and the life," should there be much evidence of the last, and still get a fair sense of the place.

Probably it will be like the fictional country with the real name in Donald Barthelme's "Paraguay," which has only one of everything. A real city—in my definition one that has either a metro or the vestiges of a medieval wall or buildings dating before the American Revolution or, preferably, all three—has dozens of everything.

But merely going to a city doesn't mean that you can breathe the air. I made my first trips to New York and Chicago in order to attend scholarly conferences, and it's inaccurate to say that I visited either because I got, at most, a few blocks from the conference hotel. At least I didn't until I got more blasé about conferences and began to leave the security and confinement of the conference to walk around or take trams to explore on my own, as when I caught a cable car in San Francisco and experienced a lifting of the heart as it crested the last hill and I saw the Bay. Even better, I sometimes was able to splice up to a week's vacation onto a business trip and become really familiar with a city and all it had to offer

There are other kinds of bubble, like the one I entered on the only bus tour I've ever taken, to insulate me from the myriad sights, smells, sounds, and movement that jumble together to create a sense of a city. On the tour, I was herded in and out of a bus with forty other tourists, told where to look and when to move, all the while in an encapsulated version of middle-class America.

I don't regret taking the tour because it allowed me to cover more ground more cheaply and efficiently than I could have done on my own. But my sharpest memories come from the times when I burst the bubble. In Barcelona, I skipped an optional dinner and flamenco performance and extended the free day to find more Gaudi work and to walk, alone, down La Rambla, seeing and hearing freely and indiscriminately. Later, avoiding another flamenco performance in Seville, I bought an empanada and bottle of water at a bodega and ate it while sitting by the Guadalquivir River. Then I went into a shop that sold Sargadelos ceramics by artists I'd met in Santiago de Compostela and had a pleasant if inconclusive talk with the clerk in my fractured Spanish and her slightly more coherent English.

On the other hand, both the conventions and the tour, like speaking engagements across North America and Europe, didn't just confine me; they provided a base to leave and return to. So finding breathing room involves a balance between security and strangeness. I'm still subject to low-grade panic in a new city until I find a map to orient me physically and learn the basic public transportation routes.

For example, on my first trip to Zagreb, I was given a tram ticket and minimal directions to a book fair on the outskirts of town and even sketchier advice on how to get back to the hotel from which my host had temporarily departed. I was carrying at least three kinds of money, but I hadn't been able to find a way to get Croatian kuna. Without money, any idea of where to get dinner, or any knowledge of Croat, I felt very insecure.

Then I remembered that I'd been told to get off at the tram stop across the boulevard from the central bus station. It was almost certain to have a currency exchange even if it didn't have an ATM. It did have a cash dispenser—no fear of a language barrier—as well as the kind of restaurants one would expect in a bus station, better, in fact, than one would find in the U.S.

My second trip to Zagreb, for a writers' conference, was more structured. Meals were laid on; we were given an information packet that included a map and an extensive guide to the city that included a number of photographs in case we couldn't read English; and a guide from the hotel to the conference site and back, dismissed when we could orient ourselves.

There was one disquieting moment when the tram hung a right well short of its usual turn. As I learned later, the normal route was closed to allow pedestrians to flood the main street and celebrate the hundredth anniversary of the city's electrical service. I have learned that when you're disoriented, the best thing to do is stop, so I got off the tram and easily found my way on foot. That walk and a stroll through the old town and the market with a Russian writer are far more memorable than any of the readings at the conference, including my own.

The Russian and I only got moderately lost because dead-end streets cut us off from the direct route to our destination. But I had a map and could read it—apparently a rarer skill than one might think. I've loved maps since I was in grade school. Unlike Joseph Conrad's Marlow in *Heart of Darkness*, I wasn't drawn to blank spots but to some place I'd never been (the only kind I saw on maps until I was almost grown). But like him, someday I wanted to go there, to a place where things were different and exciting.

Years later, I did. Sometimes I surprised the locals. I told my guide in Frankfurt by saying that, on a free day, I'd walked from my pension to the zoo. "You can't do that!" she said. But I had, partly because I didn't want to figure out the metro system for a one-time trip. Getting around Belgrade was more challenging because I couldn't read the street signs in Cyrillic script, but a pattern is a pattern, and as a part-time country boy, I can usually tell north from south.

As I gained some experience as a traveler, I began to notice other patterns, like ATMs in bus stations. And basic common sense. In Bratislava, my host pointed to a bi-level bridge over the Danube and said that one was for trains, the other for cars. "Trains on the bottom," I said. In wonder, he said, "You know everything!" "No," I said, "but unless the Communist Party discovered a new principle of physics, it makes sense to put the heavier load on the bottom."

At some point, I began to see not just sights and local patterns but larger structures. Standing on a corner in New York looking down one of the avenues, I realized that the city was an astonishing entity because so many things had to go right, and at the right times, for it to work at all.

That's true, of course, of any kind of human organization, from an ad hoc committee through a village to a vast metropolis. Any one of these is like a poem, from haiku to epic. Naturally some are more artful and impressive than others, but that they exist at all is a marvel of human ingenuity.

Borders

In the years I visited the Phoenix area regularly, I didn't exactly feel that there was no 'there there', but I did have trouble believing that at any moment I was in a particular place. The city and its many suburbs had merged so thoroughly that I never knew whether I was in Tempe or Scottsdale or Mesa—a city larger than St. Louis but undifferentiated from its neighbors for anyone who isn't a Mormon or a Chicago Cubs fan. Anyplace might have been, and to some extent still is, anyplace else.

Until I moved to Sun Lakes, a community for "mature adults" at the extreme southern edge of the metroplex, I hadn't been aware of any distinct borders in the area, but suddenly I was living on one. My reservation for old people butts against another kind of reservation, the Gila River Indian Community (afterwards GRIC). That's an ethnic border, but it is also political since Maricopa County ends just south of Sun Lakes and Pinal County begins just north of the reservation.

These facts were pressed on me during my first encounter with residents of Sun Lakes. They complained about young Indians coming across the border to steal cars, for fun rather than profit, which they then trashed and abandoned on the desert. Because of jurisdictional barriers—federal/state, different counties—it was almost impossible to catch offenders or to prosecute them if they were caught.

My future neighbors weren't just succumbing to white racist paranoia. That can never be entirely discounted, and it surfaced in complaints about casino payouts, disgust at failures to meet Anglo standards of neatness, and resentment of Indian nation sovereignty and its various ramifications. When I mentioned a few things I knew about Indians from living thirty-five years in Oklahoma and various other sources, someone wanted to know why I was so interested in Indians. Because they are interesting, I said, though I didn't voice the thought that they are a hell of a lot more interesting than your sort.

As I learned more about both communities, I saw that, like many borders, this one could seem more like a mirror than a barrier. The Saint John River dividing Maine from New Brunswick is a good example. Someone with a poor sense of direction and out of sight line to a post office might not know which side of the river he was on. That's less obvious in my slice of Arizona because south of the reservation border the population is just over ninety-seven percent Indian—dark, stocky, relatively quiet. To the north we're white by two thousands of a percent more than the reservation is Indian, pear-shaped, and noisily opinionated, mostly along the lines of Fox News.

Other differences might be expected. The poverty rate on the reservation is about fifteen times that in Sun Lakes, where the median income is about two and a half times that on the reservation. Although the population of the two communities is about equal, population density on the nearly six hundred square mile GRIC is 24 per square mile—not surprising for a people who have, since European contact, and almost certainly centuries before, lived in small groups—while that in Sun Lakes is more than ten times as high—and double even that of Sacaton, the largest population center on the reservation.

But there are some structural similarities. Both areas, the reservation by various acts of Congress, Sun Lakes by what the developer could afford to buy, have clear boundaries, and both have clearly defined qualifications for residency. Both populations are underemployed, though the figures are skewed in the case of Sun Lakes—about one-fifth of the GRIC rate—through lack of education and opportunity on the one hand and generous retirement packages on the other, since retirees don't count in the figures. Both draw significant income from government checks. Both have high incidences of drug dependency, mostly illegal to the south, mostly prescribed to the north, though people on both sides have sources over the Mexican border. Both have endemic health problems—diabetes as a result of desert peoples' reaction to Anglo foods like white flour and cooking oil; various kinds of systemic breakdown for Anglos (in the Southwest, a term that includes anyone who isn't clearly Indian or Hispanic).

Both depend on outsiders whose language isn't theirs—the Indians for medical and social service personnel, mostly white, the Anglos for maintenance and landscaping by Hispanics in Sun Lakes. Neither community does much direct yard work. To the south, the yards can't even be called xeriscaped because they look like untouched desert. To the north, gravel raked and plants tended by Spanish-speaking crews dominate except where green patches, mostly golf courses, try to ignore rainfall figures and common sense. To be fair, the Hohokam, probably the ancestors of the Akimel O'odam (called Pimas by Europeans, a practice I will follow), constructed irrigation systems that silted up and now survive in the grid of modern canals. Anglos try not to think of the Hohokams' fate.

Some borders are easier to cross than others. Physically that's not a problem in this case. Indians and Sun Lakers meet, though they don't mingle, at the supermarket closest to both communities. Although the Indians are generally wider and often accompanied by children, they take up less space than the whites, and they complain a lot less.

But psychologically, or perhaps it's anthropologically, the line seems difficult to cross. I can't speak for the Indians, but I can extrapolate from what I see in Sun Lakes Anglos and to a degree in myself. Hunt Highway—which dead ends at the west boundary of Sun Lakes—is the border, and going south one enters a different world. Sun Lakes is fenced, cultivated, the houses following strict rules about paint colors, additions, yard maintenance (no weeds or obviously *trouvé* objects) laid out by the homeowners' association and enforced by roving inspectors.

If the reservation has rules, they are to the outsider like those for Australian Rules Football—undetectable. Yards are scarcely modified bare desert; retro clothes lines are visible; objects in the yard are less *trouvé* than *abandonné*. Newer housing is as monotonously uniform in structure as that in Sun Lakes, but the colors, when they have any, tend toward green or raspberry or just gray concrete block, any of which would induce heart attacks in the Sun Lakes Homeowners Association.

In other words, to urban Americans of a certain class—and no class is more certain—the reservation looks Third World, and one can hear the Anglos thinking and sometimes saying, "I couldn't live like that." The Indians may feel the same way, but we don't consider that.

On both sides of the border, the inhabitants have only tenuous connections to their traditional cultures. Not many Pimas speak their native language, and only a few young people bother to learn tribal crafts and ceremonies. Sun Lakers try to maintain connections through associations focusing on states they've left or on increasingly vague ethnic heritages. Some, migratory snow-birds, return to their birthplaces like salmon, though obviously not to breed, before heading out again. But increasingly, through infirmity or acclimatization, they become permanent residents, though not citizens in the full sense of the term. And even those who return to northern feeding grounds are as deracinated, to some degree, as the Indians who have unavoidably ingested white culture as they have government commodities.

I doubt that many Sun Lakers have bothered to think about possible caste and class divisions in the Indian population, though some are aware that the Pimas welcomed the linguistically and culturally quite different Maricopas (who call themselves Pipatsje) without knowing much about their relationships. The Indians may regard us as homogeneous. But as with any group, the closer you look, the more differences can be seen. North of the border, Sun Lakes is divided into three communities, once numbered I, II, and III to imply a logical sequence and continuity. Now all three have different names designed to enforce subtle economic and social distinctions.

Phase I has a number of manufactured homes, and judging from the midden-heaps of estate sales, an older population. Phase II, where I live, has no manufactured houses and a somewhat younger and more mobile population. Phase III is clearly more affluent, with access controlled by guards or automated gates. Denizens of the first two areas can enter the third through guarded gates. Others, like workmen and golfers, can be admitted, but they are logged in and given an identification badge, like a disability parking permit, to hang on the rear-view mirror.

I mention these distinctions because they imply real differences. The barrier around Phase III isn't quite the Berlin Wall—the Patrol doesn't seem to be armed—but more like the newly built fences along the Mexican border, designed to keep out rather than in. But it's definitely cut off physically. And the elite's lifted noses and rolled eyes erect subtler barriers. Those can be climbed by people who have desirable qualities. For example, I'm a fully mobile self-supporting single man who has apparently deteriorated more slowly than most of my contemporaries. And if, to paraphrase an Oscar Wilde character, I am consistently underdressed, I make up for it by being immensely over-educated—a member of what Paul Fussell called, in his mischievous book *Class*, a member of the X-class. As a result, I've been allowed to enjoy the company of several princesses within the keep.

But as many fictional characters have learned, hypergamy (rising socially through romantic connection) doesn't entirely erase social stigmas. The most princessy princess, who had in the past benefited from minority status, said in a deal-breaking moment of pique, "You might be able to find a woman in Phase I who lives the way you do. My new cleaning woman lives in Phase I. She's sleeping with my yard man." Upstart duly rebuked—and out the door with a sigh of relief. (Of course, I should have left the moment I discovered that she didn't think "Blazing Saddles" was funny.)

Her remark at least let me know where I stood in her mind, and that can be an advantage, psychological or geographical, to anyone. Residents of Sun Lakes and the GRIC know where they are—no confusion or ambiguity—and in part define themselves by contrast with the Other.

The disadvantage of knowing where you are, is that you can get stuck in, confined by, knowing your place. This has not been a major problem in the mythology of America, where boundaries have been set only so that they can be crossed, re-defined, and crossed again. For John Steinbeck's character in "The Leader of the People," that process came to an end when, having reached the Pacific Ocean, he mourned that he had no further outlet for his lust for "Westering." But Walt Whitman sweeps the reader across the continent in a few lines and calls for passage not just to India but to the entire cosmos. The archetypical American would choose to go with Whitman rather than stay with Steinbeck.

On the other hand, if the border keeps moving, it's hard to know where you are, and to get back from the cosmos to the Maricopa county line, you can see physical evidence of that uncertainty and displacement if you drive east, away from the clear boundary between Sun Lakes and the GRIC to areas where distinctions blur and then, hesitantly, are re-defined.

At first you are in suburbia, where, if homeowners' associations exist, they are looser than in Sun Lakes, and where relative wealth allows for caprice not possible on the reservation. Those conditions may explain some amazingly ugly and architecturally inappropriate houses that would appall Frank Lloyd Wright, like one in a pseudo-Romanesque or perhaps Scottish baronial style, complete with an abbreviated turret.

But the developments give way to bare or cleared land, with here and there an embodied cliché from B Westerns, "Someday we'll have a church and school" as signs that Manifest Destiny is alive and well. Here the schools and churches have preceded settlers, apparently on the "If you build it, they will come" theory. For now they, at least the children, are bused in. But more will come—if the housing market ever recovers to feed megalopolitan expansion.

A little farther and you go back at least a half century to a time when Arizona boasted of the Five Cs: climate, copper, cotton, cattle, and citrus. The last two survive along these roads, but the groves are overgrown with weeds and the tree trunks are shaggy with neglect, awaiting the developer's axe and bulldozer. The biggest herd of cattle is fenced in a small, shabby dairy, a holdout from among the many north of Sun Lakes which have been moved south and west to make way for housing and tech industries, only a little of the odor remaining. A few scrub feeder cattle mingle with horses on what real estate agents would call horse properties. But these lack the marks of gentleman rancher dilettantism connoted by that term, for the yards are as bare as those on the reservation and the lawn ornaments are metal, wheeled, and functional.

These small acreages will probably hold out longer than the citrus groves against the encroachments of civilization (which a couple of miles west turns up in the form of chain drug stores and supermarkets), partly because it will be too much trouble to assemble enough of them to make a subdivision, partly because these mini-ranches jam against the foothills of the San Tan Mountains after the GRIC ends, partly because the water supply is finite and probably decreasing. At some point, even the most rabid advocates of expansion will have to recognize and respect the limitations imposed by the Sonoran Desert environment.

So perhaps Steinbeck's character was right to recognize the physical limits by which geography ended his dream. I'm not sure that this lesson applies to the Gila River Indian Community, where the river hasn't run in almost a century, because the Pimas have been in one place a long time and the Maricopas for a century and a half, give or take, and neither group shows any signs of wanting to be anywhere else.

People in Sun Lakes are by definition nomadic, but they face limits of time, though most of us resist that knowledge until the EMTs arrive at the front door or, more spectacularly, the Medivac helicopter lands on the eighteenth fairway. But as long as we are mobile, we are less bound by geography and environment, believing more or less unconsciously like Hemingway in *Green Hills of Africa* that when a country is used up, we can move to another one. As one of his characters says in another book, "Isn't it pretty to think so." Or trust in our boundaries to keep out all but a minuscule percentage of darker people, children, and signs of socialism like universal health care.

Recoveries

ST. FRANCIS'S CLEANING BILLS

Browsing in the gift shop of the Center for the Arts in Tubac, Arizona, I saw a small statue of St. Francis of Assisi with birds perched on his shoulders and wrists. This was not surprising, since Tubac lies between two missions served by the Franciscans after the Jesuits were thrown out in the eighteenth century for being pains in the ass. And of course, as a cradle Catholic born in 1934, I have been familiar with the iconography for nearly seven decades.

Suddenly I wondered, aloud, if his birds had ever acted like normal birds. My companion, raised as a Southern Baptist, now a member of some less exacting heretical sect, and in any case bemused by most signs of Popery, was shocked. "I can't take you anywhere," she said reproachfully. But the woman behind the counter snorted in surprise and what sounded like delight.

Looking back, what strikes me as odd is not the fact that I raised the question but that it took almost seventy years for it to occur to me. Anyone raised Catholic in my generation could probably come up with a number of reasons for that, all of which reveal a good deal about Catholic education and practices up at least until the mid-1960s and, in some enclaves, beyond. For example, a near-contemporary who went to a Catholic girls' boarding school said, speaking for the nuns who taught her, "Of course the birds wouldn't do that to St. Francis! God wouldn't allow it!" Made sense to me: His eye is on the sparrow, and presumably on the other species as well. Including the backside.

Of course, neither my friend nor I nor any of our contemporaries would have put such a question to the nuns, or to each other, because it would never have occurred to us that anything connected with a saint or even with the clergy could have had anything to do with bodily functions. Sure, in saints lives people got eaten by lions and torn on wheels and fried on griddles and a whole lot of other things that would make Stephen King retch, but the pace of the narrative was as swift and painless as a Roadrunner cartoon; the distinction between bad guys and good made Gene Autry westerns seem by comparison as complex as *The Brothers Karamazov*; and the resolutions glossed over any possible internal conflicts or questionings. No time for zits, wet dreams, flatulence, or any of the minor grossness that makes adolescence seem purgatorial.

Even worse than the brief saints' lives were the pious stories printed in *Manna*, I think it was called—anyway it was the magazine given to us in fourth or fifth grade—about supposedly real people. In the only one I can remember, a very pious boy drinks holy water in order to better himself spiritually and dies —though not, unfortunately, as a result—in an odor of sanctity. If this was supposed to move us to emulate him, it failed. No one we knew, even the good kids, would be that much of a dork, a term we didn't have, though we understood the concept intuitively.

As this story illustrated, in the 1940s and 1950s almost everyone we encountered who was officially connected with the lower rungs of Church hierarchy seemed to assume that profane, everyday experience had nothing whatever to do with the sacred world. Actually, the sacred was pretty much overlaid by a wide and heavy stratum of piety, and piety precluded not only questions about St. Francis but about the stories in *Manna* and everything else having to do with religion and religious people. This attitude was fostered implicitly by the visual and narrative art we saw and more or less explicitly by priests and especially by nuns.

The pictures and statues available in Catholic churches and schools in my youth would have had to struggle to rise to the level of kitsch. The term is all the more apt because the style was heavily influenced by nineteenth-century German sculptors and painters, though the Italians, debasing the style of Tuscan Renaissance painters, also contributed, and in the mid-1950s I heard a rumor that distribution of pious art was controlled by the Mafia before the organization discovered that pornography was more profitable.

Pious religious art was pastel, genteel, unthreatening, unremarkable. Even depictions of Christ's passion and death in the Stations of the Cross were sanitized, the graphic reality of the Gospels undercut by the style.

Fortunately, ecclesiastical pseudo-art was easy to ignore because it was, literally and otherwise, put on pedestals above the common gaze. The statue I saw in Tubac was by comparison to the art I saw in my youth—and in a recent newspaper story about a Catholic school—worthy of Maillol or Moore.

Music was another matter. Some people apparently can shut out tunes they find banal or offensive; others, like me, are doomed to listen to anything remotely rhythmic and melodic. Anyway, school children in my parish, regardless of desire or talent, were expected to sing in the choir. It was possible to sing, with aesthetic as well as religious fervor, Benediction hymns like "Tantum Ergo," "O Salutaris Hostia," and "Holy God We Praise Thy Name." But most hymns in English, like "Daily, Daily Sing to Mary," strained credulity as well as the larynx.

And it wasn't only statues and other forms of art that were pedestalized, raised above the common view of experience. Members of the clergy were regarded as special, above criticism, reproach, or, as recent events in the Church have shown, criminal investigation. When I was in high school, a youngish assistant priest came into the men's room and complained that lay people didn't think that priests went to the bathroom. But his colleagues and predecessors had done a great deal to foster that illusion.

Nuns were a bit lower on the scale of ethereality, partly because some of them were likely to go upside our heads when annoyed, but even had we high school boys known anything at all about menstruation, it would never have occurred to us that nuns menstruated because we never thought of them as women. (On the other hand, PMS would have explained the behavior of some nuns we encountered.)

Nor, as the reaction to the priest in the men's room shows, did many of us think of them as real people. They seemed removed from ordinary concerns, sorrows as well as joys, untouchable and out of touch. I can think of perhaps a dozen members of the clergy whom I found really attractive as human beings, and in all cases I did so because they were intelligent and well-educated and sensible and aware of human as well as pious values.

Jacques Maritain held that piety is no substitute for technique, and it took me a long time to discover art that confronted the complexities of human experience. When I did, the pious art and legends formed a useful backdrop. At the very least, they prepared me to enjoy the fake hagiographies in Norman Douglas's novel *South Wind*. One tells the story of an impossibly precocious ascetic virgin; the other of Saint Dodekanus (etymologically speaking, a name derived from twelve inglorious parts of the human anatomy), clearly based on an earth-deity of an island with twelve noxious mineral springs, in which the saint is led into the woods by a figure who may be a man (later a woman) "or only an angel."

And when I finally read Graham Greene's *The Power and the Glory*—almost condemned by the Vatican before common sense prevailed—I empathized with the young boy restive at his mother's reading of a pious legend who responds to the real pain and martyrdom of the whiskey priest. Years before, I had read Morris L. West's *The Devil's Advocate*—probably a selection from my mother's membership in the Book-of-the-Month Club—in which the central, absent figure being considered for beatification had problems and passions and conflicts that I was beginning to be able to recognize. Years later, Ignazio Silone's *Bread and Wine* showed me how someone technically a non-believer, in fact a Communist, could respond to others' need for the world of the spirit.

Still later, I was able to experience the remoteness and mystery of Byzantine art, the sense of real and compelling temptation portrayed in Cranach's diptych of Eve seductively offering the apple to Adam, the vision of the unknown artist whose Crucifixion hangs in the museum of ecclesiastical art in Esztergom, Hungary, or the practical sense of Flemish and Dutch painters who made the job of prophet seem like a really tough hustle, unlike the Tuscans who painted aged holy men with foreheads as smooth as those of praying virgins.

Obviously, not everyone feels this way, and in fact can't imagine saints looking any other way than pastel and dehumanized. This exasperates real artists like Sister Giotto, who found money to restore and redecorate the church in San Ysidro, New Mexico, and who painted Santo-like murals above the altar only to discover that many parishioners preferred the nineteenth-century blond Madonna and her plaster companions to the style of their Hispanic heritage.

Other styles and rituals came into the Church after the Second Vatican Council—not always or, in my experience, often for the better. Sometimes, like the concept of "disposable art" advanced in the early 1970s by a religious education director who liked to have kids blow up balloons to demonstrate the action of the Holy Spirit, it was often for the worse. So, it seemed to me, were borrowings from popular music like "Kumbaya" or from Protestant hymnals, especially songs proclaiming to God that He is great. Come on! He's *omniscient*! He *knows* that. Why insult his intelligence? And of course, when we started singing Martin Luther's "A Mighty Fortress Is Our God," I figured that it was all over. But perhaps the religious education director was right to reject my suggestion that, to welcome the newly imported bishop, we sing "I've Never Been to Heaven, But I've Been to Oklahoma," though that might have reminded the bishop that he was coming into a real context among real people. Still, in the ceremony celebrating the religious education director's departure for a new job, I did manage to slip in a passage from *Bread and Wine* extolling the virtues of the communist disguised as a priest. He and the congregation loved it—perhaps because, as the Virginian says in Owen Wister's novel, it was about something.

It was also heartening to see that children even younger than mine are able to let practical good sense override piety. In the 1970s, I attended a children's Mass where a hippy-dippy priest was giving a dialogue homily on the theme of freedom. Imagine a bird in a cage, he said to the children in the front pew. What do you have to do for the bird? "Feed him," one child said. What else? "Give him water." "Good," said the priest. "And then what does the bird do?" The answer, based on experience rather than sentiment, convulsed the whole congregation. The last I heard of the priest, he was selling antiques in Colorado.

Unfortunately, some members of the clergy seem immune to even stronger doses of reality. For example, the former bishop of the Phoenix diocese plea bargained his way out of charges of obstruction of justice for concealing evidence that priests under his care had molested young men and in some cases young women. In this he was clearly following the practice of many bishops, if not stated Church policy, as many other cases have shown, based on a clerical culture that put loyalty to the institution above concern for the laity supposedly in their charge. I'm reminded less of the injunction to "Feed my sheep" than of the joke about Montana, where the men are men and the sheep are terrified. Even after the Phoenix bishop signed the plea bargain, he denied doing anything wrong until the district attorney threatened to abrogate the deal. The bargain itself should have meant instant disgrace and dismissal, but the Vatican refused to accept his resignation.

It did allow him to retire when, two weeks later, the car he was driving struck and killed a pedestrian. The bishop did not stop. Told by a trusted aide that the police wanted to talk to him, he not only did not call them but refused to answer the door when they came to interview him and asked his secretary how he could get his windshield repaired. In fact, testimony in his trial indicates that he acted as he had done in the molestation cases: hoped it would just go away. It turns out that some eighteen months earlier he damaged another car in a parking lot, got out to look at the damage, and drove away without notifying the owner of the other car. Although he never admitted responsibility, the incident didn't quite go away, for his insurance company paid for the damage. In his trial on the charge of leaving the scene of the fatal accident, his defense attorneys contended, unsuccessfully, that he thought that he might have hit a dog or been hit by a rock. One can't know what was in his mind, but from the outside his actions portray a man who never had to confront a serious moral issue—at least one that involved him directly. Certainly not much evidence of heroic virtue in him or in his fellow bishops who allowed priests to run over at least 11,000 lives—and those only of the victims who were willing to bring lawsuits. Nor, come to that, much evidence of manhood.

Running away from or refusing to acknowledge the consequences of one's actions doesn't sound much like St. Francis, even in the account wavering between piety and dryness from an early edition of the Catholic Encyclopedia that I found on-line. He was often dirty and ragged, hungry and ill, not always from choice. Perhaps, however much he loved the birds and even sentimentalized them, he knew something about the ways they lived and acted. Another question bubbles up from early training: if they did leave souvenirs on his habit, would their feces be accorded the status of relics of the second order (that is, anything not bearing the saint's DNA)? And would he have brushed them off in annoyance, or would he, in the phrase notorious in my youth, have offered it up and worn the stains in honorable acceptance of the nature of birds? I like to think so. And I'm pretty sure that he would have stopped to see if he had hit a dog.

Born Again Skeptic

When I see television ads urging lapsed Catholics to return to the Church, I understand the motive behind the campaign—one in ten people in the US, some reports say, are part of that very loose group. I wonder how well the campaign is working and even have a mild and momentary response to the concern about my condition. But I'm not really interested.

That may seem odd to people who know my background. I spent fifteen years in Catholic schools and three more teaching in one. Somewhere in the detritus of history is the medal I won for having the highest grades in religion in four years of high school. I served regularly as an altar boy for seven years and occasionally during my college days. I led rosaries and English versions of the Latin Mass. I sang in the choir all during high school and voluntarily during summer vacations. Even in graduate school, I presented the orthodox line in arguments with Protestants and unbelievers. The husband-to-be of a now prominent novelist asked my advice about Church law regarding marriage.

I'm not sure whether, under canon law, I'm excommunicated *a jure* as a person divorced without Church permission and as someone who hasn't fulfilled the Easter Duty (confess and receive communion during the eight-week window between the First Sunday of Lent and Trinity Sunday) or simply an ordinary sinner. The first option seems more satisfying, on a variation of Groucho Marx's remark that he wouldn't want to belong to a club that would have him as a member.

Concerned Catholics have asked how I came to leave the church. Gradually and suddenly, I answer. The gradually is probably more interesting

For one thing, my family had a built-in schism. My maternal grandmother was a devout German-American Catholic married to a devout anti-clerical atheist—whose family, my sister discovered, is buried in Catholic cemeteries. Their daughter did not go to Catholic schools, but was on her mother's side a practicing Catholic and on her father's a maverick according the rigid standards of small-town mid-America. My father, technically a Protestant, was less vocally anti-clerical than his father-in-law, and he went to church only for baptisms, first communions, confirmations, weddings, and funerals. But he had promised to raise his children as Catholics, and he rousted me from bed for weekday Mass throughout my schooldays. I came to suspect that he just liked to see me get up early and that his promise gave him a good excuse.

During my years in a small-town Catholic school in the 1940s and early 1950s, I dutifully memorized my Baltimore catechism, sometimes drilled by my father, and was for the most part dutiful and biddable until my senior year, when my maternal heritage surfaced. What's interesting, in retrospect, is that the nuns never tried to foster in me a vocation to the priesthood. That's odd, because generally they regarded as priestly material any boy who could read without moving his lips. But perhaps they weren't as innocent or ignorant as my classmates and I suspected.

Our pastor, who seemed as immutable as Pope Pius XII and FDR, was certainly not ignorant, and his sophistication, towering in that setting, offset the pieties of the simpler nuns. He offered an alternative that I now see as fostering a kind of estrangement from conventional practice.

Rockhurst, the Jesuit college I attended, was designed less to foster vocations than to turn its students into Prominent Catholic Laymen (capitals required) who would support the Church intellectually, socially, and (though this was never quite made explicit) financially. Philosophy and religion courses relied so heavily on cookbook formulas that two of my brightest classmates are still angry about the lack of intellectual rigor. That's because they paid attention, I told them. Those familiar with the underside of Jesuit education maintained that if a member of the order was not very bright, he was assigned to teach philosophy. Less bright, he taught theology. Still less, he became an administrator.

More important than the official line was the atmosphere created by a few professors, Jesuit and lay, who did not belong to what seemed the conventional Church. The Jesuits ran the local parish, its form like that of a fish, seemingly as unusual as some—well, a few—of the sermons preached there, but we could also attend Mass in the college chapel, simpler, more austere, and somehow more attractive. Sermons and practices in ordinary parish churches came to seem drab and conventional, and I at least became further estranged from the general body of American Catholicism, encouraged, I now realize, by the Jesuit who became my confessor and spiritual advisor.

That became obvious when I went to graduate school in Lawrence, Kansas, a place without a university parish. The local parish seemed so drab that the only thing I remember was a stint in the confessional where the priest asked if I wrote to my mother often. "Oftener than she writes to me," I said, and left, absolved but disgusted. For those two years, I had to rely on the momentum provided by my early indoctrination and by my conception of myself as a Catholic intellectual, sustained by the company of several other Jesuit-educated students whose vocabulary was familiar and comforting and in some cases, even odder and more doctrinaire than mine along the lines of the main character, also Jesuit-educated, in John Kennedy Toole's *A Confederacy of Dunces*.

The situation in Madison, Wisconsin, was considerably better. For one thing, many of my fellow graduate students were Jesuit-educated Catholics, and many of those who weren't were Jewish. One of the most distinguished scholars in the department, Helen C. White, was a Prominent Catholic Laywoman. Therefore, when my mother warned me that people would discriminate against me because I was Catholic, I said—truthfully, I think—that almost no one cared anymore. That certainly didn't figure in the atmosphere I lived in. Furthermore, the university chapel was reassuringly forward-looking. That formed a welcome contrast to the church nearest my apartment. It was run by the Dominicans, whose official name was Order of Preachers. I would squirm in my pew during sermons, muttering to myself, "Order of Preachers—hah!"

More because of the other graduate students than most of my professors, my intellectual horizons were growing broader, or at least I had begun to see how limited they had been. Moreover, I married a woman who after being raised as a Methodist, studying the Anglican priest-poet George Herbert, deciding to work on John Donne, and spending some time as an Episcopalian, converted to Catholicism. Both my undergraduate spiritual advisor and my mother were suspicious of her conversion—or perhaps of my marrying someone they hadn't vetted—but it seemed like a good idea at the time, made me more disciplined as a student, and even reinforced my attachment to the university chapel.

When it came time to apply for full-time teaching jobs, I concentrated on Jesuit and a few other Catholic universities because they promised a familiar atmosphere in which I might be able to compete with what I rightly regarded as my limited knowledge and ability. I did have one interview, unsolicited in those long-gone days of a seller's market, with the chairwoman of Luther College in Decorah, Iowa, who said, "We never have hired a Catholic," so in a sense my mother was right, but here prejudice worked in my favor by closing a very unattractive door.

In 1962 I chose the nearest Jesuit university, Loyola of Chicago, over the University of Detroit, the University of Portland, and an east-coast state university, partly because it was closer to my dissertation director. Loyola turned out to be familiar in many ways, not least in the World War II temporary buildings that housed the English department, some classrooms, and the cafeteria, larger but with food in no way better than that at Rockhurst. I even had a couple of colleagues from Wisconsin. But most of the older faculty members had degrees either from the University of Chicago or Northwestern, had lived in the area all their lives, and if they weren't single and living with aged parents, were married to women named Mary Ann or Mary something. One exception had moved to Chicago from the west coast, and he had the kind of panache that made his desire to own a sword cane seem reasonable.

But most of my new colleagues seemed to lack the intellectual range and intensity of my Wisconsin contemporaries. In a departmental discussion of a selection from Thomas Merton's *The Seven Storey Mountain*, I argued that the style was prolix and repetitive. The man senior to me who taught advanced courses in my field wondered what I had against "the man Merton." Not a thing, I said—just the way he writes. (Years later I discovered that Evelyn Waugh felt the same way and had cut Merton's book by about a third for English publication.) At one meeting, I shocked the group by saying that my ambition was to write as well as a Jewish-American critic.

Although the church on the main campus was the newest and architecturally the most interesting building there, for some reason I can't remember, we often went to the local parish a few blocks away. It wasn't as big as a contemporary megachurch, but it was larger than anything I was used to. But the sermons were if anything worse. The only one I remember dealt with vocations to the priesthood in which the preacher exhorted mothers to dedicate their sons because then they would never lose them. I didn't know much about Freud, but I knew enough to be shocked. But it would be wrong to say that I was alienated from the parish because I never felt connected.

Partly this was because I was trying to finish a dissertation and then to begin to try to publish scholarly work. This was difficult to do while teaching four courses a semester, three of them freshman composition, as well as summer school, and I decided to look for a job that would give me more time for research and writing.

My time at Loyola, 1962-65, coincided with the Second Vatican Council, but except for some tremors of excitement about the possibility of a greater role for the laity, not much filtered down in the Chicago diocese, fairly liberal for those days. But that had no bearing on my applications for a new job —none to a Catholic school—and I wound up at the University of California, Santa Barbara, in the archdiocese of Los Angeles, under the authority of Cardinal James McIntyre, one of the staunchest opponents of the reforms of Vatican II. I don't know that his control of the diocese accounted for the twitchiness of the pastor of the parish into which we moved, but he would have made Woody Allen look like Clint Eastwood.

Once again, I had little sense of community with the parish, now because I had a number of interesting new colleagues in the cadre hired with me and with those hired just before and after. Most of us were ambitious; none of the others were, as far as I could tell, religious. The only prominent Catholic among the senior faculty was remarkably unprejudiced, since he identified me and the most obviously Jewish member of my group as "too visible and too audible" and, from what we heard, arranged for us to be told that we had no future there.

So I moved to Norman, Oklahoma, hardly a major Catholic center. A few years earlier, my wife and I had spent an Easter morning there on a trip from Chicago to Texas, and we had been struck by the fact that the church building looked more suited to Congregationalists than to Catholics and that the parishioners looked healthier than Chicagoans made sallow by the long northern winter.

Two of my new colleagues had degrees from the University of Wisconsin, and one was still a practicing Catholic. My mother would have felt justified by the attitude of the department's senior scholar, a classicist raised as a Scots Presbyterian, who distrusted all of the children of the Scarlet Woman. But he was conflicted because the most prolific scholar of the next generation was an Italian-American Catholic, and it soon became clear that I was going to fill that role in my generation.

No one else seemed to care whether or not I was Catholic. The real surprise came when we became involved with the local parish, which we chose because, although the parochial school had closed because of shortage of nuns, it had better Christian education facilities than the Newman Center. When I told my Italian colleague that we went there, he scoffed that the congregation was just a bunch of plumbers. I should have said, "And carpenters," but I didn't think of it at the time.

In fact, there were a number of professional and even academic members of the parish, and the priests seemed to have a good rapport with the laity. My wife got involved in teaching Sunday School, I volunteered at an adult education center in Oklahoma City to help people get their GEDs, we worked to build a playground for a day-care center, and I was asked to serve on the liturgy committee. Probably they didn't know what they were getting into, since I took a casual attitude towards things that I thought weren't important like a new version of the Lord's Prayer. But I wasn't kicked off, perhaps because the pastor seemed to enjoy talking to me.

The local parish seemed to be in tune with the spirit of Vatican II, and there were signs that old practices were waning. The pastor told me that the number of confessions had dropped precipitately, though he didn't seem to think that this was a bad thing. My son was born in 1966, and his kindergarten class in Sunday School filled two rooms. The following year, the class needed only one room, so, figuring backward, one could see when Catholic adherence to the Church's position on birth control had undergone a similar erosion only seven years after the Pill became available. Kindness, good works, community became more important than group rosaries and other pious practices I had grown up with.

I don't know when this spirit crested, but some of the clergy found it disconcerting. One Sunday, at the folk Mass, a visiting young priest attempted to lead a "dialogue homily." One respondent was a local lawyer of the type who never went to court. His wife later told mine that she hoped that he and I never got into an argument because I was always right and he had never been wrong. In this case, we both took issue with the young priest's position and, in effect, each grabbed a leg and made a wish. He tried to fall back on his clerical authority, and we just pulled harder. That was the last dialogue homily we ever heard. Not as serious as the suppression of Worker Priests or the followers of Liberation Theology, but an ominous indication of things to come.

Then the hippy-dippy layman hired as liturgy director left for a better position. He was replaced by an old-fashioned nun who tried to make Sunday School more traditional and orthodox. My children refused to attend any more, and we moved to the university chapel where they were no happier. Then my wife refused to go to church on the irrefutable grounds that the Church was run by male chauvinists.

I continued to go to Mass and take my reluctant children with me. The collapse of my marriage probably had nothing to do with this, but, out of the house, I had even less influence over my children and in any case was reluctant to alienate them further by dragging them to Mass and Sunday School.

After an interval, I went on with my life, social and sexual, and was astonished to find that I didn't feel guilty. But I continued going to church until I went to teach in Hungary. My first Sunday there, I went to Mass at the Cathedral. It was in Hungarian, of course, and when the priest began to deliver the sermon, I realized that neither the Mass nor the Church had anything left to offer me.

Back to my earlier distinction between gradually and suddenly. The nuns who indoctrinated me would say that I was guilty of the sin of pride, of thinking so highly of my intellect that I looked down on others, including the priests to whom I should have listened. Almost any priest would say that my cutting myself off from the sacraments led to my loss of faith—a point made in Graham Greene's story "A Visit to Morin." My mother would say that my mistake was marrying a convert. My surviving undergraduate professor, a layman, asked what happened to me. The best answer I could give was "I ran out of momentum"—the momentum provided by fifteen years of being trained to give answers which seemed increasingly to have little to do with my needs or with the spiritual life. Perhaps, like both sides of my family, spirituality was not a significant element of my makeup.

Or maybe the problem was that, except for sporadic moments, I have never had a sense of belonging to a congregation. An Italian-American friend who regards the Ten Commandments as the Ten Suggestions asked, on a visit to a Benedictine monastery, the difference between a monk and a priest. I said that monks lived in a community, not exactly isolated from the secular world but not as much a part of it as parish priests necessarily are. "You would have made a better monk," she said. Actually, if I had ever had a vocation, it might have been as a hermit. That always gets a laugh, since I have trouble keeping my mouth shut or staying in one place, but it's as good a description as I can come up with. Perhaps it's that I'm not a joiner, and that my association with the Catholic Church was first enforced and then habitual. On reflection, however, and remembering an essay I wrote about my lack of qualifications to inhabit a real Hermitage, I realize that I'm more like a pilgrim, though less like the foot-weary people on the road to Santiago de Compostela than like Chaucer's group who are along for the ride and for some new stories and never, even in Chaucer's "Retraction," getting to the shrine.

Now, unless a church leader does something unusually offensive, my attitude can be expressed in a line from another lapsed Catholic, Ronald Firbank: "It is wonderful how I am not interested." I'm not interested enough to call myself an agnostic or an atheist. Friends who regard me as essentially Christian seem confident that I will return to the church, but I don't even doubt that I won't. Others have wondered why I haven't joined another church, perhaps the Unitarian, but I respond with Stephen Dedalus's "I said that I had lost my faith...but not that I had lost my self-respect." A college contemporary, disenchanted with the Church in some of the same ways, continues to profess because, quoting Peter in John 6:69, "to whom shall we go?" My answer was that I felt no need to go anywhere—except to continue my personal pilgrimage.

On the other hand, I look more with sorrow than anger at attacks on the kind of religious training I received like that in *Sister Mary Ignatius Explains It All,* and a Baptist friend who took me to see *Late Nite Catechism,* replicating an old-fashioned parochial school classroom, was surprised that I left the theater more depressed than amused. But I can still see some jokes. A friend reported that when she asked a friend how long to grind coffee beans, she said, "As long as it takes to say a Hail Mary, reverently." Anyone who gets that comes from my world.

So does the priest whom I interviewed in the presence of a scientist raised behind the Iron Curtain. We Westerners discovered that we had had the same Jesuit teacher at different universities, and our conversation was easy and cordial. When my scientist friend and I left, he said, "You and he seemed to have a real rapport." "We should," I said. "We speak the same language." As I later told my daughter, who has drifted in and out of various churches, "He's the kind of priest who almost makes me wish I were still a Catholic."

Of course, according to the catechism I was taught, I can't stop being a Catholic because baptism left an indelible mark on my soul. More practically, the training and rituals in which I was immersed stay with me, as indicated by my unconventional use of capital letters. While teaching D. H. Lawrence's novel *Women in Love*, I mentioned that his wife finished reading the manuscript and said that he should title it "Dies Irae" after the beautiful but, if you understand the Latin, bloodcurdling hymn in the requiem Mass. (At my mother's funeral in 1966, it had been translated into English, still in tetrameter triplets, which work well in Latin and jingle badly in English.) My students looked blank, as they did at mention of anything religious, so I sang the first few lines. Later, wandering alone in Seville, I dredged up the Latin words to two verses of "Tantum Ergo" before I happened to pass a church, not on the tourist circuit, where Benediction was being held. But "Tantum Ergo" was in Spanish. And I shocked both my atheist and my Baptist friends by testing the acoustics in empty churches by intoning the opening lines of "Pange lingua." Perhaps I am one of the few living people who knows why, in the Nighttown episode in James Joyce's *Ulysses*, Stephen enters singing not the liturgically correct Benediction entrance hymn, "Aspereges me" but "Vidi aquam," proper to Eastertide. Both deal with water, but the first asks the Lord to sprinkle the singer—and Stephen is a confirmed aquaphobe.

Now almost nobody knows this, which is a minor loss. But according to articles occasioned by Pope Benedict XVI's visit to the U.S. in April, 2008, a great many Catholics know very little about anything else. Kenneth L. Woodward quotes in the New York *Times* a Methodist theologian teaching at Notre Dame (say *what?*) as saying "Before I teach my course on marriage I have to tell them first what their own church has to say on the subject." In *USA Today*, Stephen Prothero generalizes that "Young Catholics are shockingly ignorant of the most basic tenets of their faith. Many cannot name any of the four

Gospels, or identify Genesis as the first book of the Bible. To educate American Catholic youth, however, is to tell them that their church opposes premarital sex, condoms, abortion and the ordination of women...." And apparently, judging from an editorial in the student newspaper of the Catholic University of America, students aren't taught the difference between canon law and cannon law.

I don't have anything to say to these people, many of whom are engaged in laudable good works, now called community service. Those elders and conservative juniors of the kind who served on Bush's Council on Bioethics who used the vague concept of "dignity" to oppose stem cell research and other technical advances on what seem to be fundamentalist readings of the Bible are people I have no interest in talking to. And it isn't just me. My old professor, still a professing Catholic, said that at his advanced age the closest he came to a near occasion of sin was going to Mass.

Therefore, televised appeals to return to the Church (inescapably capitalized) don't give me much direction about where I'm to go. The Church I grew up in has gone—not altogether a bad thing. The hopes of Vatican II have evaporated as successive Popes have tried to restore traditional authority, rather like Canute commanding the sea to halt or, in terms more understandable to modern readers as ignorant of everything else as they are of theology, a man trying to put toothpaste back in the tube. The spectacle can be momentarily entertaining unless you are the toothpaste. The real problem, I realize, is that I was taught to believe not in God but in the Church. And I can't do that anymore.

And so on....

But obviously I can't stop thinking about the Church. After I wrote all this, I did go, as a tourist, to a pair of basilicas. The first was in St. Louis, where my oldest friend gave a tour of the mosaics on which he'd done a documentary, the second that of St. Anne de Beaupré in Quebec. In St. Louis, I encountered the family of one of the Shriners having a convention there (we saw some actual Shriners at the Old Cathedral). A woman asked, diffidently, if I were Catholic. "Close enough," I answered. She wanted to know the difference between a cardinal, an archbishop, and a bishop because her son was going to a Catholic school in the fall and needed to know the difference. I hated to disillusion them, so I drew the proper distinctions and threw in monsignor as well.

At the basilica of St. Anne, everyone except me and my Southern Baptist-raised partner seemed to be Catholic, so I only had to explain the numerous artifacts in the museum to her. I was simultaneously stumped and embarrassed by the dioramas depicting scenes from the life of St. Anne and her daughter, the Virgin Mary, until I saw the explanation that most of the details were derived from the Protogospel of James and Gospel of the Pseudo-Matthew which couldn't even make the Douay Version of the Bible with which I was raised. Obviously the faithful of early centuries were anxious for details about the girlhood of the Virgin, so they were duly supplied—rather as in the eighteenth century James MacPherson filled the Scots need for a national epic by passing off his pastiches as the poems of the bard Ossian which fooled Napoleon and many others. From the depths of my memory, the phrase "pious fraud" surfaced, but I didn't mention that to my companion.

In the basilica, a priest in a red skull-cap (bishop? what?) visible on the pulpit and on several monitors was giving, in French, what seemed to be an eloquent sermon about Jesus. All around, worshippers were listening, I assume raptly, and some, including a woman in a Harley shirt, knelt knelt at a pillar bearing the statue of St. Anne. The only words I understood were "Superman" and "kryptonite," about as canonical as the Pseudo-Matthew. This, I realized, was symbolic of my place outside the Church: I still understood some of the vocabulary, but the syntax no longer made sense.

Dry & High

Listening to Diane Rehm's Public Radio interview with Robert Goolrick about his book *The End of Life as We Know It: Scenes from a Life*, I was struck by his description of his parents' life in the 1950s atmosphere of "cocktails and hairdos," when everyone in their circle drank hard and often. (For that matter, so did a lot of people in the small Midwestern town where I grew up.) In that decade, I couldn't afford to drink that much, but by the mid-1960s, in a California academic circle that drank a good deal and later in Oklahoma, not far removed from prohibition laws that practically demanded that everyone consume a lot of alcohol, I was in a culture like that.

And increasingly, as my older colleagues retired or died and the atmosphere became less cordial and collective, I did most of my drinking at home, falsely secure in the assumption that because I didn't, like my father, disappear on periodic binges, I couldn't possibly have a drinking problem.

But it was obvious to my wife and, I learned later, to my children that I did. After my wife said that she wouldn't leave me if I didn't quit but that I was damaging my older daughter by continuing, I set a date—as I had for quitting smoking, much harder than quitting drinking turned out to be—for my return from a working vacation to the East Coast. On the plane, I had two splits of wine. That was in mid-June, 1978. I stopped drinking, permanently, because moderation doesn't seem to work for me or my family, all of whom seem to have only two switch positions: "off" and "test to destruction."

I didn't go into treatment or into AA, partly because I hate meetings and partly because I didn't want to center my life on alcohol or its deprivation. Unlike Goolrick's mother, who returned from alcohol rehab saying "My life will never be wonderful again," later resumed drinking, and died of alcoholism, I didn't overtly or as far as I can tell unconsciously mourn the loss of alcohol in my life. Probably I should have had counseling; certainly I needed dietary counseling. Having given up alcohol, mostly beer, I thought that I wouldn't have to fight weight gain. But that was a lot of sugar to replace, and for the first time since my early teen years, I began to gorge on sweets, especially ice cream.

My wife and therapist daughter later claimed that I had become a "dry drunk," physically sober but having the same behaviors and attitudes as when I was drinking. Then and now, more than thirty years later and still sober, I sometimes regard the term as a way of labeling people who don't follow the route dictated by alcoholism professionals. One of them, pushing therapy on me, said "You've admitted that you're an alcoholic." I replied, "I said I was an alcoholic." If it's a disease, as the popular view has it, one no more "admits"—asking, in effect, for absolution—to being alcoholic than one does to having cancer.

In both cases, of course, the problem has to be recognized and dealt with as efficiently as possible. I didn't go into a program, but I had the benefit of seeing horrible examples among my colleagues. One, in a public meeting, read through his notes twice without realizing it. Another, who finally got fired from another department for his drinking—an unprecedented feat—slobbered all over a famous visiting lecturer. Their behavior kept me from succumbing to the common fallacy, central to "Harvey" and other narratives with comic drunks, that drunks are charming, witty, and somehow special.

Going cold turkey affected both my personal and professional lives. I had finished the manuscript of the book I'd been working on—while I was drinking—for almost a decade, and whether I was in a natural lull or my brain was adjusting to the absence of stimulants, I entered an uncharacteristically unproductive period. But I could enjoy my colleagues' being threatened by my new sobriety, not that they followed my example. Others, especially some graduate students whose experience almost made me ashamed to call myself an alcoholic, began to ask my advice about and help with their own problems. All I could say was that the only effective way of dealing with alcoholism is whatever gets you to the point where you could imagine yourself never taking another drink. Dealing with my personal life was more difficult. Perhaps I felt that I deserved more credit for doing something that was supposed to be difficult than I was getting from my wife and children. Probably I was more annoying because I was more alert and because I was trying to assume a role that apparently I had abdicated. And there were other major stresses in the family having nothing to do with my alcoholism.

Eighteen months after I stopped drinking, my wife asked me to move out. This was a shock but not a surprise. Less surprising, but shocking, was her announcement ten months later that this was not a separation but a definite split and that she could never live with me again.

After an intense emotional reaction, I realized that I had to pick up the pieces of my life and move on. I had already returned to competitive swimming and was in better physical shape than I'd ever be again; I'd met some single women who seemed to find me interesting; I'd begun to write again; and before long I had the possibility of traveling to Canada and Europe to experience whole new worlds.

Before I left the country, I was invited to participate, along with my wife (we were well into divorce proceedings) in an intervention with a colleague who had a serious drinking problem. In a meeting preliminary to the actual confrontation, the group leader asked each participant, in turn, whether she or he would be willing to go to rehab with the person. Some said yes, some no. I said yes. Then she asked if we would be willing to go to AA meetings with the person. Some said yes, some no.

When it was my turn, I asked "For how long?" "Indefinitely." I said no, since I was in the habit of keeping promises, therefore tried to be careful about what I promised, and could not commit to "indefinitely."

That may have been when I was supposed to admit being an alcoholic. The counselor added, "After all, alcoholism is a family problem." I smiled and said, looking across the circle at my wife, "Got rid of the family. Got rid of the problem." Not true, since the family got rid of me, but an irresistible line.

The next stage, which took years, was to put my family life back together—at any rate, to repair the breaks with my children, since my ex and I both realized that each of us was better off without the other. It was easier, or at least more obvious, with my daughter the therapist. Early in her professional training she resented the fact that I wouldn't go into therapy and talked about our family as dysfunctional. That was before she saw some real dysfunction, before her friends started saying that they wished they had a father like hers, and before she realized that we functioned better with some distance between us. Later she decided that she didn't want me to go into therapy because I might change and she wouldn't recognize me. But she still maintains that I'm the only person she knows who used alcoholic behavior, by which she apparently meant yes/no, black/white reasoning, to stop drinking. That may be a variation on her mother's response to someone who said that I'd start again if I didn't get help. "No," she said, "he's too stubborn."

Getting back in touch with my son was harder—not surprising. Years later he saw a therapist and realized that he was angry with me because of my drinking. All he wanted was an apology, and I hope that mine was convincing and as helpful as such things can ever be. Both later thanked me for trying to act like a father in the face of their rejection. Unlike Earl in the TV show, I haven't gone around trying to make amends or gone through the other twelve steps. I'm sorry that people were hurt, but there's nothing I could or can do about that except to try to act differently—which, I was taught, was the point of going to Confession. Perhaps my early and prolonged Catholic training has led me to what is called acknowledgement of sin—though one moral theologian holds that one is guilty of drunkenness only when one loses consciousness—and to a firm purpose of amendment, or, as the Act of Contrition puts it, "to sin no more and to avoid the near occasion of sin." In Catholic theology, even after absolution there are some dues to be paid—called "temporal punishment due to sin" and supposedly resolved in Purgatory. I'm too far removed from the Church (though not enough not to capitalize it for fear of being whacked with a ruler) to worry about that. And I've never had a near occasion. A close friend, visiting me in a remote mountain village, was surprised that I was willing to go into a bar. Since, I told him, that's the only place open for dinner every night, if I didn't go there, I wouldn't go anywhere.

So far I have stayed sober, and to people who hint, or insist, that I should have done differently I can say that, according to statistics, ninety percent of people who do seek treatment relapse to some degree in four years. I'm not better than they are, just luckier. And, as my close friends and family agree, I'm too stubborn.

Not too long ago, my daughter called me "a recovering alcoholic." "When can I be recovered?" I asked. "When you can drink moderately." "Well," I said, "then I guess I'll just have to go on recovering."

One of my daughter's friends, knowing that I'm a writer, said that I should write a book about my method of quitting. I said that it would be the world's shortest book: "I quit." My daughter said that I could write about the psychological make-up that enabled me to quit. I think that's too simple to warrant much discussion, though people who have read other pieces in this book might disagree.

My unconscious mind doesn't seem to be involved. For years after I quit smoking, I had dreams about lighting up. But there've been no dreams and no waking temptations that involve drinking. I've sometimes been asked if people urge me to drink. "No one who knew me when I did." In a lighter mood, I say that I'm naturally so noisy that no one realizes that I'm not drinking.

Perhaps my daughter is right and I'm still psychologically an alcoholic. But, dry or sober, I've traveled over much of Europe, branched out into several new areas as a writer, and discovered, unlike Goolrick's mother, that life without alcohol is a lot more wonderful than life immersed in it. And for a pragmatist, going past thirty years sober may not be as good as it gets, but it's going to have to do.

Doing Times

I discipline my body like an athlete, training it to do what it should. Otherwise, I fear that after preaching to others I myself might be disqualified.

1 Corinthians 9:27

I don't know if St. Paul could swim, although he did escape at least one shipwreck, but judging from the number of times he talks about competing for a prize, he was one competitive dude. Of course, he was talking about a heavenly prize, which was not, he seems to keep reminding himself, the outcome of a zero-sum game. But even if I don't always agree with Paul, I understand something about his personality because athletic competition was an important part of my life.

Like many would-be athletes of the pre-boomer generation, I grew up playing team sports and couldn't imagine that any other kind of exercise could be fun as well as healthy. As a result, when faced with the onset of middle age, I decided to try to get back into some kind of shape by playing basketball at lunch time. That lasted until an old knee injury flared up.

Although I had done a good deal of recreational swimming as a youth, I never thought of it as serious exercise because, as a colleague said and I believed, nobody keeps score. And for someone used to competition, numbers and results are important.

Fortunately, I acquired a copy of Kenneth Cooper's *New Aerobics*, which has an appendix full of charts calibrating how many points you can get for almost any type of motion and how many more you can get for doing it longer or in less time or both. So I began to swim, consulting Cooper every day to total up my points.

Then my children joined the local swim team, and I discovered other ways of keeping score. Not just racing, which in any case seemed beyond my awkward freestyle form and my age, but anaerobic or interval training: swimming the same distance progressively faster. Warming up and swimming down. Swimming different lengths and strokes. Kicking and arm drills. (Also, after some resistance to the fact that competition suits reveal middle-ageing spread, discovering that they dry faster and thus are more comfortable to pull on than more modest trunks.)

Still, my knowledge of competitive swimming was theoretical until I learned that Masters Swimming was coming to Oklahoma. It was consoling to learn that "Masters" meant not mastery but merely attaining the age of 25. I had no more thought of competing than I had of playing professional baseball when I used to bounce a ball off the steps of my childhood home (well, that's not true), but I began to time myself on the pace clock and to do modest variations of my children's workouts. And to work on getting my weight down so I would look a little less ridiculous in a Speedo.

When my splits and my weight had reached acceptable or at least not embarrassing levels, I got the number of a Masters group in a nearby town and accepted an invitation to one of their workouts. They were a genial group, and they didn't laugh at me, though they did look skeptical when, at the beginning of time trials, I said that I could swim a 50-yard breaststroke in about 38 seconds. After I did, someone remarked that it was a very good time for the 35-39 age group. Since I was 41, I was more pleased at their mistake than at my accuracy.

The rest of the workout was less gratifying. Like many natural breaststrokers, I wasn't very good at the other events. But I had enjoyed the company, and though seventy miles round-trip was too far to commute for workouts, I looked forward to my first meet, which was also the first Masters meet to be held in Oklahoma.

That was discouraging, for the competition was as stiff as anything I encountered in national meets. The sponsors had shrewdly billed the meet as an opportunity to set a record, since all you had to do was win your event, so a lot of people traveled long distances and swam discouragingly fast. I didn't win anything, and I don't think I even placed, but I did learn something about the internal dynamics of Masters swim meets.

Like my children's meets, these were obviously stratified according to ability. At the top level were people who had been world and national class swimmers. One of my teammates was the first to use the flip-turn in the backstroke and won the national championship the year he placed second in the Olympics. Two men in my age group were also Olympians, and a friend of theirs was and for a long time was still swimming within a second of his medal-winning time in the 1500 meter freestyle at Helsinki in 1952. This top class shared a discipline and a past from which the other groups were excluded.

Next were the ex-jocks or, since I never encountered a top-level competitor from another sport, would-be jocks who were too beat up to practice the sports of their youth. As I got used to competition and discovered what events not to enter, I eased into this class, whose members could usually place in or even win some events, especially the less popular ones, more especially if the meets were not too large. Some might train harder than people in the first group and wanted to win at least as badly, but they could never overcome the advantage of years of coaching and workout in the past.

The third group was comprised of people who can be called recreational swimmers. They seemed to enjoy working out with a group and they certainly enjoyed swim meets, especially the social side. As competitors, they were the purest amateurs. Though they never won, they did what all swimmers are told to do and practice imperfectly: compete against yourself; try to better your times.

To non-swimmers, all of us looked equally insane. A new romantic interest came to her first meet as I was about to go off the block in a 200-yard breaststroke event. When I joined her after the race, she said, clearly reconsidering what the relationship might entail, "You do this for *fun*?" And I had thought of myself as fairly normal, at least as compared to one club's "Brute Squad," composed of people who entered the 1650-yard freestyle, the 400 individual medley, and the 200 butterfly.

Anyway, I hadn't thought of swimming in terms of pleasure, but obviously I did enjoy it. And there were many different kinds of fun. Going off the block was a major rush. It felt good to be able to enter —and finish —a 400 individual medley at the last minute because a woman from another team asked me to pace her. It was highly enjoyable to swim a personal best time. It was even more enjoyable to beat younger swimmers. The keenest pleasure of all came after a two-year layoff when I didn't quite catch a man ten years younger in a hundred-meter breaststroke and thought, before we hit the wall, "I'll beat him tomorrow in the 200." And did.

Just being at the meets was fun, though only if I was swimming in them. Masters meets, I discovered, were not at all hierarchical. Former Olympians might get together to reminisce, but in the rest areas and at social events they hung out with less proficient teammates. I enjoyed the unfamiliar sensation of being one of the smaller and quieter members of a group, for I discovered the principle that the better and more physically exuberant the swimmer, the more primitive the sense of humor. This was often manifested in the t-shirts they wore. My daughter's team shirt read "Swim Fast, Not Half-Fast." A fiftyish woman at Nationals sported one which said, in large letters, "I Am a Virgin" and, in much smaller letters, "This is a very old t-shirt." One national-class swimmer, asked how old he was, said, "I have an 18-year-old mind and a 72-year-old liver." The jokes, insults, and by-play took me back to the locker rooms of my youth.

And the meets were arranged to encourage mingling. Except at Nationals, races were seeded not by age or sex but by entry times, so that I might race against—though not compete for places or points with—a 25-year-old woman and a 70-year-old man in the lanes on either side of me. The system led to the friendliest kind of competition I encountered. Olympians stood up and cheered for beginners. People in adjacent lanes congratulated or consoled competitors in a way I'd never seen in team sports. Strangers held the waterproof cards which tell swimmers in longer races how many laps they have completed. Coaching tips were offered and even asked for.

Some were more welcome than others. For example, as I finished my 200 individual medley race the morning after a particularly strenuous social, a teammate told me that I was breathing too often in the freestyle. A matter of perspective, I said; it hadn't seemed nearly often enough to me. And a first-time woman swimmer who lost her bikini top in mid-race was loudly enjoined by a male teammate to keep swimming and not worry about minor details.

But meets happened only rarely. Those who train even fairly seriously at anything have to convince themselves that the journey is more important than the arrival, that practice is an end in itself. In the context of team workouts, that is not too difficult, for most drills and sets have competition built in. Sometimes there is too much. At a workout with my son's 11 and under group, the coach called for three 200 butterfly swims on an interval I have now forgotten but didn't make any difference because I didn't think I would survive. However, since my son was in the next lane, I knew I had to try or set a horrible example. So I churned eight lengths of the pool and tried to convince myself I could do it twice more. My son, too short to stand on the bottom of the pool, hooked his elbows on the gutter and announced, "I'm not doing any more." For once I was not inclined to lecture him about persistence. The coach said, "Well, John, when you swim it in a meet, you'll be hurting." "I'm hurting now," he said. The coach relented and let us swim freestyle.

More often, though, I was pleased to be able to complete the assigned workout. On July 4, 1976, for example, my son's coach had us swim bicentennial 200 fifty-meter sprints at two-minute intervals. I was at least thirty years older than the other swimmers, and I was tired for a week afterwards, but as my mother used to say, it was a good tired.

It was harder to push through solitary workouts because the only standard of measurement was the pace clock. Once, swimming in a pool without lane ropes, I bashed into a casual swimmer who had wandered into my lane. Experience had taught me not to pause or argue, so I reared up, said "Jesus Christ" in a loud voice, and prepared to go on. "Don't be angry," she said, and I thought, "If I wasn't angry, I couldn't do this to myself."

But most of the time I had to find other kinds of motivation. There was, of course, the sense of accomplishment. Less creditable but equally gratifying was the fact that my land-bound colleagues and friends expressed amazement at my dedication. And finally, besides the obvious benefits of conditioning, consistent training and some attention to diet occasionally got me down to the light heavyweight class for the first time in twenty years. I didn't look as good as the younger swimmers we enviously called "flat-bellies," but I looked very good for a man in his mid-forties and later. After my divorce, that proved to be an advantage—though not at swimming meets, where most people were surprisingly chaste.

Or at least I was, since I didn't have enough energy for more than one thing at a time. Throughout the seventies I looked forward to competing as long as I could manage to pull on a suit, though I wasn't as optimistic as a teammate who announced his plan to keep improving his times until he hit sixty and then to hold them. Both of us retired long before that.

Since then most of my cadre have also quit. A friend who went to her last Masters club Christmas party reported that she knew only one person from the group that competed from the mid-1970s into the 1980s. I saw my teammates only at meets, so I haven't talked to them to find out why they quit.

My reasons were at the beginning fairly complex and then became simple. For one thing, as Masters swimming grew in popularity more and more ex-swimmers came out of retirement and the competition grew stiffer. There are now qualifying times, none of which I could have made, for the Nationals. To put things in perspective, the first Nationals I attended in 1976 didn't seem much larger than my first meet in Oklahoma, and I placed fourth in both breast stroke events. In 1978, the field was larger, and I placed sixth in the 200 and seventh in the 100. In 1982, I swam almost as well in a higher age group and finished so far down that I didn't bother to count. The man who won the event swam a casual 50-yard warm-up lap two seconds faster than I had ever done in competition.

Of course, I had done some of my final training for that meet in the pool at the Purple Sage Motel in Snyder, Texas. As my personal life grew more interesting, my training schedule was interrupted more frequently and my incentive to go to meets for social purposes grew less compelling. The less I trained, the more arduous competition became, and the slower my times, the less I wanted to work out.

But that was less important than the uncontrollable physical factors that my ambitious teammate and I had not counted on. Swimmers are used to discomfort—a non-swimmer said he didn't want anything to do with a sport where "pain threshold" was part of the normal vocabulary—but parts of my body began to hurt in unfamiliar ways. I had thought that swimming butterfly was a cheap way to pick up points until a sports medicine specialist suggested that taking up the stroke at 41 was probably a bad idea and performed arthroscopic surgery on one shoulder. Eighteen months later the knee that had driven me to swim in the first place gave out, and the same man removed the damaged cartilage. When I asked him if I could still swim breast stroke, he said, "You can if you can stand it." When I got out of physical therapy, I tried one length and decided that I couldn't. Since I was hopelessly out of the running in backstroke and freestyle, my competitive career was over.

I don't know why my teammates quit, but two other members of our relay team got divorced since our last Nationals, so there may be a correlation between a failing marriage and dedication to Masters swimming. One very active woman had to quit because various parts of her body gave out. Some younger teammates moved away to other jobs; some older ones died. Many, like the former Olympian who said plaintively during workout, "I don't think I want to be a competitive swimmer," just got tired of the effort.

For years after I gave up competition, I continued to swim to try to keep my lungs and arteries cleared out, and I continued to time my splits and record them and my yardage, which got, respectively, higher and lower compared to those I used to record but that at least gave me the illusion that I was competing, if only against myself.

After experiencing back pain, I was told to take up water exercise, especially water walking. A man selling health products at a convention in the same hotel as my meeting said that it was a great way to meet women. He had no answer to my response: "Have you ever seen women who water walk?" Or men, for that matter. But I was still in search of a challenge, and I worked so hard that my hip joints began to complain, so that I may be the only person ever to be injured by water walking.

About then I moved to a retirement community in the Phoenix area which has two pools, one for bobbing up and down and one for lap swimming, so I resumed swimming, sometimes next to a former Navy Seal, who could swim twice as far in half as many strokes. Then my back complained again, and I was advised not to swim freestyle. So that left backstroke. Everything being compared to what, I still outpaced everyone —the Seal had moved out of the community—until the other shoulder popped and my orthopedics man counseled against backstroke and suggested breast stroke. Knees won't let me, I said. Well, he said, I guess you'll have to invent a new stroke. However, he did say that freestyle would be ok if I was careful.

What with caution and being out of town a lot, I didn't even do that for months, and when I got back in the pool, so many people were passing me, even using lousy technique, that I tried to take refuge in the illusion that they were younger or better trained. Or something.

I finally realized that swimming consecutive laps with any kind of effort was just too hard, and I began to alternate two or three lengths with a length of water walking. I still hit the interval button on my watch, partly to keep score but mostly to keep count of laps and of total time, which I hold to thirty minutes. But on the whole I get slower and slower and identify more and more with older people who swim even more slowly than I. I'm not sure whether I'm encouraged by the man, 85, who looks a lot like the comedian Buddy Hackett and gets in the pool wearing a snorkel mask and tube and bobs up and down for whatever time he prescribes. Perhaps we can take comfort in Dr. Johnson's remark on another subject that "it is not done well; but you are surprised to find it done at all."

One consolation is that my vital signs are close to what they were when I was working out seriously. And I still feel a little guilty when I miss a workout. Perhaps that is the real legacy from my Masters days. The prize is the effort itself.

LADIES' MAN?

On a recent visit to Budapest, I sat with a woman writer and good friend enjoying tortes and coffee at Gerbaud, the famous and ridiculously overpriced confectionary on Vörsösmarty Square, when she asked, apparently out of nowhere, if I were a ladies' man. That may have been because I'd published a book titled *Mid-Life Mojo: A Guide for the Newly Single Male*, much of it based, as the social scientists say, on extensive field experience. But probably she wondered because a woman whom I'd met in line at Charles de Gaulle airport a few days earlier had just spoken to me. I stumbled through some kind of evasive and inconclusive answer. But the question stuck in my mind and increasingly demanded an answer.

A former president said, notoriously, that it depends on what the definition of "is" is. As a product of Jesuit education, I started by trying to define terms. If "ladies man" means something like a hand-kissing, tango-dancing lounge lizard, then no, I'm not. I can't tango and can barely do a simple two-step, and there are parts to kiss that elicit a much more gratifying response. If it means "womanizer," "seducer," or "exploiter," I don't think I fall into that category—not that, in younger days, I didn't have that unrealized ambition. Now, much older and somewhat more experienced, I doubt that age-appropriate women can be seduced, though they can certainly be seductive. But I will accept and sometimes may even fit the Answers.com definition: "A man who enjoys and attracts the company of women."

The distinction between ladies and women is crucial. Having been raised on the fringes of the American South, I have always shied away from any female who proclaimed herself a lady because that implied that she demanded rather than earned respect. None of that "girl that I marry" softness, cuteness, and cultivated dependence.

Perhaps I can call myself a woman's man, though not exactly a male feminist. Somewhere I have a newspaper clipping in which I'm holding one end of a banner supporting the passage of the Equal Rights Amendment. My ex-wife thanked me, and I said that it was a great place to meet chicks, but that was for shock value. In fact, I had for years longed for women to achieve equality because I wanted them off my back financially, culturally, and in the broad sense politically so that they could stand up and take a real share in adult affairs.

I did start with one advantage: it never occurred to me to doubt that women could be intelligent, competent, and self-sufficient. My mother, some aunts, a sister, my wife, and later my daughter all have demonstrated that women were at least equal to men. That set a standard—brains, independence, good sense—from which I was unwilling to depart.

Well, mostly. In any case, I worried about how to relate to women. Raised as a pre-Vatican II Catholic, I grew up with the usual religious inhibitions about sex as well as shyness and a belief that my looks barely rose to the ordinary. Furthermore, the male culture of the time fostered a kind of casual misogyny reinforced by writers like Philip Wylie in the essay on "Momism." Jesuit suspicion of women in general and of predatory, i.e. marriage-minded, females in particular didn't make me any easier in the company of college girls, as they were then called.

But in my doctoral program, some of the most compelling professors and many of the brightest graduate students were women, including the one whom I eventually married—or perhaps, on reflection, married me. I assumed that marriage was for life and didn't seek or enjoy the company of other women—rare and not all that tempting in my professional career—and illustrated the truth of the interchange in *The Importance of Being Earnest*:

> *Miss Prism*: No married man is ever attractive except to his wife.
>
> *Chasuble*: And often, I've been told, not even to her.

Once divorced, I entered a new world. A woman maintained that I had cornered her at a social function. When I reminded her that I didn't move from my seat against a wall, she claimed some other kind of compulsion. Another didn't bother to protest but, after we had just met, pulled me, quite willing, in her wake to a series of functions. The mother of a former student called and was clearly—it took me a while to realize—interested in pursuing a relationship. Another time, stopped at a gas station along the interstate next to a van filled with teenage girls and two adult women, I was startled when one of the women said she'd remarked to her friend, "You take the girls and me and him'll run off." Outside the academic context, clearly brains had nothing to do with it. Inside academia, I got a second-hand report that a woman whom I barely knew said that I had a nice ass. I found it hard to object to being objectified then or, in more graphic terms, later.

Nor did I mind a male colleague's saying, with mixed wonder and envy, that recently he'd seen me with three different women, and they were all good-looking. I wasn't quite as pleased but couldn't reasonably object when a visiting male Hungarian poet wrote a squib about my being seen with various Susies, Marys, and so on because even I thought the situation funny.

Neither man seemed to think that brains had anything to do with my activity. In fact, brains or at least volubility were sometimes a handicap outside academic quarters. One very attractive woman said that she never had any idea what I was talking about and declined further involvement, so that I was forced to apply my standards despite my baser inclinations.

Another woman told her mother that I might be the only man she'd dated who was smarter than she was. She cut me loose after a few dates, but then, a mistress of catch-and-release technique, she did that to everyone.

On the other hand, one woman was initially attracted to me because I not only knew about Hungary and Vlad the Impaler but had read the rather obscure novelist on whom she'd written her dissertation. At last all those years as a graduate student and voracious reader had paid off. Another woman's daughter encouraged her mother to pursue a relationship with me, partly because it was like having a good-looking encyclopedia around. Later, I encountered a woman on a transatlantic flight who thought I looked adventurously like Hemingway.

This was after I had to give up seriously working out—two major joint surgeries—and had begun to flab up. So why was I still attracting women? One answer was that everyone was getting older and that demographically—single, straight, solvent—I was becoming a rarer commodity. Furthermore, I had learned to listen to what a woman had to say if she had an interesting story or comment. And to wait for her to make the next move rather than pounce. And realize that a relationship doesn't necessarily end when romantic involvement does.

Another reason was that in my mid-sixties, I moved to a retirement community, partly to get out of a town I'd lived in for half my life and was tired of, partly to be near the one of my children who was likely to stay in one place. Both the realtor who sold me a house and the woman at the title company inquired about my marital status—divorced—and about any commitments I might have—none. Both of them said that I ought to do very well in the community.

I didn't find a series of casseroles on my doorstep like the widower in the film "Dancer, Texas," but I did find that it was an advantage to compete in my age group, as in Masters Swimming. I had also learned not to move very far outside it. When a much younger woman assumed that I was ten or twelve years younger than I am, rather than trade on her ignorance, I told her the truth and asked if that were a problem. It was, and we've remained friends. But apparently I could still pass, for when my son-in-law returned from a retirement party in a Scottsdale bar, he said that it was a pity I hadn't been there because the place was full of after-market blondes.

It was just as well, because I've learned that sometimes I don't want to pounce—or be pounced on. The woman who asked the question which started all this once said that her husband had called her "an intellectual polygamist." That's a marvelous description of the ability to form relationships that may have a good deal to do with gender but little or nothing with sex in the vulgar and interesting sense. My friend is one of several women who are European literary intellectuals and who have become regular correspondents and useful friends.

Some former lovers have commented, only a little wryly, that I have a harem, and in the sense that I have multiple friendships with women in various countries, some former lovers, some not, I suppose that I do. That shouldn't bother anyone, and if it does, I'm sorry but unrepentant.

My attraction to and sometimes for women does disconcert some men. Recently, at a conference dinner, I was coaxing a baby girl to smile and laugh. A male friend said "There you go, charming everybody." (This is not a universal estimate of my character.) One rejected suitor—we shared the same rejection, but I didn't take it as personally—looked sourly and accused me of surveying a gathering for attractive women. Why not? I've been through enough break-ups to wonder, not as long-married people might, "What if?" but also "What next?" if the "if" materialized. I merely said that I was old, not dead.

I'd argue that this may be the most normal thing about me. Thank God I can still respond to an attractive woman—intellectually as well as physically. I've been attracted to a number of them, and some have, in various ways, been attracted to me. So if that makes me a ladies' man, I'm happy to wear the label even if I realized some years ago that I didn't have the energy to sleep with all the women I wanted to sleep with—and perhaps, and increasingly, not even all the women who wanted to sleep with me. However, judging from the personals ads in "Lovin' Life after 50," caveats about age, religious commitment, dancing skills, love of RV travel, and other impossible or improbable criteria means that their number is rapidly diminishing.

BOOKS: AN ADDICTION

When I told non-academic friends that I need to get rid of a large number of books, they asked, in wonder, how I could bear to part with them because they know how many I have and how important books have been in my life. But they don't understand how serious my problem is. I gave up both alcohol and tobacco years ago. Moderation is harder. This makes food and books a problem because I can't entirely do without either. But prudence and the expansion of my waistline and the jamming of my bookshelves dictate that I needed to learn how to do with a lot less.

I didn't hear the term "deaccessioning," librarianese for getting rid of books, until I was well into my professional career —until, in fact, I began to realize that it was a necessary concept and process. Like many addictions, mine started innocently enough and was probably genetically linked. My paternal grandfather was reportedly a book junkie; my mother and her father read voraciously and had shelves of books in their homes; and even as a child I had a modest collection of my own, some provided by an aunt who knew I liked to read and some purchased from the stock kept in one corner of my home town's lone stationery store. But if I had been given an association test, I would have responded to "book" with "library." I only bought books —Hardy Boys and other juveniles —that were too undignified for the local public library to stock and too embarrassing to take with me when I left for college in 1951.

There I bought the required texts, and occasionally—less often than I had at home—I went to the library. I was really interested in off-the-syllabus fiction available in paperback at the local drug stores like the novels of Aldous Huxley and other writers who, if not in the Catholic Index of Prohibited Books, were anathema to Jesuit educators in the 1950s. I also found *Discovery*, the slightly avant-garde paperback periodical which made me feel like a daring young intellectual. (You can't find anything like that in today's drug stores, sad evidence of the dumbing down of American taste.) Seduced by the thought of a free book, I sent for an introductory no-obligation copy of *Crime and Punishment* from a "fine editions" club after a Jesuit assured me that it was perfectly licit not to buy anything from the company.

I still have a few of these books. Some have been replaced by more authoritative or less tattered versions. Others didn't have to be consciously deaccessed; they just disappeared.

I didn't take many more books to graduate school than I had to college, but there I was able to use a major research library for the first time and began to realize how many books existed and how far behind I was in reading them. But I still regarded library books as a different species from the kind that one might actually own. Textbooks, by now mostly the primary literature, were, for the first time, something to keep for future reference, but critical and scholarly books you got from the library because in the first place they were too expensive and in the second a peripatetic graduate student couldn't house them or move them around. There were a few exceptions, notably the multi-kilo, multi-authored *A Literary History of England* referred to as "Baugh" which, we believed, contained the sum of all knowledge, or at least all the knowledge necessary to get us through our degree programs.

And I began to see that it was possible to own a lot of books, first by looking at the shelves in professors' offices and, more dramatically, when one of them was preparing to move and set out rows and rows of books for the graduate students to pick over. I found it hard to believe that anyone could have that many books and then that he could bear to leave them behind.

Although I was far down the graduate student pecking order, I managed to get a few, including a source-book on backgrounds of Elizabethan literature which, forty years later, I gave to a younger colleague.

Then there were textbooks—at first, only the desk copies provided for the classes I taught. Then the director of composition gave me a copy of a textbook I didn't have to teach from, and though the book itself was very dull, despite its pastel cover, the discovery that publishers gave away books was exciting.

When I moved to a larger university for the Ph.D. program, the first signs of addiction began to appear. The library was even bigger, the other graduate students seemed ferociously well read, and written preliminary examinations, a five-day ordeal covering most of English literature, lay only three years ahead. Everyone had to read certain key books in each field, and, some disgruntled students claimed, the library was so inadequate that even faculty members had begun to acquire collections of books important to their research. (It didn't occur to us that they might be too lazy to go to the library or just wanted important books to hand.)

Fortunately, the paperback revolution had accelerated, and I wandered through the Co-op making mental and even physical lists of books I knew I ought to read and wanted to own. My since-abandoned copies of Edmund Wilson's *Axel's Castle*, essential for intellectual respectability, and William York Tindall's *Forces in Modern British Literature*, crucial for the preliminary examination in this field, date from this period. So does the copy of a Francoise Sagan novel I passed on to my son, who knows a lot more French than I do.

When I got engaged and was officially out of my parents' house, I was given the sets of Dickens and Bulwer-Lytton novels that had belonged to my paternal grandfather and even read a couple of the latter, though I can't explain why. And when I married another graduate student, my wife and I joined not only lives but books, and those grew in number as we acquired primary and some secondary texts for our dissertations. We joined book clubs and subscribed to scholarly journals.

Dickens and Bulwer-Lytton did not survive the move to our first jobs, but most of the books did—and then to the second and third jobs, by which time our children's books were added to the load. Then the serious influx of books began, not only from desk and examination and review copies but from garage sales, especially rich in university towns, where each year for a decade I acquired fifty to a hundred books, not only about things I was interested in but in things I might conceivably become interested in, and uncounted children's books. Older colleagues retired and left their libraries to be shared among junior faculty and graduate students. Professional journals piled up relentlessly.

In late 1969 I settled into a large office and began to line it with bookshelves acquired through midnight requisitions. With 77 shelves, totaling about 230 linear feet, and at least another thirty feet in my library study and about twice that at home, there seemed no reason why I could not expand my private library indefinitely.

Losing the domestic shelf space in divorce ten years later didn't convince me that I had a book problem on top of the more obvious ones. Splitting the library was the least painful part of the process, for my wife's interest had shifted to social science and feminism, and the only books by male authors she wanted were the Readers Subscription sets of Eugene O'Neill and George Bernard Shaw, more for how they looked than for what they contained. I left the O'Neill without a pang but missed the Shaw until I got over it. The books that fell between we donated to a private school and the local Women's Resource Center.

I continued to be bullish on books for another ten years, though I did let some journal subscriptions lapse either consciously or through omission while I was out of the country. Still, my office seemed to afford room for infinite expansion — until, faced with the possibility that I might put together a Fulbright fellowship and a sabbatical leave for as long as three years abroad and with the certainty that I was going to have to provide shelf space for the visitor who would occupy my office in my absence, I had to face the consequences of my addiction.

Double shelving went only so far, and I had to make the first major and conscious decision to get rid of some books. Some of the decisions were, if not easy, at least not difficult. I had belonged to the Modern Language Association since 1961, and I had kept religiously all 108 regular numbers of *PMLA*, the scholarly journal it publishes, something over three feet. This doesn't count the annual Program issue, which I discarded, or the bulkier annual bibliography, which I had been taught to revere as an essential research tool.

As a result of too much time on my hands and some bad faith, I went through all 108 issues to see if there was anything I might use in my teaching or research. I kept just under half, not one of which was disturbed over the next eight years. The others I gave to graduate students under the illusion, more theirs than mine, that I was doing them a favor. They were also grateful for the copies of obsolete textbooks, some with commentaries I consulted less and less as I grew more confident or careless in the classroom.

Some books I sold. The copy of *A Literary History of England* I had carried through graduate school under the illusion that memorizing as much of it as possible would help me pass my Ph.D. examinations and moved several times out of sheer inertia now seemed superfluous, partly because there was a lot more literary history than there had been when I bought it, partly because I seldom read and never taught material written before the twentieth century, and mostly because nobody was going to ask me any questions about its contents. I also got rid of a number of duplicate copies of books, some of which I'd owned since the 1950s.

How much did I get rid of? It might seem simple to estimate: just measure the blank space on the shelves. That would be simple if there were any blank spaces, but of course there weren't. However, by double-shelving, I did manage to clear a half-dozen shelves for my visiting colleague and departed happily for Central Europe.

After I returned, I re-shelved my books and thought I could resume the status quo ante. But one day I noticed, on the shelves devoted to modern American novels across the room from my desk, my ex-wife's copy of William Faulkner's *A Fable*. And thought, "How many of my fingernails would they have to pull out with red-hot pliers to get me to read that again?"

That was the first time I'd asked myself the question in quite that form and in reference to a book I already owned. But now it seemed obvious, applicable not just to *A Fable* but, at least potentially, to every book on my shelves. Refined a little, it expanded into three related questions: "Do I ever intend to write about this book?" "Do I ever intend to teach it?" "Do I ever intend to read it again or for the first time?"

The first question was relatively easy to answer. After four decades in the profession, I might not have known exactly what I was going to write about next and still less what I was going to say, but I knew enough about my limitations to state that I would never write about Faulkner or Conrad or Lawrence or any number of other novelists I admire because I didn't have enough time left to master the body of their work and the mounds of commentary about it. And I would never write about some other novelists because in my view there isn't enough time for anyone to spend on topics that boring.

The question about teaching was almost as easy to answer. After years in the classroom, I knew what I'd be teaching. True, there was almost twice as much of the twentieth century novel as when I first studied it, but I felt obliged at least to think about adding new novelists rather than cycle through the complete works of old ones.

The third question I could avoid for the time being. Occasionally a student would gaze in awe at the crammed shelves and ask, "Have you read *all* these books?" "No," I'd say, "but I've read some that aren't here." And I still thought I might read some I hadn't read and others that I hadn't touched in years.

So, with the first two questions in mind, I began to run my finger across the books on all 77 shelves, turning on their spines those which got a "no" on all three counts. Whole categories and sets of authors went. Science fiction I had gotten bored with years ago, and my older daughter was willing to take it off my hands, though I didn't want to corrupt her taste with Vonnegut. The novels of Walker Percy, whom I'd never been able to read after *The Moviegoer*, went to the daughter of a friend. Her other daughter got the art books I had collected and rarely looked at. Chunks of secondary material about Renaissance literature and about drama theory went to a young colleague. William Styron, on the grounds that we'd already had Faulkner, just went. So did all of Nabokov except *Lolita* and *Pale Fire* because they were the only works of his I had read or was likely to read. Joyce Cary, who wasn't quite funny enough. Angus Wilson for the same reason. Iris Murdoch because I had despaired of trying to keep up with her output. The fiction of Norman Mailer, who has always reminded me of the Pope couplet: "Obscenity with dulness still must prove / As shameful, sure, as impotence in love." Mailer's essays keep getting pulled off the shelves and put back.

The books I managed not to change my mind about or to give away filled seven boxes on the floor of my office because I couldn't figure out what to do with them, though I later managed to donate them and many others to small Catholic colleges which needed all the books they could get. Occasionally I would dip into a box and give a book to a student, feeling rather like a recovering addict who is fostering someone else's habit to mitigate his own.

But these measures didn't begin to deal with my real problem, which was retirement. Since I was a college professor, I never had to retire, but I frequently thought about it, especially after I had acquired enough years to get full benefits. But I had to wait until I could think of what to do with myself afterwards. The department would probably allow me office space, but nothing as big as the office I'd inhabited for three decades. And that's even if I decided not to move to someplace that sounded more exotic than Oklahoma—meaning that the world was all before me, where to choose. So, despite the deaccessioning I'd already done, I still had more than two hundred linear feet of books either to move or to dispose of.

Some decisions weren't easy. I wouldn't move the long runs of three journals. That was two shelves and a bit. Two more shelves were full of *PMLA* and *Journal of Modern Literature* bibliographies, and now that the *PMLA* is widely available in electronic form, I'd have been an idiot to keep using the year-by-year hard copies even if I were still interested in that kind of research. So that was four shelves down and seventy-three to go.

One day, sitting in the recliner in my office, I looked at the four shelves—William Golding through Nancy Mitford on the modern British novel bookcases—that I could scan without moving my head uncomfortably. They held about 140 books. Then I applied my three test questions: will I write about it, teach it, read it? And a fourth, learned from experience in culling my record collection: Do I like it well enough to move it?

When I retired, the second question became moot. Even if it hadn't been, some of the writers—Golding, Margaret Laurence, T. E. Lawrence, David Lodge, Katherine Mansfield, Aubrey Menen, Mitford—could be consigned to the memory hole because I'd never taught them or would no longer teach them, never planned to write about them, and was not interested in re-reading them. But that was only a dozen books; not much of a dent.

The other two questions were harder to answer about the rest of the writers on my four shelves. There were eighteen titles by Aldous Huxley. My M.A. thesis satisfied my lust to write about him, but I might enjoy rereading *Crome Yellow* and *Antic Hay* and maybe even *After Many a Summer Dies the Swan*. But everything after 1939 could go, and that was seven more books.

Joyce had been a duty, sometimes a reward, seldom a pleasure. Nineteen books by and about him. I was old enough to admit that I was never going to read Richard Ellman's biography again or *Finnegan's Wake* the first time. I did keep *Ulysses* and one edition of *Portrait of the Artist as a Young Man*. Seventeen down.

D. H. Lawrence I have enjoyed, and still do, but how had I ever acquired twenty-eight books by and about him, plus several more I'd already boxed? Sixteen—minor novels, secondary works—went without a pang.

But things got touchy when I looked at my collection of Henry Green, Graham Greene, Christopher Isherwood, and Wyndham Lewis and thought about the still unwritten book on British fiction of the 1930s on which I've amassed stacks of notes and xerox copies and even some preliminary drafts. Would I write the book without implied pressure from annual performance evaluations? Still, even if I managed not to answer that question, I could get rid of almost everything they'd written after the thirties and, in the confidence or arrogance of long experience, some of the critical books about them. That was at least two dozen more books to dispose of.

In all, that was eighty-two of 140 books, or fifty-eight percent shrinkage —not bad for an hour's consideration. But that was four of seventy-seven shelves, and, assuming that I could maintain the same percentage across the other seventy-three, I'd still have well over a thousand books left. And the farther I went, the tougher the choices would become.

In one bookcase, the one within reach of my computer desk that contained most of my Evelyn Waugh collection, it was impossible to effect even a two percent triage. I was writing about Waugh during my engagement, during the loss of a job, during a divorce, and during many less dramatic occasions. He's gotten me invitations to Paris, Spain, and a London club, brought me friends, some of whom I've never seen, from all over the world, formed the center of my professional identity for my entire scholarly career. I could deaccess some duplicate copies of paperbacks and critical books, and I could certainly do without bound copies of dissertations which have been sent to me in the authors' forlorn hope that I could advance their careers even if I wanted to, but most of the books and all of the contents of two file drawers went on the moving truck.

Then there are books by friends and the dissertations of former students, some inscribed, which took up at least one shelf. Their fate depended on how sentimental I felt when I was ready to clear out my office. Friends, mostly yes; students, no.

One whole bookcase was taken up by copies, mostly multiple, of my own publications. I sorted out extra copies of most of the articles into neat piles. One I palmed off on my older daughter, who has a house and a sense of family; the others should have gone to research libraries with large Waugh holdings, but none offered to take them. For a while, I couldn't bear to throw them away, but finally I sorted out single copies and asked the janitor for a large trash barrel.

As I thought through the process, I realized that I was dealing with several different questions. One is practical: if I got rid of a book, would I be able to find another copy readily when I needed it? Another was professional: how long would I retain an interest in doing the kind of scholarly writing I'd done for thirty-five years? Or would, increasingly, scholarly work give way to the creative work I'd edged into during the 1990s?

The real question, though, was psychological. How much of the work, represented in the books I've used and in those I've written, that has defined my adult life could I bear to leave behind? Some day—an uncomfortable thought—I'll have to leave all of it. But not yet, the mind keeps saying.

When I retired and was, as kindly as possible, turfed out of my scholarly cave, I moved some books to my study in the library and some to the larger apartment I'd rented in order to have a home office. The others had been sold, donated, or just given away, though I couldn't bear simply to abandon any of them.

Then, on an impulse almost as sudden as my decision to retire, I bought a house a thousand miles away and had to deal with moving a little furniture and a lot of books. The last had become complicated by the fact that, without abandoning modern British fiction, I had been publishing on the literature of the American West and on Central European writing after the collapse of Communism. (I'd made the mistake of donating a good deal of Hungarian literature in English translation to the university library—the only decision I've really regretted.)

Waugh and his contemporaries went into boxes I'd scavenged from a newly arrived colleague who'd just emptied them into his office. So did much of the Western stuff and a fair bit of European literature. The books fit into the set of spring-loaded pole bookcases given me by my ex-wife, whether out of charity or malice I wonder every time I erect them. Then I bought an entertainment center with some shelving for books and found matching shelves at an estate sale. Finally, I hope, I inherited a bookcase from my daughter. Now they have pretty much been filled.

How did that happen? Most obviously, and honorably, from reviewing books in three different areas for a variety of journals, as many as two dozen a year, some of which cycle into my current writing projects. A few I've bought on-line because that's cheaper and more convenient than driving fifty miles round-trip to the nearest university library and paying for parking. Too many have come from the shelves of the friends of the local library—mostly stuff I might be interested in some day and am too lazy to find out if I am. Happily, almost nothing from garage and estate sales: the inhabitants of my retirement community don't seem to read many books other than those dealing with hobbies, health, conservative politics, and lower-middle-brow fiction. But still the books accumulate.

When I first quit drinking, other alcoholics would ask me how they could stop. I said that they had to be able to imagine themselves sober for the rest of their lives, and that whatever helped them to do that was the right program to follow.

Thus far, I have not been able to imagine myself without books, and a lot of books. A colleague who also gave up alcohol looked alarmed when I mentioned the idea and said, "Why would you want to?" So perhaps I need to go back to the analogy with food, which we can't give up if we want to live. But at least we need to keep paring away at the bibliographic love handles.

LEFTOVERS

My maternal grandfather was at one point in his varied career a horse trader, and my father would buy, sell, or trade just about anything animal, vegetable, or mineral. Both anticipated Woody Allen's family motto: The unforgivable sin is paying retail. Their influence may account for my compulsion to scrounge all kinds of sales for whatever I can find. But both men were adept at turning a profit from their acquisitions, whereas I couldn't sell ice water in hell. So what I acquire, I tend to keep until it's pried from my increasingly arthritic fingers.

During the thirty-five years I lived in a university town, I spent many weekends checking want ads for promising-looking garage sales and plotting efficient itineraries. So did many other people, including pick-up driving dealers who showed up an hour before the sales opened and ordinary people, some of whom I came to recognize, engage in casual conversation, and even share tips on where to find specific items. As one casual shopper remarked, there was nothing else to do until the movies changed at the local theaters.

Pickings were especially rich at the end of the school year, since departing students were leaving behind excess books, recordings, furniture, and appliances, like a victorious army on the march toward new conquests. More permanent residents also had garage sales, and these were a great indicator of the fads of two or three years ago. For example, at various times it seemed almost illegal to have a sale without a single-burger cooker or an ab-exerciser wheel with two handles. Sometimes odd items would show up in series, like steamer trunks or map-holders for small-plane pilots. Shifting tastes in music showed up in the sudden glut of Beatles albums. University-area books tended to be heavily intellectual or pseudo-intellectual; farther out, best-sellers and self-help books dominated.

I learned to avoid estate sales, where you'd pay only slightly more than new retail for used goods, and to learn that the posher the neighborhood, the better the merchandise and the more reasonable the price.

My children came to react to garage sales in reverse Pavlovian fashion—seeing a sign at a corner, they would yell, in chorus, "Dad! No!" But though they didn't enjoy the process, which involved their standing around sullenly or waiting even more sullenly in the car, they liked some of the results. All of the family's bicycles came from this source, as did a black and white TV for each child. (When I bought a color TV, my children wouldn't believe that it was new until I showed them the box.) Once my son, about eight, accidentally ripped his gym bag and worried wondered to his mother what Dad would say. "Probably," she said, "that there's another one just like it in the garage." His attitude changed even more when his friend from across the street looked at his room and said, "Where did you get all this neat stuff?" He mumbled, "My dad got it at a garage sale." Much later, when someone asked him if he needed a binder, he said, "I'm the son of Robert Murray Davis!" as if that were a sufficient answer. His older sister was more resistant, but after she left home, she admitted, sheepishly, that she shopped garage sales for various items, including the antique headboard I'm now using until she can find a place for it.

A lot of the stuff I accumulated was swept away in my ex-wife's final garage sale, including tools that I discovered, as a renter, I no longer needed. But I continued to attend garage sales because I needed to furnish my own place with kitchenware and some furniture. Some of that, too much, survived a thousand-mile move into the first house I'd owned in more than twenty years.

The new place is in an over-55 retirement community, a reservation for old people that offers nothing like the rich and varied garage-sale booty of my former home. For one thing, the homeowners' association severely limits or in some cases prohibits garage sales. People, or more commonly heirs, have to dispose of excess goods by hiring professional estate sale managers. For another, the analogy of an advancing army wouldn't work because people come here to hunker down, the longer the better, between working lives and assisted living quarters. An estate sale here is more like an archeological dig into a midden left by a long-departed society of folk who never planned to move.

In all but a few cases, books and records reflect commonplace tastes from years past, especially books about politics whose views would embarrass all but die-hard right-wingers, of which my community has a plentiful supply. Much more medical equipment, including a collapsible cane that I take on travels just in case a knee gives out, and that agitated German security personnel who thought it might be a rifle or a blow-gun. Lots of kitchen-ware and decorative items for all or no seasons. Some furniture, sometimes a whole houseful. The quality and state of preservation depend largely on where the sale takes place—the more recently the section of the community was built, the higher.

It's probably not fair to characterize the contents of an estate sale, laid out on counters and card tables, as outward and visible signs of a whole life, but that's what archeologists, especially amateurs, tend to do.

And people even moderately reflective should wonder with a chill when—not if—their own stuff will be exposed to the analytical view of strangers, what these observers will think of it, and what the heirs will do with it.

I've already given my kids the family heirloom pieces that my sister didn't get. As for the rest, even if they wanted some of the stuff, they don't have room for it. Not only does my son live too far away to make transporting it uneconomical, but he and his wife are still in a rearguard action to accommodate furnishings, many of them far more valuable than anything from my family, let alone my house, from her father's and grandfather's houses. Several pieces of my furniture—the headboard the least bulky—come from my local daughter's house and office, and she would take them back only reluctantly.

Some of the rest reminds me of a Los Angeles friend's reluctance to extend an invitation to visit because, he said, a friend told him that he lived like a graduate student. I reassured him because, while I had seen his apartment, he hadn't seen my living quarters. I don't think that I actually have any furnishings left from that period of my life—one divorce and many moves have cleared out that layer—but a couple of dressers from the unfinished furniture store date back forty years, the large and useful desk slightly farther.

Some of the books are useful if not particularly valuable. Anyone whose interests coincide with mine would welcome some twenty-five linear feet of books by and about British writers of the 1930s and another twenty feet or so of material about the American West and perhaps, if someone is really obsessed with one of the topics, drawers full of drafts, notes, and photocopies. But I doubt it. And the market for copies of the two dozen books I've published and edited is very slim. My son-in-law might want some of the books, but he will have to battle his wife to get many of them into their house. Maybe they can con a large library into taking some of the books.

For the most part, however, the estate sale manager will have to deal with my house pretty much as it is. I doubt that my children will be able to sell it as what is called locally a suitcase or turn-key deal—all the furnishings along with the structure, so that all you need to move in is your suitcase. (Speaking of suitcases, there's a large pile of battered pieces in the garage and a smaller pile of carryalls in the closet, since I'm the Imelda Marcos of luggage.) Very few people will want to devote one of the two bedrooms to an office crowded with books and file cabinets, two from garage sales, two from my daughter's office. Even fewer prospective buyers will share my taste and want to make room for several hundred jazz LPs, almost as many audio tapes, a fair number of CDs. Perhaps someone, probably a single male, would want the relatively new couch and easy chair and maybe even the kitchen and dining room table sets, the latter from an estate sale, though the former may be a loan rather than a donation from my daughter. But the oak shelving should get a fair price.

Electronics? One of the kids might want the newer laptop and printer, and maybe one of the grandchildren would like the old one until his or her tastes become more sophisticated. I know it works because, unlike its successor, it is compatible with the serviceable laser printer that has about 3,000 copies' worth left on the toner cartridge. My son-in-law might want the portable XM radio set, and a grandchild might want the portable boom box or even the portable CD players. But everything else is old or becoming obsolete.

That's not to speak of the storage box in the garage full of old telephones, many of them working, that I've picked up at various garage sales, and various cords that link to long-discarded computer hardware. An estate-sale manager would have a great time with those.

Kitchenware? The generation after mine doesn't even know what to do with their forebears' fancy dishes. My daughter has her maternal grandmother's and perhaps her mother's, as well as whatever she and her husband acquired in the early flush of homemaking. I need to get rid of the flatware that my ex let me take and the dish set I acquired from a garage sale when I set up my own place—it's been replaced by better but not valuable sets. Perhaps the kids will want to hold onto the metal cereal bowls they used as children and even the Corning ware set I picked up for $8, though it might, as my father used to say, hold their money together in a sale. But the miscellaneous collection of coffee mugs would go only at reduced prices.

A dozen or so 4x6 file boxes full of photographs might occupy young grandchildren for an afternoon or occasion a little guilt in my children for throwing them away. I've seen other people's photographs on display, and they are reduced to a depressing generic anonymity, faded ghostly presences that, it is hard to believe, were ever embodied.

Clothes? They seem to me an even sadder part of any estate sale, shells emptied of their owners, limp, sometimes shabby, mostly out of fashion, almost always, except for jeans, destined to clog the donation boxes at Goodwill. Men's clothes may seem even shabbier; we throw them away only under the severest duress. My closet reflects my moves across several climate zones. The good leather jacket comes out once a year, the topcoat not at all, and rain gear only for visits to Seattle. The one suit, bought for the last family wedding I'm likely to attend, fits or not depending on my will-power and exercise regime, and I have sport coats, slacks, and jeans in at least three different sizes, or did until I gave my fashion Nazi the run of closets and drawers. Even now, the survivors mark, like tree rings, the expansion and rarer contractions of my waistline. Some of the clothes are almost unworn because I bought them in an unwarranted spirit of optimism and keep in a kind of hope chest—hoping I'll be able to wear them again.

The saddest of the sad are the ties—I may wear one or two a year, and the youngest is at least five years old—and even more the underwear. I doubt that either item has ever moved off a garage sale table. In fact, I ought to get up from the computer and get rid of half a drawer full to avoid exposing myself posthumously.

The one advantage to having all this stuff is that it imposes a restraint on my making new purchases, since for any object that comes into the house, something will have to go out. At some point, as I've said, all of it will have to go out, and I think it would be wrong to burden my children with disposing of it. "Dad! No!" Therefore, I'm thinking of making a deal with them: if they take care of me in my decrepitude, I'll promise that, with my dying act, I'll set fire to the place.

Discoveries

Research & Recovery

When I began to do research as an undergraduate, I thought of it as a sedentary activity. At most it involved a physical journey to the library and around the stacks and then a mental journey around the material. I didn't get very good at it, mostly because I wanted to be a journalist and thought that all I had to do was go out and talk to people and watch and write down what happened.

In graduate school I learned about charts called bibliographies and later, having done some rudimentary work as a bibliographer myself, I discovered that some research libraries contained unique or very rare material that almost nobody knew about.

But until the early 1970's, I had only dealt with dead writers on whom scholars and librarians had done the preliminary work of collection and annotation. Then I assigned my graduate students the task of accumulating information about Donald Barthelme, a writer very much alive and my near-contemporary. As far as my students and I could tell, no one seemed to know much more about his career than we did.

At some point, I saw a biographical note about a critic named Jerome Klinkowitz that suggested he might be doing bibliographical work on Barthelme. I wrote to him, offering to give him my material, and since Jerry was and probably still is a highly energetic scholarly entrepreneur, before long, as part of a team working on a book-length bibliography, I was headed to Houston, Texas, to find whatever there was to find. The only clue I had was Jerry's assurance that Barthelme had published at least some undergraduate and professional journalism before he moved to New York to become a major writer of innovative fiction.

I checked into a motel near the University of Houston campus. As always, in a strange place with no immediate task before me and no reference points, I felt isolated and uncertain, wondering if I would be able to accomplish anything. To establish contact with a familiar structure, if not a familiar place, I headed towards the nearly deserted campus and located the administration building and the library. At least I knew where to go, but I realized that nobody had charted this territory, and I suspected that the Houston library was not going to be of much help.

I had worked on manuscript material by dead white males at the Humanities Research Library in Austin and the New York University and New York Public libraries in Manhattan, and I had found that special collections librarians, however old and crusty, were inclined to help people who exhibited some knowledge of their topic. Covington Rodgers, the assistant librarian at the University of Houston's Special Collections, was younger than I and not at all formidable. In fact, he seemed pleased that someone—anyone—wanted to use their materials and apologetic that they didn't have more.

They did have the files of the *Cougar*, the undergraduate newspaper, for which Barthelme had served as writer and editor between 1950 and 1952. The issues had an odd familiarity, especially Barthelme's columns written from the persona of "Bardley," and I realized that, from 1952 to 1955, I had written columns with much the same tone, though with less range and talent, for my undergraduate newspaper. It felt odd to have even this point of contact with a real writer.

But the printed sources were soon exhausted. Fortunately, I remarked casually to Rodgers that I had never been able to discover when Barthelme graduated from the university. He said, "That's simple enough," and called the registrar's office. (This obvious move would never have occurred to me, for I was twenty years away from newspaper work.) I could hear his end of the conversation: he insisted that "a major scholar" needed to know when Barthelme graduated. After checking, the official reported that he hadn't. He had accumulated more than enough hours for a degree, many of them in philosophy, but not enough of the required courses.

Once I realized that living people could give me information, and that Rodgers knew who some of them were, I realized that I was going to have to do what, in my brief journalism career, would have been called leg-work. First a lot of time on the telephone lining up people to talk to, which turned out not to be that difficult; then to the AAA map to find out how to get around Houston, which was.

My first stop was at the offices of the *Houston Post*, where, the *Cougar* had informed me, Barthelme had gone to work in 1951, though it didn't tell me for how long. Unfortunately, the newspaper didn't maintain an index, and the public library didn't begin to compile one until 1965. But the personnel office did give me the dates of Barthelme's employment, so that I would have to reel through only four years of microfilm in search of by-lined items.

The *Post* files contained stories about Barthelme's jobs as acting and then permanent director of the Contemporary Arts Museum, and that was another lead to follow.

But I decided to begin as close to the beginning of the written records as I could imagine. The secretary at St. Thomas High School, which Barthelme had attended for three years, said that they did not have files of the school paper, but that I could see the yearbooks in the principal's office, The faculty was on vacation and unavailable. Having spent fifteen years in Catholic schools, I was not inclined to push the matter.

The visit to Mirabeau B. Lamar high school, where Barthelme spent his senior year, started with even less promise. I could not be admitted past the office without a pass, and the beefy vice-principal who could issue it was busy haranguing a large young black man who was kneeling on the floor, arms outstretched in penance for some malfeasance.

Free to deal with an unknown adult, the vice-principal was guarded to the point of paranoia because he couldn't place me. I clearly wasn't a cop, and I wasn't dressed flashily enough to be a drug dealer. Clearly no outsider had ever wanted to visit the school library, and obviously he could not imagine that any Lamar student had ever amounted to anything. About to give up, I decided to show him my faculty identification card. Oh, he said, and signed a pass.

Upstairs, the librarian, Mrs. Renee B. Feeney, on the verge of retirement, was obviously delighted that someone was interested in an alumnus. She dug out copies of *Sequoyah*, the literary magazine in which Barthelme published poems and stories, and the school newspaper, which noted that Barthelme had been named Texas Poet Laureate "for his poem 'Inertia' on the subject of world cooperation." I had written some shameful things in my own high school days, but I couldn't recall having sunk that low.

Then south to the Contemporary Arts Museum, though not the building that Barthelme had worked in, to see what traces he had left. The files were in some disarray after fifteen years and a move to new quarters, but the staff was quite cordial. If they had more than one copy of a brochure or press release, they gave me the spare. Unique material? Take it away and copy it. To someone used to the rigorous security of research libraries, this was even more unsettling than the museum's current exhibit of George Greene's paintings of chastity belts for cockroaches and another artist's auto-wreck sculptures.

By the time I returned to the University of Houston campus, I felt more at ease talking to live people, perhaps because Farris Block, head of the News Bureau, was adept at managing interviews. He clearly regarded Barthelme as a protégé and told a series of anecdotes about Barthelme's editorship of *Forum*: soliciting money, battling with the editorial committee, authors, and printers, finding then-emerging writers like Walker Percy, William H. Gass, and Alain Robbe-Grillet, almost being fired for telephoning Jean-Paul Sartre in Paris without first asking permission.

One of the people Barthelme fought with was S. Wayne Taylor, still head of the university's printing services. I mentioned that I had worked briefly as a printer on a small-town weekly newspaper and then tried to steer the conversation away from my massive ignorance. Taylor, even more expansive than Block, still marveled at the energy and enthusiasm of a man, still in his mid-twenties, who was unhappy unless he was doing something useful or pumping people for information, often over ham sandwiches and frosted mugs of beer at the Algerian Cafe.

One thing Barthelme learned was typography. When he began, Taylor said, he did not know what a serif was, but he pestered the printers until they gave him the run of the shop. Taylor believed that Barthelme had been through every type-book ever published. In one he found the style he wanted to use for *Forum*'s title and pestered Taylor to order the five letters from Holland. He also learned to hand-set type, and would set a line, pull proof, study it, change the type, and repeat the process until he was satisfied.

In fact, Barthelme learned so much that Taylor asked him to teach a course in typography, and he produced a brochure, "Graphic Arts & Your Future," which he wrote, designed (insisting on 14-point rather than 18-point type), and set and reset perhaps a dozen times to get the layout exactly right. Then he fought with Taylor about the photographs. Barthelme did not like to have people in the photographs; Taylor insisted that a recruiting brochure should have pictures of students. They compromised: Taylor agreed to show only hands in the photographs of printing equipment; Barthelme agreed to show faces on the back cover.

Dr. Marjorie McCorquodale, one of Barthelme's English teachers at the University of Houston, also provided information, some of which, like that fact that Barthelme was color-blind, was of little use to the bibliographer. But she also said that while he edited *Forum*, he showed her a story without telling her he had written it. Published as "Pages from the Annual Report," by "David Reiner," it attracted the notice of editors of little magazines and of the *New Yorker* and, she said, was the real beginning of his career as a writer of fiction. Then, although I was some I.Q. points shy of eligibility, she took me to a Mensa meeting which was pleasant but not unendurably stimulating.

Then it was back to the University of Houston to do the kind of research I was used to: unreeling microfilm of the *Post* to find Barthelme's by-line. By the end of two weeks, I had discovered more than four hundred items, sufficient justification of the research funds I had received, which duly appeared in the bibliography. I drove back to Oklahoma, the day after Bob Wills died, listening to the Texas Playboys on almost every AM station across the dial, a dip into the popular culture of my teenage years in a small Midwestern town.

I was even more deeply immersed in the pop culture of my youth during my stay in Houston. Artifacts from my own past kept popping up: John Payne and John Wayne and Wayne King, Ma and Pa Kettle and Abbott and Costello, John and Bing Crosby. Even the columns of the *Post* that Barthelme hadn't written took me back to a world in which Texas had baseball minor leagues of its own, polio was still a threat, and the Dodgers heartbreakingly lost the 1951 playoff and marched triumphantly to victory in the 1955 World Series.

In many ways, I realized, Barthelme's early career anticipated my own. I entered college just after Barthelme went to work for the *Post*, our careers as columnists for college newspapers overlapped a little, and at times we expressed similar attitudes towards women, jazz, and non-canonical writers. Even our portraits, emphasizing crew cuts and glasses, could have been assembled from the same parts of an Identikit. By the time that Barthelme went to work for the University of Houston News Service —the same month that I began graduate school —he had already done, at the *Post*, what I thought I had been preparing to do during my undergraduate days and had tried, briefly and ineptly, to do during my brief career as a reporter for the Great Bend (Kansas) *Daily Tribune*.

I didn't spend much time regretting that I had not followed Barthelme to fame in New York, Instead, I took pleasure in the fact that I hadn't lost some of the skills I had learned as a reporter about finding sources and extracting information in the world outside library walls.

These things mattered only to me, but they did matter because, I realized for the first time, I shared them with a writer whose work I admired. I too had struggled, with more modest success, to acquire the skills and discipline which would enable me to move from the provinces to a larger world. But I had been slower to learn the value of my own past and the possibility of interpreting it.

This realization, more or less unconscious for some years, began the process of reconnecting me with the time when I had wanted to be a writer rather than a scholar. Perhaps the goals were not incompatible. Perhaps my professional journey was not finished, but as so often in my life, I had to wait years and travel thousands of miles before real change could take place.

"Stuff a Wife Can Understand"

Long ago, in the days before poststructuralist jargon really took hold in American universities, a colleague besotted by the plain style movement, perhaps because he was baffled by polysyllabic words and complex sentences, was condemning critical jargon. He pointed to me and said, "Now take Davis. He writes stuff a wife can understand." Since I don't think that any women were present—certainly not my wife, several parsecs brighter than he—he was not immediately shredded like an out-of-tune Orpheus.

A few years later, of course, directness and clarity came to be regarded as a handicap, and insistence on them a source of contention for members of an editorial board I served on until the new fashions prevailed, well before their followers, especially at Duke University, grew weary of them. By that time, however, I had shifted my own emphasis away from unfashionable scholarly pursuits like bibliography and textual study, first to what's now called creative nonfiction and then to cultural commentary or reportage or something I haven't bothered to name that may fit my father's category of "something a normal person might read" (as in "When are you going to write" that kind of thing).

But for a long time my style was hopelessly out of date in the academic world. Thinking back, I can see where I went wrong: I grew up wanting to be a writer. There was a price to pay—in 1950, I quit a job at the local Dairy Queen that paid fifty cents an hour to take one at the local weekly newspaper for twenty cents in the hope that I might learn something about writing. (This proved to be a prophecy of future income.)

E. J. Melton, the owner, editor, advertising salesman, pressman, and part time novelist, was the first author I met. He wasn't a great writer, but as someone pointed out, writers who had been printers in the days of hand-set type—Mark Twain is a prime example—acquire a physical sense of the value not just of words but of letters. Things probably started to go to hell with the invention of the Linotype, in time for Henry James' late style, which led to Twain's bankruptcy when he bet on the second-best technology, and can only get worse now that everyone can publish from electronic files. I set only a little type—headlines too large for the Linotype to handle—but Melton taught me to get to the point in the fewest words possible.

Later, when I began to write for my college newspaper and thought that I had to be fancier for a more erudite audience, the editors shook the big words and circumlocutions out of my stories until I saw their point and could try to pass it on when I became an editor.

By the time I worked—briefly—as a professional journalist, I had learned several important lessons. First, writing is before anything else a craft. If you can't manage the tools—grammar, vocabulary, syntax—you will never attain clarity, let alone grace, no matter how lofty your aspirations might be. Second, every day brings a new deadline, and there is no room for writer's block. Third, artistic temperament is a luxury whose price is too high. Later, a former student and now friend, novelist, playwright, and agitator Frank Chin, enunciated a fourth, especially applicable to formulators of theories in whatever school: "Don't start believing in your own bullshit."

Every semester I spent in graduate school reinforced the second and third lessons, and the example of the best scholars like Frederick J. Hoffman and Madeline Doran as well as the most promising graduate students, showed what one could do with mastery of the tools.

And of the material. Without knowing Evelyn Waugh's family motto, *Industria Ditat*—hard work pays off—they understood the concept. Of course, most of my peers then and some of my colleagues later worked hard, but some had trouble escaping the consequences of what seemed to be a fear of putting something in writing and standing behind it; some got distracted by serial domestic entanglements; some moved into fields—real estate, law, computers—more suited to their talents, and some fell prey to what Brother Antoninus/William Everson (and so on, not quite ad infinitum) called "the fallacy of the perfect work." One colleague felt it necessary, before writing a 500-word review of a scholarly book, to re-read all of the primary and many of the secondary texts involved. Some, of course, wrote or thought so poorly that, in a department meeting on criteria for annual evaluations, someone suggested, not quite seriously, that certain people be given credit for not publishing.

Some valuable lessons from journalism are echoed in Elmore Leonard's ten rules, with some corollaries, for keeping himself invisible as a writer and "to help me show rather than tell what's taking place in the story. If you have a facility for language and imagery and the sound of your voice pleases you, invisibility is not what you are after, and you can skip the rules." One sentence sums up his approach: "If it sounds like writing, I rewrite it."

These rules did not carry over to graduate school, though perhaps they should. Nor did the journalist's basic tools: look at the visible world, listen to people, take down what they say, prompt them for information, remember it, synthesize it, and put it into words. (Also, of course, to sound more expert than you are, but that is also essential in the scholarly world.) Well into my teaching career, I began to see that material from my life outside academia could be useful in dealing with literature —and, not incidentally, in disconcerting people who didn't share my background.

But I did learn something from books. For example, John D. Gordan's *Joseph Conrad: The Making of a Novelist* taught me how to look at a text as evolving, at a writer as someone who struggled not just with plots and characters but with nuance and rhythm in every word. More important, though, were the primary texts of Evelyn Waugh, the writer on whom I have worked most diligently since Kennedy was president.

It might be interesting, or at least revealing, to ask scholars of my generation, in which almost everyone wrote a dissertation on a particular writer, why they chose that one and how that choice affected not only their future careers but their attitudes towards writing and towards life. For example, my graduate school contemporary Harold Fromm began his career with a dissertation and book on George Bernard Shaw and is now writing about evolutionary neurobiology in *Hudson Review*, among many other things and in many other places. My former colleague Bill Holtz began as a Laurence Sterne expert, then published a biography of Rose Wilder Lane (daughter of Laura Ingalls Wilder of the *Little House on the Prairie* series), then a fine volume of autobiography. (Ex-poststructuralists like Frank Lentriccia and Jane Tompkins seem to write only about themselves and how they got famous and then disillusioned.)

I first became interested in Waugh when I reviewed *The Loved One* for a contest and won. In 1954, his irreverence and satiric edge seemed unusual in a living writer, especially in a Catholic writer. My affinity for his work was obvious to one of my professors, who said, "When I knew what you'd picked, I knew you'd win." But I wrote my MA thesis on Aldous Huxley, who expanded my vocabulary and range of general knowledge but did nothing for my style, and I didn't return to Waugh until the leader of a Conrad seminar was unable to continue and the students were farmed out among the faculty to do independent study. And then, as I said, I stayed with him for more than forty years.

Chasing Waugh down his nights and days, his visions and revisions in thousands of lines of manuscript and variant editions, had some interesting consequences. When my older daughter was in college, she reported that one of her professors had mentioned Waugh. Until then, she had regarded him as something like an adult version of an imaginary friend with whom I seemed to spend at least as much time as I did with the family. (At least she was kinder than the daughter of a friend who worked on Willa Cather—during a trip through Nebraska, the girl asked if they were going to stop every place Cather took a crap.)

For anyone interested in the craft of writing, Waugh is an excellent model. Unlike Huxley, who wrote as if he were being paid by the word, perhaps because his eyesight was so poor that he couldn't readily revise, Waugh is so terse that, as I found when I tried to summarize his letters for a catalogue of the holdings at the University of Texas, it is impossible to say things more briefly. Furthermore, although he had many personal idiosyncrasies, there were none in his style, which is why he has never successfully been parodied. And though he had many intractable positions, he never lost the ability to look and listen, however oddly he processed what he took in.

I'm not sure that the philosopher and novelist William Gass would think Waugh serious enough to be counted as one of the writers who

> chooses subjects, adopts a tone, considers an order for the release of meaning, arrives at the rhythm, selects a series of appropriate sounds, determines the diction and measures the pace, turns the referents of certain words into symbols, establishes connections with companionable paragraphs, sizes each sentence's intended significance, and, if granted good fortune because each decision might have been otherwise, achieves not just this or that bit of luminosity or suggestiveness but her [he's speaking of Katherine Anne Porter] unique lines of language, lines that produce the

desired restitution of the self. ("Go Forth and Falsify: Katherine Anne Porter and the lies of art," *Harper's*, January 2009)

Waugh did say that "what makes a writer, as distinct from a clever and cultured man who can write, is an added energy and breadth of vision which enables him to conceive and complete a structure." Probably neither Waugh nor Porter nor anyone else could keep all of Gass's caveats in mind and write even a sentence, though Gass admits that the process might be unconscious.

Anyway, both Gass and Waugh are talking about so-called creative writers rather than critics, and I was setting out to become a critic. Still, hanging around a great stylist all those years was probably good for me as a writer, at least sentence by sentence. Of course, I also read critics, biographers, and even some theorists in the innocent days when Wayne C. Booth was cutting edge. Some wrote and thought better than others, and in those days it was easier to distinguish sense from nonsense. Or, to paraphrase Hemingway's view of Pound as a mentor, they were often right, and when they were wrong, they were so wrong that it was obvious and didn't hurt you.

Potentially more harmful was the process of writing articles. Many of my contemporaries used what I called the gunfighter opening, in which every critic since Hazlitt was given twenty-four hours to get out of town—or else. Young scholars seemed especially anxious to establish themselves as alpha males or queen bees; their seniors, better established, affected a bemused pseudo-tolerance at the folly they witnessed.

One advantage to writing about Waugh, for whom there was a very short secondary bibliography when I began, was that there was very little underbrush to slash through in order to get to a clearing and begin work, so that I didn't have to kill off older rivals. I have to confess to some world-weary superiority in later years.

That might be called another story, but in fact it has a good deal to do with making the transition from article to essay. Writers of New Critical articles probed and analyzed a poem or novel, tying or purporting to tie everything into a neat, glowing whole. Essentially, they were dealing with relations between words. Their successors have done something of the same thing, though the term "interrogating" indicates their superior attitude towards texts. Neither school was officially concerned with people, reality, self-analysis (let alone interrogation), or doubt.

All of these are the province of the essayist or, to use the current and broader term, the writer of creative nonfiction. The first such piece I wrote, a quarter-century after I left journalism, was commissioned by a US State Department magazine published for Hungarians in the last decade of the Communist regime. I was warned not to deal with politics or religion or anything then controversial, and certainly nothing specialized. After some floundering, I realized that I crossed the Danube at least twice every day, that I had grown up on the banks of the Missouri River, and that looking at the two told me a good deal more about myself and my relation to my past than I had realized or was able to get into the essay.

However, I learned to look at the outside world and into myself. The effects on my writing are most obvious in essays on Steinbeck written almost twenty years apart. In 1970, Maynard Mack asked me to edit the Twentieth Century Views collection of essays on Steinbeck, perhaps because he knew I'd lived in California and Oklahoma, either not knowing or not caring that I'd never published a word on Steinbeck and had read relatively little of his work. My introduction was modeled loosely on Fred Hoffman's surveys of an author's career and accomplishments and on the subsequent criticism. It was based more tightly on my own survey of Evelyn Waugh's career, written just after his death.

Until now, I hadn't looked at the introduction in years. I stand by the judgments, and I'm rather pleased at patches of unexpected eloquence. But the only sign that it was written not by a disembodied and omniscient being from another sphere was a passage discussing Steinbeck's ability

> to show many people doing things with their hands, and do them naturally and without fuss. My mother's father, for example, could trade a horse advantageously, fix his car, drill and thread the seat for an oil plug, convert a carriage shed into a house, do all but the most complex veterinary's tasks, write guest articles for small-town newspapers, serve in two state legislatures, read voraciously, swear profusely and imaginatively, and, for recreational purposes, lie copiously and brilliantly. My father had been, among other things, a brakeman, a butcher, an oil field roustabout, and a salesman or trader of most movable objects. (*Steinbeck: A Collection of Critical Essays*, Prentice-Hall, 1972)

Of course, being a literary critic, I linked Grandpa Murray and Dad to versatile fictional characters from Twain's *King and Duke*, Orr of *Catch-22*, and various Steinbeck characters. But I did dedicate the book to my father, who sort of grunted but kept it on his bookshelf until he died.

In 1989 I was asked to write about Steinbeck in Oklahoma for an issue of *World Literature Today* celebrating the University of Oklahoma's centennial. I shrank from plowing back through stacks of Steinbeck criticism, partly because I was getting ready to leave for Canada and then Hungary and partly because the prospect seemed really boring, and decided instead to drive over to eastern Oklahoma and retrace, as far as possible, the Joads' route from south of Sallisaw to Oklahoma City. (I'd made the rest of the drive many times and in fact, having moved to Oklahoma from California, was a reverse Okie.) After some struggles with the material, I wrote

> What I found, not on any map or in any photograph I took [and certainly not in any critical book or article], but

there, between the lines of the novel where even Steinbeck could not have suspected it, was a piece of my own past and the past I share with my forebears and some of my contemporaries but not with my children. In fact, I am part of the last generation likely to read or read about the novel for whom it is not purely historical and scarcely credible.

I was born in Dust Bowl Kansas, and my family had moved numerous times—with characteristic perversity, mostly east rather than west—before settling in Boonville, Missouri, in 1939, which, as a Steinbeck character in *To a God Unknown* says, is now ours because we have some graves there. As nearly as I can figure, my father (who had died in 1988) and Tom Joad are almost exact contemporaries, and I noted that he "had a good deal in common with Tom Joad, including his suspicion of government and his attachment to family, besides their age" (*The Ornamental Hermit: People and Places of the New West*, Texas Tech UP, 2004).

Back in eastern Hungary, this time in Debrecen, called the largest village in Europe, I was preparing to write *Mid-Lands: A Family Album* (Georgia, 1992), which I described as reminiscent social history of a small Midwestern town after World War II. That book's evil twin, *Playing Cowboys: Low Culture and High Art in the Western* (Oklahoma, 1992), which began by describing my father's attraction to Tom Mix and his own early, adventurous life, was in part an attempt to explain the genre's attraction to me and to many others. (A poststructuralist said that I had done "cultural studies," and I felt like Molière's character when he was told that he had been speaking prose all his life.)

By the time I got to Moab, Utah, in 1999, on a visit prolonged beyond original plans, and had gotten weary of looking at beautiful rock formations, I became curious about the town, its history, and its inhabitants, and went around talking to people—interviewing, not interrogating—about what it felt like to live there. The result was my first newspaper feature article in more than forty years. Since then, I've talked to the manager of the Navajo Nation radio station, sponsors and vendors at the Sallisaw, Oklahoma, *Grapes of Wrath* Festival, directors and performers at the Gene Autry, Oklahoma, music and film festival, and many other people in many other places in middle and western American and in central Europe.

Some of the results appear in *The Ornamental Hermit*, my first collection of essays, published on the condition that I not use "essays" in the title. The first review I saw called me "amiable and erudite." That's the first time my name and the first adjective have appeared in the same sentence, so perhaps the transformation from scholarly articles is almost complete.

Or perhaps the essayist is influencing the scholar. In the mid-1990s, I was a panelist at a session of an international conference in England. The first panelist spoke with a heavy accent, and about the only words I could understand were "Derrida" and "Foucault." Or maybe it was "Lyotard." (Someone asked what I thought of him, and I had to say that my chief association was with dancers.) The second panelist, a Brit, spoke on Francis Bacon's influence on postmodern English painting, and since he had slides, there was something concrete to refer to.

I spoke about works by Elizabeth Bowen, H. E. Bates, and Anita Brookner dealing with Englishwomen abroad, linking themes, plots, and attitudes to each work's historical period. The panel's chair, a German, approached after the question period and said, "That was very interesting. You actually told us what the books were about!" Perhaps, like wide ties, the journalist-humanist-essayist approach may be so avant-garde that even a wife can understand it.

MUSEUMS

During my reading at the Zagreb Literature Live Festival in 2007, a member of the audience asked why so many of my poems dealt with a subject as boring as museums. Coming from a European, I found this so startling that I could only mumble that I found museums very interesting.

However, it seems a good or at least a provocatively useful question now that I've had time to think more clearly about it, and I realize that I am interested in museums because I have been interested in the past as long as I can remember, that in fact I have never been able to distinguish sharply between past and present, between my experience and that of others..

Long before I began to assimilate the experience of people remote in time and space, I listened eagerly to my family's stories about its various members. While they were not nearly as convoluted or tragic as those in William Faulkner's novels, they gave me a sense that two generations and sometimes more had been alive in a world that seemed to me both strikingly different and comfortingly recognizable. And as I learned more about history, including the history of American culture, I began to see my parents and grandparents in larger contexts. For example, my mother graduated from high school in 1927, the year that Lindbergh flew across the Atlantic and *The Jazz Singer* marked the beginning of the sound era for motion pictures. When she said that she was twenty-five years old before she knew that you could drink Dr. Pepper straight, I realized that this coincided with the end of Prohibition, an even clearer insight into what she must have been like as a young woman. This was reinforced by the story about her and Dad being stopped at a road block set up to catch Pretty Boy

Floyd and sweating nervously because they were bringing a trunk full of booze into still-dry Kansas.

These stories were plausible, unlike most of my Grandpa Murray's, which were entertaining in a fabulous way, and by making past events dramatic, this oral tradition helped to give me both a sense of period and of continuity, especially as reinforced by music from their era which taught me that the 1920s were far more lively than the sepia-toned 1950s, what with "Sparrow in the Treetop" and such drivel. (I still prefer jazz of the late 1920s—Louis Armstrong's Hot Five, almost anything with Bix Beiderbecke, Sidney Bechet, Coleman Hawkins—and am still able to place, at least by decade, most jazz and pop music performances, though I couldn't tell you how I do it.)

Another source of information and entertainment was the family archive which included my mother's high school yearbooks and, for a brief period, one of my father's until I pointed out a photo of an attractive girl signed "To a real hunk of man." Somehow that disappeared. These books and family photos gave me a sense that my parents had not always been old. And rummaging in attics and drawers turned up what I didn't know were artifacts that reinforced my sense that the past could exist in the present. This stuff, as well as family, was something that we could share across generations, creating cultural as well as blood links.

I'd be tempted to say that none of the things preserved in attics and drawers was museum quality, though visits to small-town historical museums show me that I'd be wrong. And it's disconcerting to see labeled as antique stuff I clearly remember using. Of course, none of this could be called art, except in the loosest sense. The first museum I encountered was in the Missouri State Capitol in Jefferson City while visiting my grandparents during legislative sessions. I was fascinated. Since I wasn't more than six at the time, I can't remember much about it, and since now, even in the museum's expanded state, it can be covered in one or two hours, it couldn't have been much then, but it did convey the sense that a whole lot of other people had been alive. And Thomas Hart Benton's murals, completed only a few years before my visit, must have been the first murals and perhaps the first paintings of any kind that I had seen. My grandmother had the good sense to let me wander around by myself, or seem to, and stop when and where I wanted.

I didn't enter a real museum until I went to college in Kansas City and discovered what was then called the Nelson Gallery and was stunned by what seemed an enormous collection of classical art that made (still makes) Benton's murals look like cartoons. I remember only two pieces from that period because of my younger brother's reaction. We entered the galleries from the side, and the first painting we saw was resolutely modernist. I almost had to tackle him to keep him from leaving and steered him into the classical gallery where he stood a long time before a painting with a Biblical figure, probably Caravaggio's *John the Baptist*. For the first time, I experienced pleasure from art by sharing it with someone else. (About that time Evelyn Waugh dragged a friend from a Klee exhibit to the National Gallery and, standing before an old master's work, exclaimed, "The difference is that they started earlier and they worked harder"—sharing in a different way.)

After that, graduate school caused a gap in my museum-going partly because I was immersed in canonical literature and partly because neither Lawrence, Kansas, nor Madison, Wisconsin, had significant museums. I did buy my first print, of Dali's *Christ of Saint John of the Cross*, to give to my mother, and she enjoyed it enough to have it framed, and this was another kind of sharing. My first purchase of an original art work was a drawing of *Leda and the Swan*, for which my then wife and I traded a washing machine and then, because I felt guilty, another twenty dollars. It hangs on my bedroom wall, although I've become so used to it that I hardly notice it.

My literary study did introduce me to names of artists. Evelyn Waugh's first book, a biography of Dante Gabriel Rossetti, had some discussions of technique, and when I read the novels of Ronald Firbank and encountered probably more allusions to painting per page than in almost any other novelist, I learned how ignorant I was about broader culture. Like one of his characters, I didn't know the difference between Manet and Monet, let alone anything at all about Murillo or Zurbaran or dozens of other painters. And, then and now, I hate not knowing things.

When I moved to Chicago, I did manage to snatch a few hours from my first full-time job and work on my dissertation to visit the Chicago Art Institute. If I didn't alleviate my ignorance, I at least saw work by Manet and Monet, and I experienced my first non-aesthetic and definitely non-reverential pleasure from Jean-Baptiste Joseph Wicar's *Virgil Reading the 'Aeneid' to Augustus, Octavia, and Livia*, at that time hanging over a staircase landing and exhibiting a staring eyeball so thickly painted that it seemed to pop out of the canvas. Done in conventional academic style, it's not a great painting, but it showed me that even B-list art could give pleasure of a different kind from that provided by a major work.

Then came another gap during my time in California and my first years in Oklahoma. In Oklahoma, I did take my children to what museums were available between events at innumerable swimming meets, and I tried to make those visits educational as well as enjoyable—with mixed success. However, my daughter remembers the trips fondly and hopes that I will take my grandchildren as well. But most of the museums displayed artifacts rather than art, and except for the Philbrook in Tulsa, they did little to expand my experience or knowledge of art.

That began to change when Educational Testing Service invited me to read Advanced Placement essays in New Jersey, travel and a modest honorarium paid. The work was grueling—

I read as many as two hundred papers a day—but it gave me a jumping-off place and an excuse to indulge myself with extended visits to New York City, Washington, DC, and Boston, where I could see major works of art by the dozen and encounter some surprises, like a pastoral landscape from early in Jackson Pollock's career and James Hampton's over-the-top *The Throne of the Third Heaven of the Nations' Millennium General Assembly*. The first showed me something about the strange paths that lead from apprenticeship to maturity, the second that the artistic impulse, however strangely generated and obsessively or erratically followed, is ineradicable in the human imagination. Both, as well as obviously major work, showed me that art could be appreciated for its surprises as well as for its accomplishment. And at some of the lesser Smithsonian museums off the Mall, I saw that while there was a good deal of talent, there was a shortage of genius. This immersion at least began to show me what I liked, though, as with music, I couldn't say why with much precision.

In Boston, looking at the sarcophagus with a husband and wife embracing in death, I was moved by an image of fidelity that contrasted with my marriage, in the process of collapsing, and for the first time was able to see art as a reflection of my experience as well as a piece of artistic craftsmanship. (Months later, in the Metropolitan Museum of Art, standing with a very handsome woman before a Rubens nude, I heard her say, ruefully, that she was born three hundred years too soon—a collapse of aesthetic distance even more total than mine.)

A year later my first trip to Europe, a sort of wandering scholar's version of the Grand tour, took me to Budapest, Venice, Florence, Paris, and London and perhaps two dozen museums of varying degrees of fame. I learned to laugh at myself during my first days in Budapest when, at the National Gallery, I saw a very nice painting by Festő Magyar from the seventeenth century, then another in the mid-eighteenth century. Well, Impressionists lived a long time, so why not

Hungarians? Then I found another dated in the nineteenth century and resorted to my dictionary to discover that the name meant "Hungarian Painter." Oh . . Embarrassing but not crushing. And, freed from the obligation to marvel at masterpieces, I began to have some sense of period styles, especially of self-portraits.

At the Fine Arts Museum in Budapest and elsewhere, I came to appreciate work by artists largely unknown because they have been overshadowed by the big names, like trumpet players (Tommy Ladnier and Jabbo Smith come to mind) eclipsed by Louis Armstrong, especially painters like Tivadar Csontvary whose work doesn't seem to have traveled well outside his country. I learned to seek out churches and minor museums not on the usual itinerary to rest my mind from too much greatness. In Florence, faced with long stretches of stairs, I better understood the view of a character in Ronald Firbank's *Valmouth*: "I date my old age...from the day I took the lift first at the Uffizi," and had a clearer insight into the sexuality of the character in *Vainglory* described as looking "like a Saint Sebastian with too many arrows." Away from the major museums, I now knew enough to be surprised and delighted by paintings of a brown-haired Virgin and of a fully clothed St. Sebastian in Florence. I began to see humor in objects like a sculpture of a man looking as though he was shooting a fade-away set shot and in Vienna a painting of a Roman reveler reclining on a couch, surrounded by nubile nudes, with an expression very much like Alfred E. Neuman—"What, me worry?"—in *Mad Magazine*. I learned from the Kunsthistorisches Museum that there can be almost too much of a good thing and that the collection of the Art Institute a short walk away is smaller and much more manageable. I learned to ignore E. M. Forster's cautionary advice in "Not Looking at Pictures" to keep irrelevant personal memories and associations out of what he thinks should be a purely aesthetic experience. Of course, it would be silly to ignore the tutelage of experts like Clive Bell or to refuse to learn about technique, but if art is communication, what it communicates shouldn't be limited to modernist or any other puritanical, constrictive theory.

Two years later I got to spend five weeks in Paris, giving a few lectures at a branch of the university, spending mornings writing what became part of a book on the American Western, afternoons visiting a museum or just wandering around, and evenings at theaters showing movies in English. At that time, my faculty card was a free pass to the Louvre and many other museums, so I was able to drop in, fill my senses to their capacity, and leave before I was overloaded. At a major exhibition of Claude Lorrain's work, which paired drawings and sketches with finished work, I got an inkling of the structure that underlies a painting.

Back in the US, I continued to visit museums whenever I could, and once, wandering through a Remington exhibit at the Amon Carter Museum in Fort Worth and arriving at some late work, slightly blurred in outline and subtly different from earlier, hard-edged images from his years as a magazine illustrator, I said to myself, "Damn! I bet he'd been to Europe and seen work by the Impressionists." When I discovered that this was the case, I realized that I had lost, if not my amateur standing, a part of my ignorance, earning Lady Bracknell's disapproval of "anything that tampers with natural ignorance. Ignorance is like a delicate exotic fruit; touch it and the bloom is gone."

By this time, I could admit, at least to myself, preferences that were not always fashionable: Manet over Monet, almost anyone over Renoir, Picasso, and Rauschenberg, Pollock over Klee; in Western American art, drawings over watercolors and watercolors over oils (all that color is seductive and overwhelming); the Netherlands realists over the Tuscans. That a whole lot of El Greco or almost anyone else, mounted without the kind of information and structure that the French gave to the Claude exhibit, demonstrates that less can really be more. That minor museums, like the one in dour, Calvinist Debrecen, Hungary, can offer unexpected delights, like the portrait of a woman with a bare bosom and bright smile, the only one among neighboring grim matrons.

It's probably a failure on my part, but I came to prefer paintings that imply a narrative, and I remember best work that calls for a caption, like the painting of a watch in the Rijkmuseum (not *The Night Watch*) in which an elaborately dressed man, his back to the viewer, looks down over his shoulder as if to say, "Does this make my ass look fat?" Or work, like Leonardo's *Portrait of a Woman*, with brown hair, that I enjoyed more than the *Mona Lisa* because it hadn't been smeared by millions of eyeballs or the superheated prose of Walter Pater and others.

What else did I learn? That I could spot a Rembrandt two rooms away. That I felt confident enough in my aesthetic choices that a friend and I could agree, looking at an exhibit on Texas honky-tonks in Lubbock, that, given a chain saw and forty-five minutes in east Lubbock, we could mount a better exhibition. That when, on a tour of the local museum, a lecturer asked the difference between a Byzantine-style painting and a swirling, dramatic painting from about 1610 (I looked), I answered "The Renaissance," with the rise of individualism and the sense of tragedy, since the second painting was contemporary with late Shakespeare. He went to the second painting, looked at the date, and didn't ask any more questions. But another member of the audience asked, "What do you do?"

I could have answered that after forty-five years in the classroom I could make a lot out of very little knowledge, but said something more gratifying to my ego. And I have not only heard the names of the painters whom Firbank mentions but have seen work by most of them—though I can't swear that he didn't make up the titles.

Once my reach threatened to exceed my grasp. Evelyn Waugh's heirs tried to arrange a traveling exhibition of his collection of paintings, mostly from the late nineteenth century and worth very little when he bought them. They wanted me to write the catalogue. What the hell, I'm easy. It was fortunate, I suppose, that the project wasn't funded, since I couldn't possibly have stretched my little knowledge that far. But it might have been fun to try—tempering, in the words of a character in Waugh's first novel, "discretion with deceit." Or pure bluff.

Most important, however, I have learned that the painters are or were living human beings with whom it is possible to share experience, even jokes, and that, especially in portraits, we can learn a good deal about what human beings were like not only in the past, whether they be cardinals, grandees, merchants, or Rembrandt painting himself, but in people of any time. When the paintings are beautiful or striking or horrifying or affect our aesthetic sense as well as our emotions and understanding in any way, we can reach into the attic of our collective past and bring forth something valuable in a unique way. Most important, we can see that the work was created by individuals not unimaginably unlike ourselves and shed the chronological provincialism of people who marvel that, centuries ago, people could aspire, create, and achieve in ways that still speak to us.

That's one way of sharing. Another way is to introduce friends and family to work that has given us pleasure. While visiting my son in Des Moines, I took him to the art museum, where he was as captivated by Francis Bacon's *Study after Velasquez's Portrait of Pope Innocent X* as my brother had been by Caravaggio decades earlier. At the very well mounted exhibit on the life and career of Miles Davis in St. Louis, I stood next to a black man in front of the album cover of *Sketches of Spain*. He turned to me spontaneously and asked if I'd heard it. "I own it," I said, and we had a brief moment of shared connoisseurship.

And you don't have to know or even see the person with whom you are sharing. An episode of the sit-com *That Seventies Show* ends with a freeze-frame of characters in a diner, arranged like those in Edward Hopper's *Nighthawks*. People who don't recognize the allusion aren't necessarily bad or stupid, but they are missing the pleasure of a shared experience, an aesthetic sympathy, available to those who do. And, as I said, I like to know stuff.

APPENDIX:
PHILISTINE'S TEN COMMANDMENTS
FOR VISITING ART MUSEUMS

(Complied after visiting five museums in three days)

1. You are not obliged to like any particular work.

2. You are not obliged to like anything at all. But if you don't, then you should examine your life and especially your imagination.

3. If you don't like a painting, it doesn't matter who painted it and when. This tip will save you untold amounts of time.

4. No museum should be allowed to exhibit more than five works by any one artist. If they do, you can stop looking after three—even if the artist is Rubens. Especially if it is Rubens. As a Ronald Firbank character says, "The busiest man who ever lived most certainly was Rubens." (Except maybe Picasso, who didn't hit full productive stride until after Firbank's death.)

5. In looking at non-objective art, you are allowed to remember the quotation from Evelyn Waugh's *Put Out*

More Flags. It's about a woman painter, but gender does not matter. "...you can positively hear her imagination creaking, as she does them, like a pair of old, old *corsets*, my dear, on a *harridan*." Earlier painters may be no more imaginative, but at least the two hundredth Madonna gives you something to look at. And every St. Jerome shows something about the artist's and period's conception of religion—or who was paying him off.

6. The more modern it is, the truer it is that less is more. Compare Louis Morris's *The Pillars of Hercules* and Lucio Fontana's *Concept especia*l at the Thyssen in Madrid with Jose Guerrero's daubs.

7. The same truism applies to classical art. Too much paint can be stunning. Stick to portraits and small canvases until you're ready for the epic.

8. Don't be afraid to laugh. If Bosch hadn't intended you to laugh, he wouldn't have stuck a bouquet up a figure's backside in *The Garden of Earthly Delights*. And Goya wouldn't have had shown Maria Tomasa Palafox holding a paintbrush and looking as though her sitter had broken wind. The portraits, especially, are character studies, and not all characters are venerable.

9. A corollary of 8: If the painting reminds you of something or someone, enjoy the association. Bosch's *Un Ballastere* looks a lot like Bruce Willis, or vice versa. As I noted earlier, the central male figure in a painting in the Kunsthistoriches Museum in Vienna reclines on a Roman couch, surrounded by nude women. He looks very much like Alfred E. Neuman in *Mad Magazine*. It isn't art criticism, but it's fun.

10. Keep going. The more you see, the more context you have and the less strange some things will seem. But don't go in the hope that looking at art will make you a

better or more desirable or cultured person. It won't do any of those things. Go because you can find something to enjoy.

11. For those over fifty: It is better to sit on a bench in front of a painting you don't like than not to sit at all.

GET OFF MY ROCKS
OR, SUFFER LITTLE CHILDREN

There doesn't seem to be a lot of graffiti in central Lisbon, or I didn't notice it because my Portuguese is minimal. But one graffito in English showed up at various locations; only once in Portuguese. It read, "He who is without faith is the looser."

I'm used to impressionistic use of English—try a provincial Hungarian menu—but this could as easily have been a philosophical proposition. I lived for more than thirty years in the American Bible Belt, where the Congressional delegation is ultra-conservative in religion and politics even by the standards of the Republican Party and the Baptist Church. The same attitudes are tiresomely evident in the editorial and letters columns of the state's largest newspaper. So it seems self-evident that faith, at least of a certain kind, constricts and narrows. That's as true of my doctrinaire leftist acquaintances as it is of my so-called representatives in the national government.

The great thing about travel, especially alone in a new country, is that many of the usual boundaries and limits either disappear or don't seem to apply to me. That isn't really true, of course. There's gravity, economics, language, and various moral, political, and religious lessons I think I've abandoned or outgrown. But I can either forget those for a while or, in the unfamiliar context, see them in a new way. And, as I discovered when I took the train to Sintra, that's as true of aesthetic principles as it is of the more bourgeois principles.

By the time I got to the old casino that's now the contemporary art museum in Sintra, I had passed in front of thousands of square yards of framed, cased, and sculpted objects ranging from the prehistoric to the post-modern, which was often much cruder-looking, though shinier, in the museums of Lisbon.

Some of that was by artists whose work I'd seen and been impressed by elsewhere; some was derivative in depressingly obvious ways. Some, especially that of Portuguese artists new to me, had a fresh perspective on old themes, as in the Pentecost scene where an apostle at the rear of the group has raised his arm to fend off the tongue of flame like a man attacked by a bee, or in the *Birth of John the Baptist*, where maids are performing the necessary but usually undepicted task of cleaning the floor after the delivery, or in a portrait of the apostles as a very funky looking and sometimes overweight downscale group of real human beings without haloes or Tuscan gloss.

But even this kind of faith-based realism, though welcome, could not be described as loose, and it certainly wasn't unfamiliar. Nor were the classically modernist works on the first floor of the Sintra museum. But at the head of the stairs to the second floor lay stones, strewn loosely in a rough rectangle about ten by four feet or so. Just lying there. No frame or rope or anything else to separate the rubble from the rabble.

In *The Short Reign of Pippin the Fourth*, Steinbeck has a scene in which an old man is pulling statues out of a moat. Vandals have thrown them there, he says without indignation or surprise. Some people throw them in; others pull them out.

I like to think of myself as a puller-out, but that day my first and very strong impulse was to kick one of the stones—in fact, to fuck with, maybe fuck up, this unprotected and at least potentially random scattering that dared to call itself art—like Dr. Samuel Johnson dealing with what he considered Bishop Berkeley's preposterous theory that phenomena exist only when perceived.

I didn't kick anything, of course, and after reading the legend identifying the rocks as Richard Long's "Sandstone

Line," I moved counterclockwise, like a good patron, through the rooms containing the other exhibits. All were more colorful, if not garish, than what I still had trouble calling Long's scattering, since it didn't look like one thing, and many were more obviously "transgressive," to use last year's popular term, than his rocks. But all had a necessary relationship between part and whole and a definite shape imposed by framing or welding or clamps, and all looked like something.

But none stuck in my mind like Long's or raised questions as interesting. Can a work of art exist in a form that is neither accidental nor fixed—loose? If I had dislodged one of the rocks, would I have been a vandal? Was it even possible to vandalize a work that was, in legal terms, an attractive nuisance? Did the piece invite, indeed demand, action like the one I'd contemplated? Would Joyce's Stephen Dedalus say that the rocks excited kinetic emotions rather than the proper contemplative, aesthetic response?

By the time the circuit brought me back to the landing, a school group, teenagers, had invaded the second floor. They gathered at one side, looking at each other until one boy stuck out his arms for balance and hopscotched in gaps between the stones from one side to another like a broken-field runner.

That emboldened the rest. A girl used it as an obstacle course; then a slender black kid in glasses walked from end to end on the stones themselves. Then one boy reached down, picked up a small wedge-shaped stone, and made as if to put it in his pocket. A second boy grinned, gestured as if to say "Piker," picked up a stone larger than a bread-loaf, and pretended to conceal it in the fold of his t-shirt.

In any other museum I know of, there would have been guards, alarms, Dobermans, admonitions, expulsions. But either the Portuguese are very tolerant or they didn't care. And I noticed that the kids didn't molest or play with any of the other pieces.

Their horseplay reminded me of an incident from the late 1960s that I hadn't thought of in years. The Catholic grade school in Norman, Oklahoma, had closed from lack of teachers, and some of the parishioners had volunteered to help convert it into a day-care center for low-income families. We cleaned and sawed and screwed and collected equipment from garages and attics. Then the Christian Education Director, an earnest young man named Gabe Huck (even Flannery O'Connor would have been embarrassed to make up a name like that) found some very rough-cast concrete circles lying in a field at the former Navy Air Base north of town, got help loading them into a pickup, and installed them on the playground for the children to use as stepping stones.

When I unrolled the newspaper next morning, I read "Major Art Theft in Norman." A restaurant in Oklahoma City had commissioned work from an environmental artist; after the concrete cured, the circles were to be displayed on edge in some kind of pattern. The Norman police chief speculated that the thieves had to be from New York or someplace like that because locals couldn't be sophisticated enough to realize the value of the art.

Paper still in hand, I dialed Gabe. "Uh, Gabe. You might be interested in this story...."

After various gulps and "Oh, my Gods!" he called the police and fessed up. Fortunately, the artist had a sense of humor, donated his work to the day care center, and was photographed watching the children hop across his stones.

The Portuguese teenagers had the same impulse, without adult assistance. They didn't want to fuck up or fuck with the stones; they just wanted to fuck around with them. I just wanted to take a photo, and with a flash at that, though I figured that the light couldn't damage even sandstone—and no one yelled at me.

A few days later, at the Guggenheim in Bilbao, any guilt I might have had was dispelled by the legend next to another

Long installation. Long photographs "his interventions as a means of preserving what nature will eventually undo." This solved two problems: what term to use for what Long does and what to think about the teen-agers. They were forces of nature. I was not.

I was given another perspective at an exhibit of resolutely modern art in Budapest. In a darkened space curtained off from the main hall was a CD-projection of Ange Leccia's *The Sea*, shifting, fluid shades of black and gray undulating across the wall at the far end. It reminded me of a toy, various colors of sand enclosed in a thin plastic oval, I'd given a friend's grandson. Every adult who passed in front of the light flinched at seeing his or her shadow and ducked out of the way. But a boy, about eight, started in delight, waved his hand in front of the projector, and ran toward the shadow of his head, becoming, at least temporarily, in and of the work.

This is a very different impulse from that of the kind of person who throws acid on Giottos or tries to smash Michelangelos —or even paints mustaches on copies of the Mona Lisa. Those people want to dominate by appropriating or destroying something that others value. The children I saw want to enjoy it. The teenagers didn't actually take the stones, though they probably didn't put them back exactly as they found them. The boy left no mark on the wall.

Of course, this kind of interaction wouldn't work across Heroes' Square in the Fine Arts Museum. All you can do with the lovely small Rembrandt, "The Slaughtered Ox," is to look at it. And that is, as the line in the old Latin Mass went, "fitting indeed and just," the kind of thing that the Aquinas-besotted Dedalus would approve of.

And children and even adults wouldn't want to interact with the art of extreme transgression (though there might be an impulse to punch out a performance artist that could probably be exercised only in Portugal) like the cadaver in the Royal

Academy reported by a colleague. That sort of thing isn't cathartic; it's emetic.

The work of Long and Leccia is designed primarily to be contemplated. But unlike the Rembrandt or even the wrappings of Cristo, it's looser. While it may be based in a belief or even a series of tenets, it admits, even anticipates, the possibility that boundaries don't have to be constricting or confining. And in suggesting the possibility of freedom from ordinary constraints —an aesthetic holiday—this kind of art provides a kind of pleasure, even joy, not found in art bound by frames or even spot-welding.

Not everyone agrees—including, I discovered after I sent a copy of my essay to Richard Long, who responded with "My work should have the same status (and "protection") as any other work of art. It is not there to mess or play with, by walking over or through them, by kids. (or anyone). Or to be stolen."

I understand, respect, and basically agree with his position, but I also sympathize with the teenagers and remember Walter Mosley's character Mouse in *Devil in a Blue Dress* who, enjoined from shooting a captive, cuts his throat instead. When reproached, he says indignantly, "If you didn't want him killed, why did you leave him with me?" Or to recall another kind of installation, why not, practically or as an aesthetic statement, walk up to Marcel Duchamp's *Fountain*, called "the most influential work of modern art" in a survey of critics, and use it for its original purpose? Would that fit with the spirit of Dada? If not, why not? Do not, as the authors of *1066 and All That* caution, attempt to write on both sides of the paper at once.

GOING NOWHERE IN AN ORDERLY FASHION

When *The Way Things Go* (*Der Lauf der Dinge*), the short film by Peter Fischli and David Weiss, came out in 1987, I had been in Oklahoma for twenty years, and if cultural lag is not mentioned in the state's constitution, it is embedded in the culture. So when I saw it in 2008, it seemed fresh, surprising, and delightful. And it gave me a new way of thinking about art, less from the critic's than from the producer's viewpoint.

Those who haven't seen the film can find clips on google.video.com or buy the 30-minute DVD from a variety of on-line sources. For those who can't wait, a brief and inadequate description: one thing rolls into another, which tips a bottle which fills a cup at one end of a teeter-totter which raises a candle to light a fuse which ignites a flare....and so on until the carefully ordered series of physical reactions just stops. Excruciating suspense is created when a rope connected to a filled trash bag unwinds from a pole, like a tether-ball in reverse, coming closer and agonizingly closer to a tire, finally nudging it forward to create another reaction. Or as the summary at *http://www.frif.com/cat97/t-z/the_way_.html* says, the film "simply records the self-destructing performance of Fischli's and Weiss' most ambitious construction: 100 feet of physical interactions, chemical reactions, and precisely crafted chaos worthy of Rube Goldberg or Alfred Hitchcock."

I saw the film at the Hirshhorn Museum on the Mall in Washington, DC, on a screen in a corridor between two exhibit rooms. As my companion and I came near enough to see the film in progress, all of the seating was taken, and I insisted on waiting to see the whole film. As I watched, other people started to pass through, and many—most males—stopped to watch. Not everyone laughed as much as I did—women don't seem to find it all *that* funny—but no one who sat down left before the film ended. My only question was, how many cases of beer did it take to work out the whole process?

When I got home, I found a YouTube clip and sent the link to everyone who might appreciate it. Only two people responded. One, a European scientist-journalist-novelist, said, "Have no idea what to do with it. Too many options." The other, a semi-postmodernist writer in various genres with some interest in scientific theory who once wrote a short story illustrating Heisenberg's Uncertainty Principle by leftovers from the refrigerator, said ". . . and then the world comes to an end. Who spends his life thinking up —and setting up—nutty stuff like this?" For somebody who has seemed to embrace what John Steinbeck used to call non-teleological thinking, this seemed an odd reaction.

These people are very intelligent and very good friends, and in the years I have known them, we have rarely disagreed, so I turned to Google to see what other people thought. One of the first things I found was by Arthur Danto, a widely published and respected philosopher and art critic. He praises the film accurately and eloquently, but he and fellow viewers also found "meanings that touch on waste, violence, pollution, exhaustion and despair" that somehow imply "the pointless horror of unending war" (*http://www.postmedia.net/999/fischweiss1.htm*).

Thirty or forty years ago, this analysis would have left me abashed by my naiveté in simply enjoying the process. Now, more confident or more stubborn, I decided that Danto had to be very well-educated to be that wrong. But he did raise, consciously or not, a kind of corollary to Stephen Dedalus's question in *A Portrait of the Artist as a Young Man:* "Is a finely made chair tragic or comic?" Looking at the materials—mostly junk—Danto sees tragedy. Looking at what the creators do with them—get everything to work in logical but surprising ways—I see comedy and consolation. In the same vein, Godfrey Reggio in *Koyaanisqatsi* sees the procession of clouds as lyrical but seems to scorn, by speeding up the film, the procession of car lights on a freeway. I marveled that the freeway traffic manages to work at all.

To check my reaction, I called up a clip of *The Way Things Go* for my four-year-old grandson—who crowed in delight, said "Bang" when a fuse sputtered, and demanded more.

That was interesting, because he is currently obsessed with Thomas the Tank Engine and his companions and accessories, an enthusiasm his parents use as a way to reward approved behavior. The official narrative is also teleological—cooperate, live for your job, obey Sir Topham Hatt, the slightly bloated capitalist who owns the Isle of Sodor which the railroad services. The official web site has various games and puzzles, all of which have definite and prescribed outcomes, with recorded regrets for failure and congratulations for success.

My grandson enjoys the on-line games, but in playing with his trains, he is primarily interested in connecting one piece to another and moving them around—or, in the case of the ones with friction motors, in watching them move back and forth. They don't have to get anywhere. Perhaps, as someone said of George Bernard Shaw, he cleverly coated the pill of his lessons with the sugar of comedy—and the public even more cleverly licked off the sugar and left the lesson.

But some people need a moral, or at least a destination. Destination clearly matters to my two friends and to the amazon.com poster who "can't begin to understand how [Fischli and Weiss] could go to all this trouble and NOT have a punch line for it." I decided that these responses stemmed from Aristotle's dictum that

> A whole is that which has a beginning, a middle, and an end. A beginning is that which does not itself follow anything by causal necessity, but after which something naturally is or comes to be. An end, on the contrary, is that which itself naturally follows some other thing, either by necessity, or as

a rule, but has nothing following it. A middle is that which follows something as some other thing follows it. A well constructed plot, therefore, must neither begin nor end at haphazard, but conform to these principles.

"The Way Things Go" is all middle, and Aristotle would not regard it as a whole. But if one can accept the idea that the journey, not the arrival matters—it sounds Zen but is actually Montaigne—then the film itself can be considered an entity and a conclusion.

Not everyone can see it that way. Of the thirty-four people who rated the film for Amazon.com, twenty-two gave it five stars, eight four stars, 3 three stars, and only one two stars. That reviewer was "somewhat disappointed" and thought the much shorter and more polished Honda commercial "Cog" (*http://www.videoclipstream.com/akamai/h-l/honda/*), which moves a series of parts in a sequence which ends with a completed car rolling off a ramp, "better in pretty much every way." However, another commentator maintains that while "Cog" is "slick and perfect," *The Way* is rough and ready, chaotic and a little bit insane"—perhaps "the madness of art" Henry James spoke of.

Since the purpose of the commercial is to get the viewer to want to buy a Honda, it is not only teleological but, in Stephen Dedalus's distinction, kinetic rather than static, and therefore an inferior work of art because it arouses "desire or loathing." But *The Way Things Go,* though by one definition kinetic since it shows the transfer of energy from one thing to another, is aesthetically speaking static, so that "The mind is arrested and raised above desire and loathing."

Danto admits, paraphrasing Kant on art, that *The Way* "seems purposive while lacking any specific purpose." But *pace* Dedalus, is the film a work of art? Would Aristotle be satisfied with the idea that the film itself is a kind of end? And even if he wouldn't be, would Aquinas, via Dedalus, see it as satisfying his definition of beauty as "the apprehension of which pleases." It certainly pleased me and most on-line respondents, some of whom say to those disappointed by roughness or cuts or inconclusiveness, "Lighten up!"

But my postmodernist friend's question remains: why bother doing this, or, as he refrained from asking, for that matter any purposive rather than purposeful work of art or anything else? Why, to take an immediate example, am I writing this essay? In "Why I Write," George Orwell offers four succinct purposes: sheer egoism, aesthetic enthusiasm, historical impulse, political purpose. Danto might strain to place my motive in the last two, and I have been conscious of the second in dozens of revisions, physical and mental, for precision and rhythm, and I did want the result to be a logical and harmonious whole. Egoism—of course. I was pleased at my ability to dredge from memory various allusions, some of which had to be verified by Google.

But my real motive, which Orwell only hints at, if at all, is to see if I could do it, bring the task to completion. I began and have continued over several days without any idea of what I'm going to do with the essay once it's finished. For years, a rhetorician friend, told of work in progress, has asked about my intended audience. I always replied that I'd worry about that when I was satisfied with it. Perhaps I was relying, unconsciously, on the advice of Professor Helen C. White: "Just keep sending it out. Someone will publish it."

Since I retired and no longer have to file an annual report to justify my existence, I send things out less and less frequently. Instead, I use e-mail to circulate material among a few private friends, like Shakespeare's "sugared sonnets" before Francis Meres assembled them for print, though I have no—or only a few—illusions that someone will do me the same service.

Perhaps, by not rushing into print, I have regained my amateur status in the root sense—doing something for love rather than for gain. I'm able to do so for two reasons. First, I have been able to afford to, earlier because of a tenured professorship, then because of a (thus far) adequate retirement income. Second, the internet has freed me from the tyranny of hard type. It's easy to circulate what I write, and if I am desperate to go to hard copy, there are dozens of alternatives. Or not alternatives: for some book reviews, I have been able to choose electronic over hard copy publication in a small literary magazine because that form is easier for possible readers to see, and my second book of poems is available both in .pdf file and on-demand publication. The fact that there seems to have been no demand doesn't bother me.

Between the Renaissance and the electronic age, between the security of inherited income, sinecure, and, less surely, patronage, came the domination of hard type, a period in which the often unspoken motto was Dr. Samuel Johnson's "No man but a blockhead ever wrote, except for money."

Today, few writers would turn down money, but far fewer have the chance except for the genre writers who churn out a book or two a year, leap to the *New York Times Book Review* list, give way to other members of that cohort, and resurface in turn. Almost all so-called serious writers have to have some kind of day job—often teaching appointments supplemented by lecture or reading tours. This has some advantages, perhaps dubious. Anthony Burgess, who lived by writing, noted with a mixture of scorn and envy that John Barth was able to write books like *Giles Goat-Boy* because his professor's salary gave him time and security.

That cushion between artistic desire and economic necessity gives the writer, and perhaps other artists, a place to play, to test his or her capabilities, and to take pleasure in completing the process. That's the kind of satisfaction I'll feel in completing this essay, perhaps something like the satisfaction that greater writers felt in completing even works with the most depressing implications like "A Modest Proposal" or *Nineteen Eighty-Four* or, if Danto is right, *The Way Things Go*. That pleasure can be regarded as an addition to Orwell's four reasons.

The work, then, can give pleasure to the creator as well as to the audience. Sometimes the audience can find nothing pleasing, for as Sturgeon's Law maintains, "Ninety percent of everything is crap." That's because some people aren't careful enough about the details of the craft. Of course, there is always the eye of the beholder. When John Steinbeck was asked why he wrote, he told a story about a woman whose children asked about the process of making a baby. When she began to explain about sperm and eggs, they interrupted with "We know all that. But *why* do people do it?" The mother thought a minute and said, "Because it's fun."

If You Don't Like My Peaches...

*"... they invented new notions ideals and points of reference
as well as new anxieties and disgraces..."*
—*Ottó Orbán, "Poets"*

Heading west from the Yakima Valley in Eastern Washington, I could see that the land had begun to slope too steeply for vineyards and orchards and that I would soon pass the last of the roadside stands filled with plump fruit. Although I wasn't really hungry, I stopped to buy cherries, far cheaper and incredibly tastier than the ones available in supermarkets in the Sonoran Desert. I hadn't planned to buy anything else, but the peaches were so tempting that I added them to my basket.

Back in the car, I ate, as usual, more cherries than I'd planned to, but I could tell that the peaches were at the peak of ripeness and juiciness. Suddenly, like a pop-up ad on my computer screen, a line from T. S. Eliot's "The Love Song of J. Alfred Prufrock" flashed across my mind. "Do I dare to eat a peach?"

I hadn't thought of the line in years, but it took me back to the mid-1950s, when I first encountered Eliot's poem and it seemed to embody not only my response but that of a whole generation of would-be intellectuals to a complex and intimidating world.

Anyone familiar with Kansas City in 1954 might think it odd that my contemporaries and I would be affected by the poem narrated by someone with an acute testosterone deficiency—hardly our problem. The atmosphere and setting were nothing like Eliot's smoky, fog-bound, winding, and almost deserted London streets. Kansas City's air seemed clear and often more than crisp; the streets seemed, to a small-town boy, full of traffic and exotic-looking people or, late at night, stretching into the night with endless promise. We could see "one-night cheap hotels": one north of downtown had a sign reading "Rooms 25 cents. With electric light 30." But none of us ever went there or even to the Kay Hotel, which purportedly rented rooms by the hour for sleazy, illicit, and disturbing purposes. The cafeteria spoons we used to stir our coffee would have disgraced the tables of Prufrock's hostesses. Some of us might have heard of Michelangelo, but I'm sure that none of us had ever seen any of his work.

For that matter, we didn't know any women who talked of Michelangelo—though if we had, we'd have been even more intimidated than Prufrock was. We tried not to look it, as I can see in a photograph from about 1953 that my first serious girlfriend sent to me fifty years later, in which, 50 pounds lighter than I am now, cigarette dangling from my mouth, I look rather like a cross between James Dean and Buddy Holly, though the body language looks tight and defensive.

At any rate, the women I knew at all—"best" would be a gross exaggeration for any of them—were probably not mature enough to have much hair on their arms, though I was surprised, the first time I got that far, to see fine hairs between the first breasts I had a close look at. (Unlike John Ruskin, who had an emotional meltdown on discovering that his bride had pubic hair, I survived the shock. By now, when a woman talks about showing her true colors, we know where to look for them.) We had heard about mermaids, and the Catholic girls most of us encountered might as well have been as unbifurcated as their sea-born sisters as far as we were concerned. And as far as our Catholic educators wanted us to know. (As George Carlin, a couple of years younger than I, said, in response to the 1950s line, "I'm not one of *those* girls," "Where *were* those girls?") And according to the subtext of some Jesuit advice—not always that sub—girls were to be respected but on the whole avoided.

In those days, being ignorant of or, alternatively, shocked at the simpler anatomical facts, let alone the more complex and interesting social ones, was, in a phrase I hadn't yet learned, *de rigueur*. So was being sensitive, diffident, and, above all, modest. Those of us who were at all sensitive knew all about "wriggling" with embarrassment at or fear of saying the wrong thing, of having a woman respond to an overture by saying that she hadn't meant to encourage us, and of fearing to disturb the universe—even if we had any idea of what the universe was. As Stephen Dedalus thought, in James Joyce's *A Portrait of the Artist as a Young Man*, a book we weren't encouraged to read even though he too was Jesuit-educated, thinking about everything was very hard.

Mostly we didn't try. My contemporaries and I had far more to be modest about than our fellow Missourian Eliot. We didn't know that he had a far more prominent lineage than any of us. We could see that he was far more intelligent and better educated—we not only didn't know that many languages, we didn't even know that some of them existed until we read the notes to *The Waste Land*. But "Prufrock" was most of all a psychological challenge, for it introduced us to the concept of ennui, the sense that our lives were over without ever having happened. *The Waste Land* was just plain intimidating, and I doubt that many of us even tried to read it.

Like many of my contemporaries, I first encountered "Prufrock" and *The Waste Land* in the 1951 printing of Cleanth Brooks and Robert Penn Warren's *Understanding Poetry*—and not only the poems, but page after page of very daunting New Critical explication. Harold Bloom may not be right about everything, but his theory about "the anxiety of influence" describes very well the attitude that many of us had towards Eliot's poetry because it seemed obvious that if one was going to write poetry at all, that was the way to do it. (Much later I found that poets older and more talented than I like Robert Lowell and Richard Wilbur thought so too. Later still, I discovered that they were able to recover from that illusion.)

Brooks and Warren did include poets from older traditions, but William Carlos Williams was represented by only one poem, "By the road to the contagious hospital"—no commentary—and Walt Whitman not at all. Wallace Stevens was represented by two poems, Dylan Thomas by one. W. H. Auden had five poems in the anthology but no commentary, and since he seemed perfectly understandable even to a nineteen-year-old, there was some question as to whether he and Eliot could both be called poets because he didn't require that much explication (another word of many that was new to me).

I'm not blaming "Prufrock," which after all used language far more interesting about emotions far more complex than any poetry I had been taught in high school (Bliss Carman and Richard Hovey are names that stick with me, though none of their poems do. A little repression might not be all bad, in poetry and sex, as long as the words are accurate and the emotions genuine). Nor Brooks and Warren, who showed me new worlds of the possibilities of language. But the poems they chose, and the commentaries they provided, convinced me that poetry was just too hard, at least the kind of poetry that their commentary seemed to value above all others.

Some of my elders and contemporaries were quicker to see that there were other traditions and ways of operating, but it took me three decades to find that out—partly by reading but mostly by meeting, talking to, and reading poets more or less contemporary with me. Allen Ginsburg's *Howl*, which I now see as the prophetic poem of his generation, as *The Waste Land* had been for Eliot's, came too late to speak to me psychologically, though poetically it had a delayed effect on many poets of my generation and older. Looking at other poems—many of them in the *New Yorker*, for example—I often wondered "Why bother?" Reading poems by friends and colleagues like Arthur

Oberg, some of the many post-Wintersians in Santa Barbara, and some experimentalists in Oklahoma, I began to think, "Hell, I can do that!" Or if not precisely that, something of my own not impossibly different. So Harold Bloom was only half right: influence can occasion resistance, confidence as well as anxiety.

Although I resisted Wordsworth's poetry from the moment I encountered it, I have to agree that the kind of poetry I write and, at least from my own period, am most likely to read comes in the language of common men. Not all readers agree. In fact, when a friend copied one of my poems for his class to analyze, the students wondered why it could be considered poetry, since they not only recognized the words but could understand what the poem said. Maybe they were right. Judge for yourself.

> Long Distance Love
> There is no news, and there is never much:
> one slept, one didn't, what s-he did instead;
> the mail was this or that; the weather such
> and such; what separate, scattered children said;
> what's on TV, or will be; who was here
> for lunch or talk; films showing or to come;
> consoling word that children of a peer
> are faring somewhat worse and staying home;
> the office gossip; scandals of both states;
> the paper shuffled, work there is to do
> before one even thinks of setting dates
> to come together. Nothing really new.
> Phone lines, like final couplets, bear the strain
> of longing's burden they cannot sustain.

My friend asked the students how many lines it had. Lots of pencil-tapping produced the answer, fourteen. Did anything rhyme? By god, it does! So what has fourteen lines and a rhyme scheme like that? Oh, crap! It's a sonnet! So: does that make it a poem? Does language have to be "poetic" to be a poem? Does it have to have esoteric meaning or lots of footnotes and allusions (anyway, obvious ones)? Well....

I don't know if his students were convinced, but I take some consolation in the fact that another friend, a specialist in Renaissance literature, says he likes it a lot, though he remembers best a much briefer poem recounting three of my grandfather's maxims, ending with "Three squares of toilet paper will suffice." That's about as far from *The Waste Land* as one can get both in language and spirit. Sometimes it's fun just to screw around.

That goes for life as well as art. It took me a long while to stop worrying, like Prufrock, about presuming or being, or not, Prince Hamlet and to learn that when a woman compares you to a fictional figure, she has only aesthetic and psychological interest in you as a specimen. Anyway, Hamlet dies. Screw that! Some of us learned that being the Fool isn't necessarily bad—he generally had the best lines—and that we didn't have to swell anyone else's progress, unless, of course, we had organizational ambitions. There were other roles, of course, but as John Barth pointed out in *End of the Road*, one of his earliest, shortest, and most interesting novels, we could make a choice among dozens in what a character called a spirit of "cheerful nihilism." By the time I had stopped worrying about or even wearing ties, a friend observed that I seemed to walk into a room as though I owned it. That came from over forty years in the classroom. Long after giving up the Prufrock role, I continued to think of myself as brooding and Byronic until one of the brightest students I ever had told me that he enjoyed my classes because I was always so cheerful. And until other students told me that I was intimidating. Me as Apeneck Sweeney? At any rate, I stopped being as diffident as I had been in 1954. One day, probably in the 1980s, I discovered that I had assigned, in two different classes, *The Waste Land* and *Ulysses* on the same day. Earlier in my career, I would have wept and prayed if not fasted. Instead, I went into the classes and told them not to worry but to read the one as a poem and the other as a novel, just roll with the feeling and not worry about footnotes.

That may have been after my encounter with Allen Ginsberg, who was giving a reading at my university, at a potluck dinner given by some graduate students. I was closest to him in age of anyone at the party, and we fell into conversation that had nothing to do with Michelangelo but seemed to be one man speaking to another rather than disciple approaching guru. He seemed pleased with the conversation and asked if I were going to stay for dinner. "No," I said, "I have to go to my yoga lesson." Since then, people to whom I've told the story have asked, "Did you really say that?" Yep.

I don't know what writers inspire or intimidate twenty-year-olds in the twenty-first century. There are plenty of very good poets, but Ginsberg was the last Leading American Poet. My creative writing students in the 1990s seemed to be fascinated with song lyrics by people whose names I don't recognize. Eliot and even Ginsberg have pretty much receded into the anthologies—in one of which *Howl* has an average of a half-dozen footnotes a page—and the memories of people fifty and older. In the department I retired from, students seem to be taught more theory than poetry or even than fiction, which is far more amenable to deconstruction, interrogation, or whatever the current fashionable term may be. The poet is no longer even, as Shelley put it, the unacknowledged legislator of humankind. I don't know how the young learn what is really important to them—but the ignorance of my generation is probably crucial to their learning it for themselves.

Meanwhile, back to the outskirts of Yakima. Prufrock worried about women seeing the bald spot in the middle of his hair, and I had had a bad moment when my former wife, climbing the stairs in our house, called attention to mine over a quarter-century ago. Since then, I have learned to regard any hair day at all as a good hair day, and experience has taught me that men don't need to presume because, past a certain age or kind of conditioning, women know exactly what they want, when they want it, and how and where, not being mermaids, they want it.

So I took a bite from the peach. As the juice ran into my beard, I realized that this was the very best peach I had ever eaten or ever hope to eat. Do I dare? As we used to say in my youth, "You bet your ass!"

WHEN WAS POSTMODERNISM?
OR, OUTLIVING A MOVEMENT

I wasn't formally invited to join writers and critics from seven countries who gathered at the International Center for Contemporary Art for the Bucharest meeting of Café Europa in November, 2000, supposedly to discuss the "Flavour of Postmodernism." But the sponsor of my visit to lecture and give poetry readings didn't have enough scheduled to occupy all of my time, so she brought me to the venue, introduced me, and plopped me down. I was eager to join conversation of a kind I encountered all too rarely in my years as an academic. As one might expect from a highly diverse and polyglot group, postmodernism seemed to have almost as many flavors as Baskin-Robbins. But the speakers and respondents spent far less time discussing what postmodernism was than when it happened. As I realized over the course of several days, it sprung up as I was learning to participate in the cultural life of my milieu and ebbed as my interests turned elsewhere.

No one at the conference seriously disagreed with the notion that postmodernism was a thing of the past. Chris Keulemans, the youngest participant, said that the topic made him nostalgic for the bookstore discussions he remembered from the Amsterdam in the 1980s. (And on the flight back to the U.S., the thirtyish woman seated next to me, director of adult education at the Chicago Art Institute, asked, "Are people still talking about that?") Several Romanians agreed that the term described for them a state of mind and kind of writing that subverted official Communist aesthetic by avoiding politics, overt commitment, and formal closure. Antonje Zalica, a Bosnian émigré novelist and filmmaker, dismissed the term by contrasting "post" with "ex" and remarked that concentrating on the first was like climbing a mountain backward in order to see where you'd been rather than where you were going. People from the Balkans tended to be impatient with too much emphasis on undecidability and detachment.

Peter Jukes, a dramatist from England, and Krzystof Czyzewski, a Polish writer and publisher, articulated most clearly a wide-spread objection to postmodernist tendency to value aesthetics over ethics. Only David Antin, an American theorist and performance artist, seemed to regard postmodernism as a living movement that had released art from the intellectually-formulated cage of modernism.

More interesting were Antin's distinctions among postmodern experience, postmodern art, and postmodern theory. He was able to do so, and I was able to understand him, because he and I were the only people at the discussion who remembered World War II—that is, who had direct experience of the pre-postmodernist world. And, on reflection, that many of the prominent writers of American fiction—called, variously, absurdists, surfictionists, black humorists, metafictionists before the term postmodernist was coined—were roughly our contemporaries: John Barth, 1930; Donald Barthelme, 1931; Robert Coover (and Alvin Greenberg, less well known but in some ways more interesting because less programmatic), 1932; Thomas Pynchon, 1937; Ishmael Reed, 1938.

To our juniors, who don't share the experience, and to our contemporaries, who may never have thought about it in these terms, it's necessary to historicize ourselves, as my younger colleagues would put it.

In the first place, as I once told a contemporary talking about our generation, nothing really happened to us. Too young to remember much about the Depression, too young to serve in World War II, we entered our teens (though teenagers as a class didn't exist) before Eisenhower became president. Only Barthelme went to Korea, and the armistice was signed the day he arrived. Coover and Pynchon served in the Navy between Korea and Vietnam.

Some of us were the first in our families to go to college because of the expectations and opportunities created by the G.I. Bill. There we encountered not only the texts and artifacts of high culture but also those of what was not yet termed underground or alternative culture. (I described this process, more or less unconsciously, in my memoir *A Lower-Middle-Class Education*.)

God knows, we needed an alternative. Think of the official culture of the late 1940s and early 1950s as sepia-toned: various shades of brown. Popular music before rock and roll (c. 1955) was saccharine and bland, scarcely leavened on radios and select juke boxes by be-bop and, slightly later, rhythm and blues. (And even Charlie Parker played with lush string accompaniment in order to reach a larger audience.) "L'il Abner" was as subversive as comics got. And when popular culture wasn't sappy, it was terribly, terribly earnest. Popular fiction was dominated by capitalist realism, highbrow fiction and its criticism by post-Jamesian psychological realism, poetry by the example of T. S. Eliot and the New Critics. The critic Steven Marcus, younger but formed by the *Partisan Review* school, confessed to enjoying Evelyn Waugh's novels, even though they were funny. In politics, we experienced what Pynchon's Oedipa Maas knew, in *The Crying of Lot 49*, as "a time of nerves, blandness and retreat among not only her fellow students but also most of the visible structure around and ahead of them, this having been a national reflex to certain pathologies in high places only death had had the power to cure."

No wonder, then, that some of us looked for alternatives to what Pynchon called "the exitlessness...the absence of surprise in life, that harrows the head of everybody American...." The future writers of fiction began to find it, of course, in books. John Barth read a lot of trashy paperbacks before turning to vast compilations of stories like the *Arabian Nights* while supposedly re-shelving books in the Oriental section of the Johns Hopkins University library. Donald Barthelme explored the by-ways of official literature, reading non-canonical writers like Ambrose Bierce, and also reviewing dozens of movies for the *Houston Post* and listening to what modern jazz he could find in early 1950s Houston. Thomas Pynchon took Vladimir Nabokov's course in the novel at Cornell and somehow discovered what Northrop Frye termed "Menippean satire," work based on the root meaning of satire, "satura," medley, mixture.

My introduction to the nascent postmodern experience came from *Mad Comics*, precursor to *Mad Magazine*. I remember where I first saw it: at the rack to the right of the front door of Foster's Drug Store on the northeast corner of Main and Chestnut streets in Boonville, Missouri. It was like a blow from the hand of God on the road to Damascus. And to every smart-ass boy (this was a guy thing, as was the golden age of literary postmodernism) looking for an escape from the dominant culture. I can't prove that Pynchon read *Mad*, but his first three novels offer convincing evidence that he did.

You had to have been there. Suddenly, a whole anarchic world was revealed, one which wasn't merely critical or subversive of conventional pieties or didn't just assume that popular and even more revered icons could be toppled. *Mad* taught me and many like me that these things could be played with. Superman became Superdooperman; Tarzan fell in love with Little Orphan Annie in a musical comedy, singing "The girl that I marry will have to be / As light on her feet as a chimpanzee." Irving Berlin sued; the Supreme Court ruled that iambic pentameter could not be copyrighted. The gates were opened to the gleeful barbarians, and thousands of young WASPS were introduced to Jewish humor and Yiddish words in the pages of *Mad*. (Chicken fat? What was that?)

The breakthrough in fiction came in the early 1960s with *Catch-22*, *V.*, and the early collections of Donald Barthelme's stories and continued with Coover's *The Universal Baseball Association, J. Henry Waugh, Prop.* and with Barth's stories in *Lost in the Funhouse* and *Chimera*, experimentally more concentrated than work like *The Sot-Weed Factor* and *Letters* which parodies or transmutes earlier forms. They wrote stories about writing stories, even sentences about being a sentence. They constructed stories according to mathematical formulae like the Fibonacci Numbers. They used engravings and parodies of everything from *Oedipus* to Jacobean revenge plays and rock lyrics. They wrote elaborate and eloquent pastiches of historical novels, including historical accounts of events that never happened. They created self-constructed, self-contained fictional worlds that absorbed their creators. These books jolted the literary world, disturbed people like John Gardner, who attacked them in *On Moral Fiction*, and for many readers served as an antidote to "the absence of surprise in life."

So why didn't they go on being surprising? Well, when someone said to Cocteau, "Astonish me, Jean," Cocteau for a change had nothing to say. It's hard to go on being surprising time after time. Also, and this could not have been clear in the early Sixties, what came to be called postmodernism requires a great deal of freedom—economic, political, and most of all imaginative—not only for the authors but for their audience..

All of those kinds of freedom existed in the period between the end of the Korean War in 1953 and the first really serious, i.e., violent, protests against the Vietnam War about 1967. This was the period of Ken Kesey and the Merry Pranksters—neither postmodernists nor war protestors, they nevertheless illustrated a certain kind of cultural freedom. Then the Zeitgeist caught up with them. As Joseph Heller wrote in *Catch-22*, "Outside a lot of funny things weren't going on. What was going on was the war." Vietnam closed off a number of options: you were for it or against it, and in any case it was a subject that was hard to play with, though Barthelme tried in his story "Report," and Coover made some passes at it.

Another thing that happened was that they got older, and when that happens, it's hard to be entirely open to indeterminacy and undecidability. It's not just teeth and piano lessons one has to worry about, as Paul does when refusing to respond to a beautiful woman's "hair initiative" in Barthelme's *Snow White*. It's prostate exams and retirement plans and root canals. Metafiction is a young or youngish man's game, as was very clear in Pynchon's *Vineland*, which goes through some of the same motions as *V.*, but without the energy. And as Mel Brooks' later film career shows, one can run out of things to make fun of.

Also, audiences change. The first, most enthusiastic readers face signs of their own mutability, even mortality. Younger readers may be respectful, even interested, but they read the books not as revelations but as assignments, sometimes through the veils of theory laid upon theory. And as eighteenth century England showed quite clearly, it is possible to construct very sophisticated terminology to describe a form, like the epic poem, that no one is using any longer. Or, as Peter Jukes says of postmodern theory today, it has become the language of curators rather than artists, the language of the establishment.

Finally, or almost finally, the writers are canonized, or embalmed. A web-site dedicated respectfully to Barth calls him "one of the last [postmodernists] still publishing." Coover, whose parody Western, *Ghost Town*, made *Vineland* look positively vital, has been referred to as an "old-school postmodernist." It's hard to get any deader than that.

So. Literary Postmodernism, at least as a visible force, at least in the U.S., is over. The writers are dead or professors emeriti, or soon will be. It has happened before. Pope and Swift died and went out of fashion. But *The Rape of the Lock* and "A Modest Proposal" can still surprise and delight us. The *Universal Baseball Association*, *V.*, and other books and stories will probably do the same for future generations. That is the difference between a movement, which is generic, and a work of art, which is unique.

And what of us survivors? Judging from the book titles in his Wikipedia entry, David Antin goes on being astonishing. I've begun, as in this essay, to look into the past to see what sense I can make of it and to convey that sense in old-fashioned styles and modes when not provoked by younger colleagues to do otherwise. I admire Antin, but I see the job of survivor, buoyed up like Ishmael on the coffin of the past, as recounting and evaluating what I can see and understand of that past.

Valedictions

FAITHFUL SAM MARX

Until the mid-1970s, I had never run across the name of Sam Marx because I was a fan rather than a student of Hollywood films and had only read casually in the biographies of William Faulkner, F. Scott Fitzgerald, and other novelists I sometimes taught. I had heard the story about Faulkner's asking MGM if he could work at home, receiving permission, and disappearing to Oxford, Mississippi, on the incontrovertible grounds that it was his home.

Like many stories, that turned out to be amusing rather than true, but I didn't know that until sometime after I ran across letters from Evelyn Waugh to his London agent while compiling a catalogue of his papers at the University of Texas-Austin. In those files the name of "faithful Sam Marx" appeared at intervals, often when Waugh was in direst need of money, offering to renew options for the film rights to his novel *A Handful of Dust*.

But this was one of hundreds of unknown names, and it never occurred to me that any of them existed in the way that, for example, my relatives and associates did. Back home, however, I read a syndicated story from the Los Angeles *Times* about a Sam Marx who, after years in the movie business, had begun a second career as a writer. On the chance that this was the same man, I wrote to him in care of the *Times* columnist, to tell Marx of his place in Waugh's history, though I didn't tell him how unique that place was because Waugh professed to dislike all Americans, especially Jews, especially Hollywood Jews.

By almost immediate return mail came a cordial answer and a post card from Waugh inviting Marx to Piers Court, his country home. This, I could tell Marx without fear of giving offense, was unique because Waugh had put off a visit from his American publisher, the source, through the success of *Brideshead Revisited*, of a major part of his income.

But I didn't know until much later that Sam had been story editor at MGM under Irving Thalberg, where Louis B. Mayer and others complained that he liked writers (as he did almost everyone), that he had worked for Samuel Goldwyn, that he was in the middle of a fruitful career as a chronicler of Hollywood in the 1930s that was largely unchallenged because he'd outlived almost everyone, and that he was a major resource for biographers and historians of the movie industry.

It was probably just as well, because I might have been too diffident to approach him. That would have been unnecessary worry, for we had one thing in common. As Sam said, we became friends because we were the only two people left who still wrote and answered letters. The correspondence continued until 1979, when I went to a conference in Claremont, California, and arranged to stay in Los Angeles for a day or so in order to meet Sam.

The hotel I'd chosen for price and location had the tightest security I'd ever seen. Sam arrived in a vintage Mercedes, tall, straight, a full head of white hair. He spoke and moved with a kind of dignity that came to remind me, in an odd way, of two of Satchel Paige's rules of life: never look back, because someone might be gaining on you; keep the juices flowing by jangling gently as you move.

Sam was clearly nonplussed at the hotel because he'd never heard of it. But he was gracious, and after some introductory chat, he drove me to a memorial service with a buffet on the anniversary of the death of Kathryn McGuire, who had starred with Buster Keaton in *The Navigator* even before Sam had settled in Hollywood, and then to a showing of the film.

Sam was traveling to New York the next day, but at least we had faces to put with the names on letters, and after that we became friends. It was an unlikely pairing. Sam was born in New York City in 1902, and because of the people he had grown up with (Richard Rodgers, the Gershwins, E. Robert Oppenheimer, and many others) and encountered in his years as story editor and producer at MGM and other studios, he seemed to know everyone who was or had been anyone. I was to discover that it was impossible to walk down Rodeo Drive or go to a restaurant with him without his being stopped by an old friend.

I was born in Lyons, Kansas, in 1934 and didn't know anyone famous or important. Until I met Sam, I'd never been to Musso and Frank or the Motion Picture Academy or the Farmer's Market. On the other hand, Sam hadn't been to the center of the country since he drove from New York to Los Angeles in 1930. So why did Sam keep in touch with me? Perhaps I was the only academic who didn't want to pick his brains about Fitzgerald or Faulkner (who didn't ask to work at home because he would have had to ask Sam, and he didn't) or Hollywood figures from Erich von Stroheim on.

Our next meeting was in my territory. It turned out that Sam knew or at least knew of someone else in Oklahoma, for my colleague Joanna Rapf is the granddaughter of Harry Rapf, one the founders of MGM. I was to discover that talk of the MGM family wasn't idle, for the old connection was enough to persuade Sam to break a cross-country flight to talk to our film students.

Sam seemed almost as nervous about being in Oklahoma as I was about being in Beverly Hills. He wondered anxiously if there would be heckling during and after the speech. Apparently he had a bad experience in England. I assured him that Oklahomans would be grateful that an outsider was taking notice of them. I was right. The students loved his stories about actors and writers; he was interviewed on a local talk show; everyone, including the acting president of the university, wanted to meet him. He was particularly pleased at being given the Presidential Suite at Sooner House, the equivalent, at best, of a three-star hotel.

Two years later I was in Budapest on a Fulbright, scheduled to depart in December, and because I knew that Sam liked to get out of California at Christmas, I wrote to ask him where he would be on the chance that we could meet. He said that he had not decided among New York, Paris, and London. I was pleased to be able to say, for the only time in my life, that I would be in Paris to give a lecture, in London to meet with another Waugh scholar, and in New York to deliver a paper at the Modern Language Association meeting. Not bad for a life-long denizen of fly-over country.

He decided on London, and when I arrived he invited me to bring my friend to lunch at a restaurant opposite Hyde Park. As usual, he was gracious and as close to being courtly as anyone I've met. But his anecdotes were always lively. I remember only one on that occasion. He pointed to another table and said, "The last time I saw Charlie Chaplin he was sitting there with Oona spooning food into him and it dribbling down his chin."

A year later I was in Los Angeles for another professional meeting and had gone to lunch with a woman I'd met in New Jersey. From her house I called Sam to arrange to meet for dinner, and when I mentioned where I was, he invited her as well. Sam had been a widower since I'd known him, and when my friend went to the ladies' room, he asked if I would object to his asking her out. Since, I said, they were both well past the age of consent, I had no objection. It seemed that his current lady friend, about my age, didn't have the energy to keep up with him. As I was to realize later, Sam enjoyed not only the company of women but the process of courtship.

Five or six years later, Texas Tech University announced a conference on "Film and Literature: A Comparative Approach to Adaptation." I had a relationship with a woman faculty member and was always pleased with an excuse to go to Lubbock, as odd as that might seem, so I called one of the sponsors to suggest a topic. He was encouraging and went on to ask if I knew anyone who might pair with screenwriter Horton Foote as a featured speaker, expenses and fee paid. He'd never heard of Sam but was impressed by the credentials I recited and politely puzzled by the insistence that he use my name as bait.

Sam was even more puzzled by the invitation to speak in Lubbock, Texas, which I doubt he'd heard of, and he called me to find out what this was about. He decided to accept—but only if he could come by way of Oklahoma so that I could guide him across what his school geography book probably called the Great American Desert.

And back. I said that I had personal reasons for remaining beyond his stay. "But how will I get back to Los Angeles?" I said that not only was the scenery the same both ways but that it was (at that time) easier to fly direct to Los Angeles from Lubbock than it was from Oklahoma City. I'd been right about his reception in Norman, but he was obviously skeptical.

Joanna Rapf wanted him to talk to her film students, and again Sam was nervous because he didn't have anything new to say. That's the good part about my business, I told him: you get an entirely new audience every four years. And as before, the students paid far closer attention to him than they ever had to me.

Then we set off on our trip across the plains by what passes for the scenic route. We stopped for lunch at a partly restored hotel in Medicine Park, Oklahoma, that looked like a set for a neo-realist Western, and then passed through the Wichita Mountains Wildlife Refuge, with longhorn cattle and buffalo running loose. He was delighted by the confirmation of stereotypes and surprisingly tolerant of the state lodge at Quartz Mountain, undergoing renovation. Then through broad cotton fields through Altus and south through the village of Eldorado, population 688. Sam was interested in everything, but he especially enjoyed the brief glimpse of the town. "The most elegant woman I ever met," he said, "came from Eldorado. I'm glad to see it at last."

Then the back, back road, through almost uninhabited land to Paducah, Texas, past the small ghetto that reminded Sam of rides with a Tucson policeman while on location years earlier. We stopped for coffee at the Dairy Queen—the only one for sixty miles in any direction. The woman at the counter offered him artificial cream. That was too much. "You have all the cows in the world out here," he said indignantly, "and you give me artificial cream?" Pleased to have superior country mouse knowledge, I said, "Wrong kind of cows."

In Lubbock, as the crowd assembled for Horton Foote's keynote lecture, Sam confessed that he was nervous about following Foote's act. I replied that, on the evidence of past performance, he would do just fine. This obviously fell into the same category as the reassurance about Lubbock's airline connections.

Then the speech began. Foote's talk reads as well as Sam's in the volume of the conference proceedings, but he didn't have Sam's presence or skill with anecdote in delivering the speech he gave the next day. Two minutes into the speech, I leaned toward Sam and said, "Piece of cake." I could feel him relax. Later he and Foote, who had somehow missed each other all their decades in show business, enjoyed a quiet dinner together away from the conference. The dialogue consisted mostly of "Do you know so-and-so?" and "Is he still alive?"

Lubbock gave Sam one more disconcerting moment. Some of my local friends joined us for a late supper. The waitress brought, on request, separate checks while his attention was distracted. As usual, he reached the check and found that there were six instead of one. This was farther beyond his experience than the Paducah Dairy Queen, and he asked, with real wonder, "How did you do that?"

The last time Sam came to Oklahoma, in 1989, he was returning from a meeting with his editor in New York about the manuscript of *Deadly Illusions*, which was to be his last book. There had been problems, and I was pleased that he not only asked my advice but took some of it—perhaps because it was the same as his editor's.

Sam was even more eager to get me to Hollywood than I was to get him to the Great Plains. He always hoped that I would abandon scholarly books and articles and, God forbid, poetry, to write something that would make money. Once he said that I would have made a great story editor for a major studio, which I said would be like applying for a job as a maker of buggy whip handles.

He kept trying. In 1983, when MGM brought him back so that he could tell them what they had in their files that might be made into a movie, he said that he was keeping me in mind. But his role as consultant had not gone terribly well. John Derek was preparing to direct *Tarzan, the Ape Man*, and since Sam had been involved in buying the rights for the first sound version, he asked Sam's advice about the script. To ease into broader criticism, Sam pointed to a scene in which Jane's father, who has a black mistress named Africa, enters and, says "Where's Africa?" Sam didn't give the obvious answer—"You're standing on it, you twit!" Instead, he pointed out that the line would get a laugh, and Derek didn't want a laugh there. Derek said, "You shouldn't have read that script!" Why not? "That's not the final script." Where is it? "It isn't written yet." At this point Sam started edging towards the door.

He followed this story with one about a baby mogul who asked him to suggest a story in which Jacqueline Bisset would star with her Russian ballet friend. I said, "Simple. Do a flip on *Ninotchka*.

"You're a genius," he said. "And do you know how I know that?"

"No."

"Because that's what I told him. But I made him wait three days."

Then he showed the mogul a print of the original Lubitsch film in which "Garbo laughs." When the star entered, the mogul asked, "Who's the blonde?" About this time Sam realized that he no longer recognized the movie business.

But he did discover Graham Greene's unpublished story "The Tenth Man" in the archives and hoped to produce it and bring me in as a consultant. At a restaurant on Rodeo Drive he discussed some of the problems with me. The greatest was the studio's desire to set the story it on England, apparently to use funds that couldn't be taken out of the country. "Occupied England?" I said. We went on talking about possibilities—he said that Charles Bronson had expressed interest—and he said that we were having a story conference. I replied that I thought a story conference involved everybody getting paid. He seemed pleased that I was learning.

That project fell through, and he was far more disappointed than I was. It would have been fun to learn something new, I told him, but I wasn't any more disappointed than if I'd been turned down for astronaut training. Meanwhile I enjoyed visiting him in Hollywood. He took me to some members' showings at the Motion Picture Academy in Beverly Hills. Once I sat next to Angie Dickinson and Mrs. Ira Gershwin. On another occasion, standing in the lobby lined with still photos from MGM's files, I heard one man say to another, "That's Sam Marx. I wonder what happened to him." I leaned around the pillar and said, "If you go around to the other side, you can ask him." In fact, he was chatting up a retired ballerina who was to collaborate on his last book.

We did start work on a novel about Evelyn Waugh in Hollywood, where Sam had met him in 1947, but I was seeing two spectacularly unprofitable books through university presses and Sam was busy with a novel based on Irving Thalberg's life and with his job as consultant for Ted Turner's *When the Lion Roars*. In his last letter to me, he said that he was becoming such a celebrity that he would have to get out of town. Coming out of the wrap party, he said that he felt ill. On March 2, 1992, just before the series premiered, he died. One of his sons wrote that his life met the story editor's chief requirement: a happy ending.

Some months later—he had remarried a few months before his death—his widow said that I was like a son to Sam. No, I said. There was no history, no expectations, and no disappointments. But I was struck by Sam's mental and physical energy, by his willingness to meet new people—especially attractive women—and by his enthusiasm for trying new things. I used to tell him, "Sam, when I grow up, I want to be like you." I still do.

Model & Mentor

At the beginning of a visit to a former student and his family, I attended a meeting of his freshman English class. He reminded the group that if students were lucky, they would have three great teachers and pointed to me as one of his.

Naturally I was flattered, but I also doubted that if a multiple choice evaluation form ranging from perfectly satisfied to extremely unsatisfied were administered to all the students I had in forty-five years in the classroom in nine universities and three countries, most or even many would agree with him even though I wasn't aware of treating him any better or worse than anyone else.

Thinking about it later, I decided that for that student at that time, I satisfied a need as no one else was capable of doing. I don't know what his other two great teachers were like, but I doubt that there was much resemblance. That was certainly true of my three best teachers, who were not good in the same way. Their success had little to do with ambition and perhaps only a little more with intellectual ability.

In *A Lower-Middle-Class Education*, I wrote about the Rev. Joseph A. McCallin, S.J., who was not only my teacher but my spiritual adviser. He was the best Socratic method teacher I ever saw, and by those methods made me feel smarter than I was. In my high school, the teachers didn't or couldn't challenge me to think harder and read more widely. Fr. Mac did both, not always as successfully as he would have liked, by pushing both me and ideas farther than I was used to going.

When I got to the University of Kansas, I had several good teachers (and a couple of execrable ones), but they were more impressive as personalities and classroom performers than as intellectuals, and it never occurred to me that they could serve as models; they seemed uninterested in being mentors, at least to me; but they were kinder to my work than perhaps they should have been. After the first few months in the M.A. program, I began to feel more comfortable than was good for my development as a scholar.

At the University of Wisconsin, that changed drastically and abruptly when I entered the room where Frederick J. Hoffman conducted his seminar on American literary criticism. As the new boy, I didn't know any of the students, some of whom had been in the program for two or three years and seemed intellectually far more mature and better prepared than I. Hoffman was clearly on an even higher plane. I was to learn that he had probably published more books than the entire faculty of the whole English department at Kansas, and while he was not rude or condescending, he charged directly and forcefully at topics like a linebacker from Ohio State University, where he'd completed his Ph.D.

He outlined the reading we would do for the semester and asked for volunteers to give reports on each of the critical books. One of the first was Irving Babbitt's *Rousseau and Romanticism*. Since from Hoffman's brief description he sounded less complex than some of the other writers, and since I thought that giving one of the first reports would make me less exposed to comparisons if not criticism, I volunteered.

I don't remember much about my report, luckily. I hadn't realized that at the beginning of each meeting Hoffman would introduce the topic, in the process anticipating everything the student had to say and a lot more. After the presentation he would give a summary that exposed the puerility of one's approach and the gaps in one's reasoning.

There were plenty in mine. At that stage, Babbitt's conservative elitism sounded not unreasonable to me, and I was not equipped either to criticize it or put it in context. Hoffman didn't tell me how badly I'd done—he didn't have to—and the other students seemed to be avoiding eye contact.

After that, I was out of the direct line of fire and tried to keep my head down. That worked until near the end of the term. At Thanksgiving I went into the hospital for hernia repair, and on New Year's Eve, my appendix ruptured and I was unable to teach for the rest of the semester or, I think, go to many classes. Or to finish my paper for the seminar. I had to take an incomplete and was for a while in the unique position of having incompletes at two different universities.

When I enrolled for the second semester, I'd heard rumors that Hoffman might be leaving for a job elsewhere—apparently he didn't get on with the department's other Americanists, both senior to him, who were steeped or stuck in old-fashioned methods of literary history. Therefore, I signed up both for his seminar in the modern American novel and for his lecture course in the relations between European and American literary movements of the twentieth century.

I was more comfortable in that seminar because I'd read a lot of novels, if not always the right ones, and in those days there was a lot more criticism of fiction to draw upon—I'd had more training in bibliography than most of the other students—than there was criticism of criticism, so at least I could find some outside help. Also, I had learned something about keeping my mouth shut, though, as I was to learn, not enough.

As the semester passed, I became involved with and then engaged to another graduate student, less incapacitating but more distracting than my operations, and I realized that I was not going to be able to write the two seminar papers and a term paper I owed Hoffman. I knew that he could be stern; I suspected that he could be formidable. But, lacking other options, I had to throw myself on his mercy and went to his office as nervous as I had ever been before going to confession. I told him that I could finish the paper for one of his seminars and for the lecture course but that I couldn't possibly finish all three.

He looked at me almost without expression and said, "Tell me, Mr. Davis, does your income depend upon your academic record?"

I have forgotten my answer—obviously it was "yes"—but I remember my reaction. For weeks I went around as if, psychically, I had been punched in the stomach, and it took another ten years to realize that he was not threatening me but was merely curious about how serious I was about being a scholar. The immediate effect was that I managed to clear up all my incompletes and never had another one. When he got the Babbitt paper, he commented as carefully and helpfully as if I had submitted it on time.

The bright spot in the semester, besides my engagement, was the lecture course, so full of information and so well organized that in later years I could find specific information in my copious notes without a lot of rummaging. And I had been working hard on a paper on the dramas of Jean-Paul Sartre—then more highly regarded than now—and when I submitted it, for once Hoffman seemed pleased with my work, though, as his comments show, with a catch:

> This is by all odds the best paper you've yet written for me. It lacks some of the fuzziness and the willingness to bring everything into a discussion regardless of relevance that I've sometimes spotted in your talk. It shows a fine perception of dramatic values and above all avoids the mistake made by about 99.9356 of Sartreans—the failure to make the link between theory and literary fact without reams of ponderous verbiage.

He also appended a list of recommendations for further development and carefully marked errors and obscurities in the margins of the paper. Other than the (perfectly accurate) reference to my scattered mentation, there was no mention of my shortcomings as a scholar.

I think that it was three semesters later that I was allowed to sit in on the seminar in which Hoffman was developing the ideas that formed the basis of his book *The Mortal No: Death and the Modern Imagination*. It was the most intellectually stimulating experience in my graduate career. The students officially enrolled were overshadowed by the auditors who included David DeLaura and Joseph Riddell, very high-powered then and later in their academic careers. Hoffman, in pursuit of a book, was even more tightly focused than usual.

I never worked harder in my life. One week, besides teaching two composition courses, which involved grading about 50 papers, and taking courses in the history of the English language and Victorian fiction, I read *Middlemarch* and *The Brothers Karamazov*, well over a thousand pages. Apparently I had learned something about work.

By this time, I had grown less uncomfortable in Hoffman's presence. Stories about him—his revolt against the dominance of the cross in the town where he grew up; his reliance on his wife, who read his manuscripts and confined her comments to "Fix" in the margins where needed; the story that he had bought at least one book in every town where he'd spent the night; the possible exaggeration that he was on vacation because he was only working twelve to fourteen hours a day—made him seem, if not exactly human, a bit less like a demi-god. At coffee after one seminar, he even made a joke. Joe asked about the problem of grading foreign (now called international) graduate students who clearly weren't as well prepared as their American counterparts. Hoffman said, "Are you familiar with the concept of the Chinese home run?" Joe and I were—it referred to balls hit along the very short foul lines at Yankee Stadium and the Polo Grounds. "Well," Hoffman said, we have what we call the Chinese B."

By this time, most of us had some idea of his prodigious output of scholarship—surveys of American little magazines; intellectual history as in *Freudianism and the Literary Mind*; a literary history of the American 1920s; studies of individual authors; enough other books and articles to fill seventeen pages of the bibliography appended to the book dedicated to his memory. So perhaps the story about his vacations was true. And he had a sense of proportion. Once, congratulated for the publication of a book in a series that he rightly regarded as minor, he brushed aside the compliment by saying that it was minor work for hire.

In the seminar, I felt comfortable enough to engage in the discussions, and once even brave enough to challenge him. He was praising the symbol of hay in E.M. Forster's *Howards End,* where the good people can happily smell the hay and the bad people sneeze. I said that it was a sentimental symbol. Hoffman bristled. "What do you mean?"

"Have you ever bucked bales?"

He harrumphed and said that he had.

"Well," I said, "you'll notice that the people admiring the hay only pick up wisps of it? What about the farmhands who have to bale it, allergies or not?"

Grudgingly, he conceded my point, and the discussion continued.

After that year, Hoffman left Wisconsin, one of the professors swept up by the University of California system's academic press-gang of the early 1960s. I saw him only once more, at a Modern Language Association meeting in New York, where he was giving a paper. That year—1966?—the organization had decided to enforce the policy of admitting to sessions only people wearing the official badge. Hoffman had forgotten his, and was distraught at being denied entry. I intervened, showed the guard his name in the program, and saw him go in. I don't think he even noticed me, let alone remembered me.

A year or so later, at another MLA meeting, I heard that he had died, two years short of sixty.

By that time, I had learned, not everything he had to teach me, but as much as I could bear. I didn't have his intellectual range or his energy, but I had learned how to apply what I had as consistently and thoroughly as I was able. Later, when people asked how I got so much done, I'd say, "I work very hard." In fact, at one count I had published more books than Hoffman had, though nothing of their stature and over a longer period.

However, if Hoffman had been my only influence, I might have been so overwhelmed by his example that I might never have published a word. Fortunately, after I had finished official course work with him, I encountered a mitigating force that enabled me to use the tools I had acquired. To use a sports analogy, Hoffman ran me through weights and drills; Alvin Whitley taught me to loosen up, open my stance, and hit to right rather than swing for the fences.

Whitley was as different from Hoffman as a professor could be. Hoffman had come out of a big, sweaty, smash-mouth Big Ten graduate program. Although Whitley was said, very quietly, to be the son of a San Antonio barber, he had done graduate work at Harvard and absorbed the culture in which learning was worn lightly, even casually. Hoffman clearly prepared his lectures; Whitley was rumored to rehearse his before a mirror. They were certainly performances, whatever he was teaching, and one anthologist called him "one of the great lecturers in the Johnsonian tradition." In contrast to the specialists who filled most of the faculty slots, he taught all over the place.

He had published scholarly articles on a variety of authors and subjects and co-edited two anthologies, and he had received Guggenheim and other fellowships, but by Hoffman's admittedly exacting standard he was hardly a scholar at all, and he never taught graduate seminars, at least in my time at Wisconsin.

I may have sat in on one or more of his lectures, but I didn't encounter him directly until my fourth semester. The previous semester, I was enrolled in Paul Wiley's seminar on Joseph

Conrad, but when Wiley's health problems caused the seminar to be cancelled about a month into the term, the students were asked to write the name of an author they would like to study and shunted off to suitable faculty members for directed readings. I chose Evelyn Waugh and was sent to Ricardo Quintana, the Swift scholar who huffed that he didn't know much about Waugh that semester and sent me off to do research and write a paper. His comment—all of it—on the result was "Altogether first-rate, or so it strikes me (I've made it clear that E.W. is not one of my specialties.)" I'd have preferred caustic comments from Hoffman.

But Quintana did ask me if he could show my paper to Whitley, who invited me to lunch. By not trying to put me at my ease, he put me at my ease, and after he praised my paper, we talked about books like Aldous Huxley's *The Genius and the Goddess,* published a few years earlier, which, Whitley said, would have been very creditable for a beginning writer.

Looking at my paper, I find a very encouraging note from Paul Wiley, who was indisputably a specialist in twentieth century British literature, and I planned to write my dissertation with him. But when I went to him with my proposal to write on comic technique in Waugh and two other novelists, he said, "Wouldn't you rather write on irony in Conrad?" For one thing, I envisioned finishing the dissertation sometime in the twentieth century. For another, the question reminded me of Anse Bundren's question, in *As I Lay Dying,* responding to his youngest son's desire to see a toy train: "Wouldn't you rather have a banana?" Not really in either case, as my son used to say when he meant hell no, not under any circumstances.

Instead, I said that I'd like to think about it and went to Whitley's office to ask him to direct my dissertation because two friends ahead of me in the program, in two different fields, had worked with him and found him satisfactory.

(Later the more serious of the two complained that Whitley made him stop working and submit the dissertation before he felt that he was ready. This was most encouraging. So was the story one of them told about his dissertation defense. He, Whitley, and Murray Fowler, a well-known linguist, showed up early, and in conversation the linguist asked a convoluted question about the nature of metaphor. Whitley stood and said, "Murray, if you're going to start that kind of crap, I'm leaving." Clearly a man who had his students' interests at heart. And his own. On another graduate student's 50-page term paper, he had written "A. Sensitive, intelligent, and, God knows, thorough.")

Then and throughout the process of guiding me through the dissertation, Whitley's implicit advice, exactly right for that stage of my career, was "Relax." Asked about the required proposal, he said that submitting something was the goal. You could say you were working on Joyce and wind up with a dissertation on Lawrence. His premise as director was that I was going to know far more about the subject than he did. His job was to make sure that I make some sense of it. He also cautioned me that the dissertation was a stage in a process, not an end in itself. When I asked if I should begin by surveying the scholarship, he said, "Put all the guff in the footnotes. You'll have to put it there anyway when you turn the dissertation into a book."

I moved to a full-time job before I completed the dissertation and worried about communicating with my director. I needn't have. If I mailed him a chapter on Monday, I would get it back on Friday with a few pointed and useful comments and the injunction to continue.

When I returned to defend the dissertation, the last formality, I gave him the greatest pleasure in the whole process by saying that I would not return for the graduation ceremony. "Thank God," he said. "If you did I'd have to come to bestow the hood." That might be part of the ritual, but it wasn't an essential part of the process.

After I began to publish articles, I sent a few offprints to Whitley. He never responded. He had seen me through the process, and the process was over.

But he had taught me something as important as the lessons I'd learned from Hoffman. As I said, Hoffman taught me to work as hard as I possibly could, to take the work seriously. Whitley taught me not to take it or myself too seriously.

During my years as a teacher, I may have exhibited traits of both men. Some of my students said that they found me intimidating, though I never tried to be and though my taste for the irrelevant gave me a lighter touch. On the other hand, when an Honors student complained that I didn't make her feel smart, I said that I had never thought to try to remedy God's omission.

Perhaps I was more like Whitley as an advisor and thesis and dissertation director. I had more interest in the goal than in the details of the process and enjoyed cutting red tape for students. Unlike too many of my colleagues, and in honor of Whitley, I did a quick turn-around on chapters and next to final drafts, where the process often stalls. One student told me that he was advised to seek other directors if he wanted to feel smart but to come to me if he wanted to finish.

Hoffman was a good model for a scholar, but Whitley's example as mentor was equally important. Each came at a moment when I needed to, and could, learn what they had to teach. I'm pleased that at least a few of my students had the same experience.

Conventions

Until I was applying for my first full-time teaching job in 1961, I hadn't attended any kind of academic convention. I didn't feel ready to be a real college teacher, but I was termed out as a teaching assistant at the University of Wisconsin. So off I went in late December to the Modern Language Association, then and now the biggest convention in my discipline, wide-eyed and nervous. It was the only conference that even my cadre, highly professionalized by the standards of the day, had even heard of.

Nowadays, even M. A. candidates not only go to one of the many smaller conferences that exist now, but they present papers, hoping to fill out résumés to compete in a job market that has been depressed since the late 1960s. I didn't have time even to think about suggesting a paper, which would have been futile anyway, because the fat days had just hit the academic marketplace and I had fourteen interviews, some of them solicited on-site by minor colleges I hadn't applied to and some whose names I didn't know.

That year the MLA meeting had been moved from Cincinnati to Chicago because registration had grown so large that only Chicago and New York had enough hotel rooms. Chicago was the biggest town I'd ever seen—I'd only stopped there to change buses a few years earlier—and the convention alone had more people registered than lived in my home town. The Palmer House lobby was crowded with people probably smarter and certainly more sophisticated than I was. The panels featured scholars whose names I recognized, some because I'd read their books. I hardly had time to leave the hotel—just as well, since the temperature rarely got above zero.

Mostly, though, I went up and down elevators and in and out of hotel rooms to my job interviews that, even to me, were clearly generic. Had I finished my degree? If not, when would I? The teaching load and salary were such and such, and I would be asked to teach courses in the following fields. The questions didn't change over the next thirty years, even when I was asking them, though by then I had an ear for evasive and unsatisfactory answers that came from being on both sides.

When classes resumed after the Christmas break, I went to see Alvin Whitley, my dissertation director, notable for the fact that he had never been to the MLA, to give my report. He usually had good and eminently practical advice about managing my career, but I remember only his view that the conference was "all right, if you like finding out who has gone mad in Pennsylvania."

That stuck with me because, unlike Whitley in many ways, I loved finding out who had gone mad in Pennsylvania, published an article, changed jobs or, as the years went on, wives or sexual preferences or medications.

As I got further into my academic career, my interest in the job market became intermittent, piqued when I hoped or needed to make a move. The old questions still came up, especially sensitive regarding issues of equal opportunity and political correctness when I was asking them.

After a few years, I gained enough credibility to speak on panels and to speak out in those—decreasing in number as my confidence grew, my interests focused, and the topics became increasingly theoretical—I bothered to attend. My best friend, academic or otherwise, joked that the mark of a really successful conference was not to attend any sessions at all and that the real reason to be listed on the program, besides getting travel money, was to let your friends know where to find you.

This wasn't just a joke. Finding people at the MLA grew more difficult, in the days before cell phones, as attendance grew and lodging spilled out of the main hotel. Some people were predictable—a graduate school contemporary could usually be found sitting in the Palmer House lobby. But most people were peripatetic, and one of the earliest lessons I learned was to make first-night dinner arrangements before the convention to avoid being left, stranded, forlorn, and searching for someplace to eat.

That became less and less a problem because I knew more people and recognized, through shared interests or appearance on the same panels, many others. Some encounters were more illuminating than edifying. Sitting alone one night in the bar at the Hilton in mid-town Manhattan, I overheard the chairs (definitely men in those days) of two leading West coast universities, scholars whose work I'd read and admired, discussing candidates for their jobs in rather slurred tones.

One said, "The trouble with you, you old sumbitch, is that you're hiring all the best people!"

"Show me your list," the other replied. He looked owlishly at it, his vision somewhat impeded by bad lighting and good whiskey, and ran his finger down the page. "I'm going to hire him...you can have him...you don't want him...."

By that time, I was over thirty, and I guess I shouldn't have been surprised. But I was—at least until I served on a number of hiring committees, had to sort through hundreds of dossiers, and listen to hypersensitive colleagues twitch over the ranking of an obviously third-tier candidate at least ten places below the conceivable number of interview slots.

However unpleasant, if necessary, I found the hiring hall function, I continued to believe that the conferences were valuable in a number of ways. By prowling the book exhibits, I could learn about new materials in my field or, more practically, about gaps that I could fill, as when I came home from the 1969 meeting in Denver with two book contracts.

Mostly, though, I learned more about who had gone mad in Pennsylvania than who had grown jaded in the Hilton bar or who had made a scholarly breakthrough in the study of John

Henry Newman. Once, at the end of a MLA meeting, I was relaxing with a friend who stretched luxuriously and said, of a particularly abrasive contemporary, "Just think. At this very moment, he's vomiting in the back of a bus on the way to Des Moines, Iowa—which *proves* there's a god!" The same friend, told that I'd been invited to Canada as external examiner of a dissertation, exclaimed, "My God, my dear, you're a star!"

That kind of support was not unusual, though rarely as enthusiastic. When my marriage blew up, I had a pleasant dinner on North Beach in San Francisco with a friend who'd been divorced, lost a long-time partner to a lingering disease, and was so involved in a new romance that he was leaving the convention early, in mid-winter, to return to Minnesota and "her." He didn't try to console me, but the fact that he was clearly able to go on with his life, and happily, gave me the first indication that I might be able to.

The next year I met a friend from graduate school who asked after my wife. "We're divorced," I said. "God! That's the third one today." Not quite the same degree of consolation, but it did let me know that I was not alone.

More broadly, it's useful to mingle with people from other places and discover that, however hard it might be to imagine, your situation could be worse. In Denver, when the job seekers' caucus had replaced the radical caucus sessions as the focus of most intense interest, I met people who were still at the university from which most of us were, sooner or later, dismissed. They had less travel money than I; their prospects for tenure were dim while I was about to get it; my research was encouraged and rewarded.

Years later, I interviewed for a job as chair of a university in the Northeast. The composition of the interview team—an elderly associate professor and a very young, untenured assistant professor—would have put up red flags to any experienced academic. Every solution I offered to a staggering number of administrative problems was dismissed as logistically or psychologically impossible. Finally I stood and said, "You've accomplished a very difficult task. You've made me a lot happier where I am." Later I learned that the man who got the job lasted a year.

Perhaps I've sounded too cynical about the meetings. They can help young scholars to sharpen their game as scholars and speakers and to escape from the inevitably provincial culture of their graduate programs and departments. Fairly early in my career, filing a required report to justify my travel expenses, I wrote that the meeting gave me a clearer sense of the profession to which I belonged and of the audience for which I wrote. I wish I still had that report—it had an earnestness and idealism which at this distance I can admire but not replicate.

That report was for the MLA meeting. The culture of my department, most of whose members had never taught anywhere else, was oriented more to regional meetings, mini-MLAs without the hiring hall, geographical range, or talent. Serious scholars looked down on them. Told I'd been to (and enjoyed) a Rocky Mountain MLA conference, the very most serious contemporary from graduate school said, "You'll go anywhere." He was right—as was my wife who, at her first and only South Central MLA meeting, said that she kept looking for the hidden agenda and finally realized that there was none.

I, on the other hand, enjoyed hanging out in New Orleans, the Dallas area, Houston, and Memphis, eating different food and meeting people I didn't have to see every day and having a claque who listened to my papers. But I knew that while I was easy, I wasn't dense. After I returned from a regional meeting, the senior scholar in my department asked about my experience. It was all right, I said, but I didn't meet many people smarter than me. He smiled benignly and said, "You'll find that will happen more and more."

That might not have been true, but it mattered less and less. As a younger man, I would see leading members of the profession talking seriously and wearing expensive suits and wonder what they were saying. I didn't aspire to that status or fashion sense. I did get to be president of the Western Literature Association more or less by accident, and at the meeting I stood talking to one of my predecessors in Norman, Oklahoma, both of us wearing jeans. I can't remember anything we talked about, but it was probably griping and gossip and who had gone mad in Wichita Falls.

More recently, another past president said over coffee that he didn't know how many more of these meetings he would attend. When he started coming to them, he said, he listened to giants in the field and went home inspired. Now they weren't around anymore.

"Gary," I said, "we're them."

I don't think that this consoled him, and I'm not sure it consoles me. But a decade after retiring I continue to go to regional conferences in places convenient for me to see friends, to give practical if cynical advice to newcomers to the profession and sometimes useful tips for their research, and to breathe the academic atmosphere once again. But I won't go back to the MLA because, judging from the names in the last program I saw years ago, I won't know anyone and won't know or care what they are talking about. Young people say about music, "If it's too loud, you're too old." The new generation's topics are too obscure for me. I am old; and though people keep going mad in Pennsylvania, it's no fun to hear about if I don't know them.

Old Sons-of-Bitches

To the surprise of his children, our father announced that he was going to his fiftieth high school reunion in Arkansas City, Kansas. We didn't know that he had kept any ties with a place or people he hadn't seen in forty years, and he didn't appear to us like someone who lived much in the past.

But he went—and came home well before he was supposed to. When my sister asked him why he hadn't stayed, he said, "Aw, there was nothing but a lot of widows and old sons-of-bitches!"

This seemed a little ungracious because he had dropped out of high school to work in the oil fields and had only returned because our mother refused to marry a man without a high school diploma, so he was at least two and possibly three years older than his classmates. But in his mind he looked younger, and he probably did, though probably not as good as he did when an attractive girl inscribed her yearbook photo to "a real hunk of man."

My yearbook from a small-town Catholic high school in mid-Missouri contained no such testimony either because I wasn't a hunk or, as I prefer to think, the girls in my class were more inhibited. And since my college was all-male, I'm just as pleased that my yearbook contained nothing of the sort—not that there's anything wrong with that. But perhaps because I didn't come out of either school with inflated views of my qualities, I've enjoyed the school reunions I've been to.

The fiftieth reunion of the Boonville Catholic High School class of 1951 was a pleasant surprise. Over the years since graduation, the high school had closed, and I had kept loosely in touch only with Jerry Lammers, who, I had forgotten, was class president. Occasionally my brother, who lives in Boonville and seems to know everyone, would give me news about a classmate. Jerry must have had better information, for he tracked down people scattered from Florida to California.

Numerically that wasn't difficult—there were only seventeen of us to start with, and one had died. Thirteen showed up for the reunion, a good turnout considering that only four lived within twenty-five miles of Boonville. Two of those were routinely spending winters in warmer climates, and they and others do a lot of traveling. Five more lived—still do unless I missed something—in Missouri, three of them in St. Louis, which, along with Kansas City, had in 1951 seemed to us the center of sophistication.

Judging from appearances and the biographical sketches that Jerry collected, we were a fortunate group who had more or less lived the life promised in 1950s sit-coms. All but two of the boys saw military service, but only Gilbert Schwartz, who enlisted in the Marines the day after graduation, had seen combat in Korea. Six (five of the eight boys) had college degrees, a much higher percentage than in previous classes; three of those went on to do graduate work, perhaps the first from our school to do so. Two women became RNs.

None of us had set the world on fire, but by our parents' standards, and even by our own, we had become successful, some in jobs we couldn't have imagined in 1951. Only two of us did anything like what our parents had done. All were retired; I was the only one to work until sixty-five. Shirley Cochran (Christus) and her husband became Visiting Conservators of Decorative Art at the Daytona Museum of Arts and Sciences, and they wrote and mounted a ballet. Isabel Lang (Stoecklein), who had been a faster softball pitcher than any of the boys, became Director of Finance in a Kansas City suburb. Bill Cleary was information technology manager at various GM plants. Pearl Haney (Thrasher) worked with computers at a large insurance company. Jerry worked on the Mercury and

Gemini projects and on the F-15 for McDonnell. Don Vollmer helped to design and test atomic weapons at Livermore Labs. Bill Stuesse became a chemist and Key Manager for Bristol Myers-Squibb.

The number of careers in science and technology is astonishing, considering the level of training we had. There was a year of algebra, which I don't think everyone took, and an Algebra II class, taught overload by the principal, Sister Lorena, a fine teacher and the only sensible nun in the school, to the two engineers and me, an overmatched future English teacher. There was one General Science class which didn't even get to the inclined plane. The only thing we could remember about it was the boys' shooting each other in the crotch (we didn't know that girls had crotches) with water pistols under the table—generic high school nonsense common before drugs and real guns.

But we must have paid more attention than anecdotal memory would indicate. In fact, we seemed to have taken in not only the information but the spiritual values taught overtly and the social values implied in our upbringing. As far as I could tell, all but one of us were practicing, indeed active Catholics, which would have pleased and perhaps surprised the nuns who taught us. All of us married (three to Boonville women, none within the class), and there were only two divorces, one in a marriage later annulled. Sixteen people reported a total of 69 children, at 4.3 each above the national average, and thirteen reported 89 grandchildren (at least four and probably more added since then) scattered from Malaysia to Bosnia. The next generation gets divorced at a much higher rate.

No one took a survey on how many medications we were taking or the total pounds we had gained, but only one seemed to have maintained his high school weight, and I had added more than a pound a year. There were various ailments—from Parkinson's and cancer down to prostate, back, and joint problems common to our age. No one seemed to be on recreational drugs, and the one admitted alcoholic had been recovering for going on a quarter-century. Everyone seemed not only mentally functional but alert. Many had been or still were active in various forms of volunteer service, religious, civic, or health-oriented. Most unusually and most pleasing to me, since he gave me one, Jerry makes finely-balanced tops from six different kinds of wood for hospitalized children.

Most of us have lived and worked far removed professionally, if not geographically, from our roots. That is supposed by some to produce a kind of cultural guilt and unease like that John Sutherland found in Alistair MacLeod's *Island: The Complete Stories*. MacLeod, several years younger than the class of 1951, had moved beyond his Cape Breton, Nova Scotia, background but, according to Sutherland, is "haunted by a sense of lost authenticity, by the life not lived. This pathos is something that afflicts transitional generations: above all, the first children in a family to benefit from higher education. The one consolation is that education—the enlargement of mind that it brings—is a tool with which to understand what has been lost."

Perhaps this reaction is peculiar to Scots or to Scots writing about Scots. The predominantly German strain in the class of 1951 was having none of this, not even enough to bring up the topic. Our parents would have thanked God that we had fulfilled their dreams that we would lead different lives, and we were taught every year in Catechism class to honor our fathers and mothers.

We didn't talk about that either but enjoyed good food and companionship—and a lot less alcohol—with people we hadn't seen in decades and probably wouldn't see again. Except for one man, whom, fifty years later, was still irritated that Bill Cleary and I had been double promoted into his class and busted the curve, I don't think that any of us are particularly nostalgic, but it was pleasant to remember where we had come from and to take note of a benchmark that indicated where, individually and collectively, we had come. Besides, like our teenage parties, the reunion was entirely free of official control—and because, having few expectations, we could all relax.

In contrast, my college reunions looked to be very official indeed. Annually the Alumni Office sends out notice of Homecoming activities that irritate more than inspire me because they have very little to do with the life I've led since graduation and almost nothing to do with the intellectual atmosphere which my best teachers and most intelligent classmates had created. Instead, there are banquets, sometimes inductions into the Rockhurst College (now University) athletics hall of fame, a special Mass, and some fundraising initiatives of varying degrees of subtlety. Occasionally a dance. Not only did these lack appeal for me, but they seemed to preclude the chance to talk with the people who interested me then about the things that interested us now. The persistent ignoring—or ignorance—of the intellectual accomplishments of alumni depressed me, since my class, for example, produced a number of full professors but, as far as I can discover, no professional athletes.

So, a couple of years before my fortieth class reunion, I wrote a modest proposal for the kind of reunion that might bring me back to campus and sent it to *America*, the national Jesuit magazine. I didn't object to a Mass, as long as it had some Gregorian chant for us to listen to, or, if we wished, to sing in voices grown increasingly tremulous. Even a cocktail hour and dinner wouldn't be too objectionable, though I certainly don't need the calories. But a dance might bring back memories of the awkwardness of late adolescence, when dancing was the only morally acceptable reason for touching a woman.

Alumni office staffers might wonder what we would do. What we—I don't mean everyone, but the people I could reunite with—did best and most interestingly when we were at Rockhurst was talk. Argue. Sit at tables in the cafeteria over bad coffee and play with ideas and language. Remember what we took with us from college and think about where had gone since and what we had brought back. Not necessarily in academic terms, though many of us had academic careers, but put in terms that a liberally educated person could not only follow but respond to. Even a case from our ethics book, if anyone still had a copy.

The article drew some response from graduates of other Jesuit institutions and a concerned letter from the alumni office at Rockhurst. But I went on to other things and soon forgot about my proposal.

One of my classmates did not. A medieval historian, he was, and is, even more emphatic than I about the primacy of the liberal arts over vocational training and especially over intercollegiate athletic, even though he was a good athlete. By mid-summer of year of our fortieth reunion, he had persuaded the alumni office to include on the schedule something like the gathering I suggested, nominated me to lead it, and wrote a letter to our classmates urging them to attend.

Our session was listed between "Las Vegas Night" (a benefit for the athletic program) and a tailgate lunch at the women's and men's soccer matches. It was titled "Rockhurst College: A Solid Foundation," a title which no professor or contemporary of mine could have believed was mine. On second thought, the alumni office arranged two other sessions: on the alumni survey and on "Current Issues in Corporate America."

I didn't go to Las Vegas Night, which featured "an all-you-can-eat buffet, casino games, silent auction, sports memorabilia, and raffle." Instead, I spent the evening with the English professor, now retired, who had steered me to graduate school and had read a draft of the book I had written about my undergraduate years. We talked, of course, about our lives and about his and my contemporaries at the college, but much of the time we talked about our profession: where it had been, where it seemed to be headed, what kind of work was being turned out. He was disconcertingly better read in current scholarship than I, and intellectually far more active in the kind of reading and thinking I had valued as a young man.

    I did attend the other events and enjoyed them far more than I expected. Seven of my classmates turned up. None of us had been close friends forty years ago, but we shared memories, and the unpleasant turned out to be as strong a bond as the ones the alumni office probably hoped for. The weather was ideal for tailgate lunch and soccer match. We had neither women nor soccer in our day, but though one contemporary growled that the two combined were a sign of decadence, the women trounced the William Jewell team. The reception and banquet were pleasant enough, but they seemed to be designed to bring us together only to interrupt our conversation, and at the banquet we were joined by the Jesuit religion professor whose classes had alternately bored and infuriated us. Among other things, I learned that a disconcerting number of our class had died or retired. One man, who in the 1950s seemed enviably happy-go-lucky and feckless, had given the college an improbable number of millions.

    The real purpose of the reunion was, for me, the seminar about what we had learned. It was held in Conway Hall, the surviving building of the two where I had attended classes. Only the composition stone steps looked familiar; the building is now occupied by the large business program and has been much remodeled and updated with the latest instructional technology.

    About a dozen people showed up at our session: five from our class, one with his wife; the Jesuit associate chancellor; two staff members; the retired English professor; a woman from the class of 1985; and a man who was one-third of the class of 1945.

    I talked about the "manly exchanges of ideas" that the 1950 recruiting brochure had promised and paid tribute to those who had really encouraged them, including Fr. Joseph A. McCallin, the Jesuit who had influenced us most strongly and, from the point of view of the orthodox Thomists, most detrimentally.

The discussion that followed was more decorous than the ones we had forty years ago in the now demolished cafeteria, but it ranged just as freely. The alumni director said that the alumni survey showed that the graduates remembered best and valued most the courses in philosophy and religion. (Two of my classmates are still angry about the intellectual impoverishment of those required courses; my response was that they made the mistake of paying attention.) When the English professor asked, wryly, if he had those figures broken down by year, the director was wise enough not to pursue the issue.

The historian wondered if, since the major goal of our education had been to produce faithful Catholics, the survey had asked how many alumni were still practicing their faith. It had not (though gossip turned up a number of divorces consistent with national statistics).

Those who had graduated when Rockhurst was aggressively all-male were curious about the effect of going co-ed. The nurse, thirty years our junior, is a woman and a non-Catholic, but, articulate and outspoken enough to have come from our group, she made us feel better about the change even if she did value her ethics class.

The most serious issue was the effect on Jesuit education of the decline in the number of Jesuits. Someone said that it was difficult to find young men who would make a life-long commitment. ("You mean celibacy," the historian interjected.) The wife of my contemporary, having lived with a Rockhurst graduate for thirty years and seen several more in action for a half hour, decided that we were the natural replacements. "Except Davis," the retired professor said. "Him more than the others," she replied. Or at least I like to think that's what she said. Of course, much the same could be said of Voltaire and James Joyce....

In any case, she and the alumni director who had titled the seminar were more right than wrong. Rockhurst had provided the foundation for our professional and intellectual lives. The historian conceived his love for the liberal arts in his freshman English class. The son of immigrants and the member of the class of 1945 would not have gone to college had it not been for the aid and encouragement of the Rockhurst administration. I would have gone to college, but I would have led a very different and probably narrower life had I not come to Rockhurst.

It's not that I remember much of what my teachers said about any particular book or idea or even of the way they said it. But it was important that they did say it, because like my first-generation peers in college, I had never heard it said before, in that way. They taught us how to pursue a line of inquiry for its own sake and to examine someone else's premises and method of reasoning. In short, they made us aware of participating in a dialogue with people oceans and centuries removed.

That dialogue, which Rockhurst introduced me to, has continued over more than fifty years, and my modest participation in it could explain why I have not been a more loyal alumnus of the kind desired by directors of the three alumni associations I perforce belong to. And since I have lived my adult life in one university after another, my sense of institutional loyalty is not strong. Instead, my private definition of "Rockhurst" has always been three or four teachers and a half-dozen friends. But on this weekend I realized that they could not have assembled had it not been for the institution.

I didn't have a chance to learn what conclusions my classmates reached. We parted somewhat raggedly at the end of a long evening with vague promises to see each other in five or ten years, God willing. Perhaps the next morning's Mass and brunch provided some kind of closure. But some of us had come from out of town and had to leave early the next morning to deal with the Monday obligations our training had prepared us for.

Ten years later, past the age of seventy, I received the invitation to meet with a lot of other old sons-of-bitches at our fiftieth reunion. Whether through weariness or the serenity of age, I had a more relaxed if not more tolerant attitude. Part of this was the result of the arrangements for the "Golden Hawks" being segregated from Homecoming events—an evening buffet ("casual dress") and class photo (of the sixteen who showed up); next day a continental breakfast and presidential briefing, a noon Mass, and a luncheon. My best friend and co-editor of the newspaper (later famous, apparently, for being counter-cultural before the term existed) and I skipped the Mass to check out the library. It was encouraging to see one sign—literally—that the Jesuit mission had not altered. On the door to the gleaming new library was taped the notice "Wipe Your Feet." So I did.

Throughout the reunion, I had an increasing sense that we were part of a past growing less and less imaginable in current conditions, so it was comforting to hang out with people who shared some memories and historical perspective. I could not have imagined Rockhurst, now called a university, as it now exists, prosperous, expensive (almost $19,000 tuition a year, with various scholarships and rebates available), thoroughly integrated. The class of 1955 had only one African-American graduate (plus two African-Africans) and no women at all. Now, as an Evelyn Waugh character said, the campus is "pullulating with women," since Rockhurst now has more women than men and even had a woman as interim president.

Other changes are equally startling. Massman Hall, far more luxurious and much larger than the World War II surplus building which served at the cafeteria in our day—although the coffee is no better—has a Pub, unthinkable in the mid-1950s. Even more unthinkable is the fact that the pub stopped serving beer because so little was bought that it spoiled in the keg. And the first thing that one sees in the bookstore is a *Sports*

Illustrated swimsuit calendar. That wouldn't have lasted twenty seconds in the prudish 1950s.

There has been all sorts of physical expansion. The campus is about two and a half times the size it was in the 1950s and will grow further, and the full-time undergraduate population has at least quadrupled. Computers are everywhere, and they cost about $2 million a year. Security, as President Edward Kinerk, S.J. (Rockhurst '64) said, was in our day managed by Fr. Cahill, the assistant dean. Now it costs a million a year in a neighborhood that is increasingly "transitional"—code for changes in racial and economic status.

Fr. Cahill, like full-time Jesuit faculty, cost only his upkeep. By 2005 there were only five Jesuits on the faculty. Two were teaching part-time, and the other three were my age. Most of the teaching and administrative work is now done by lay people whose salaries and benefits raise costs considerably. (The situation is not unique to Rockhurst. Fifteen years ago I spent several days on the Saint Louis University campus and never saw a Jesuit.)

Recognizing the necessity for change—a Jesuit university without Jesuits—Rockhurst now emphasizes a sense of mission in the motto on the new (to me) bell tower, "Learning Leadership Service in the Jesuit Tradition." As a result of campus ministry programs, ninety percent of students participate in volunteer work in Kansas City and abroad. In our day, the yearbook photographer didn't need a wide-angle lens to include the members of the two service organizations, though in our defense, some of us had jobs for as many hours a week as we could get.

The biggest difference, according to Fr. Kinerk, is a stronger religious sense. In the 1950s, our one religious obligation, as far as the college was concerned, was noon Mass on Fridays, attendance compulsory and checked. Now there are voluntary Rosary and prayer groups.

This may be connected to increased psychological uncertainty about the future. Adolescence now lasts until 26 or 27 due, Fr. Kinerk thought, to an increasingly complex society and, I would add, to changing methods of child-rearing and to changes in the economic structure, since our generation is the last, or perhaps next to last, to feel that it could rely on steady employment in the same place for our working lives. He seemed to think that we were hopeful when we graduated and knew where we were headed.

In fact, I don't remember that we were encouraged to look ahead or perhaps, as was frequently the case, I didn't pay attention. Only one of my teachers, Fr. McCallin, spoke in terms of thinking even a decade ahead. He told us to spend our lives until the age of thirty preparing for what we would do the rest of our lives. Official pronouncements from the president tended to be monitory on the one hand or lofty and vague on the other.

Everyone assumed, of course—this being a Catholic college—that ultimately we would have to confront the four last things: Death, Judgment, Heaven, and Hell. But weekly confession—more often if one had the need and a personal confessor—was assumed to take care of that.

In practice, we were being groomed to become members of the middle, even professional class. Jesuit higher education in the United States seemed designed to catch the children of Irish, Italian, and Polish immigrants and teach them how to tie their shoes and use forks, though not, remembering the cafeteria in my day, the right fork. Just any fork.

In fact, judging from the nearly twenty "Golden Hawks"—mostly silver when they had any hair at all—who came to the reunion, we could manage forks fairly well. And judging from the self-provided biographies, we had managed to infiltrate the professional classes.

My group of English majors—there were four of us, all with Bachelor of Science degrees because we didn't take four years of

Latin—has done well. One was a college president several times over; another teaches at Saint Louis University and makes documentary films for public television; one was Acquisitions Officer and Public Programs Coordinator at the Truman Library. I've written a number of books on various subjects, including *A Lower-Middle-Class Education*, about my years at Rockhurst.

I don't know whether English majors talk more than others, but the security guard had to ask us to leave the parking lot after everyone else had gone. Of course, the Rockhurst College we attended was far more present to us, in the parking lot and elsewhere, than the Rockhurst University that surrounded us.

We might have been able, dimly, to imagine the lives of the current undergraduates—many of us having been teachers. The reverse is probably unimaginable. As I was preparing to leave the reunion of Rockhurst College's class of 1955, a blond, fresh-faced young man waited for me to go through the door. I said, "Can you imagine yourself in fifty years?"

Although he didn't say anything, judging from the look on his face the answer to this old son-of-a-bitch was clearly "No." I didn't blame him, for if anyone had asked me that in the Eisenhower era, I would have been equally nonplussed.

TWENTIETH-CENTURY MAN

Although I was born about one-third of the way into the twentieth century, I didn't identify myself as a twentieth century man until I entered the doctoral program at the University of Wisconsin. In the M.A. program at the University of Kansas, I was encouraged to fill in gaps left by my undergraduate education at a Jesuit college where some of the professors were conducting passive resistance against the Renaissance. But the Wisconsin program encouraged the movement toward specialization, and it had so many students that declaring a field—in those days identified with an historical period rather than a theoretical approach—was a way to characterize oneself as a budding scholar.

Except for American literature specialists, who had a structured series of courses with a limited number of professors, period identification was a label rather than a caste mark, a focus rather than a destiny. Because the preliminary examinations for the Ph.D. required a broad knowledge of literature, everybody, even American literature specialists, mingled in a variety of courses with the cadre defined by year of entry into the program. As a result, we knew each other and something about each others' fields, and we saw the goal of the program as preparation to teach undergraduate surveys of (English) literature without doing further research. Some of my best friends were in the Nineteenth Century, and I married a Renaissance specialist.

But we went on the job market as specialists in a period. When I got my first full-time appointment, the twentieth century seemed to stretch reassuringly far ahead. Since I'm fairly adept at mathematics that doesn't involve letters or brackets, I knew that I would be 65 a few months before the last nine rolled over. But like the national debt or a light year, that number had no concrete meaning for me because the century and I had a lot of mileage left in us.

But as we both aged, I began to notice signs that the new was wearing off. I'd been trained as a scholar and hoped, through reading non-academic critics like Edmund Wilson and Dwight Macdonald, to become flexible enough to become a critic. I'd taught myself something about textual study and how to trace the genesis and growth of literary texts. Since these were the days in which authors as well as texts existed, this required me to focus not just on a period but, for much of my career, on a specific writer.

About the time I became a full professor, these skills were becoming obsolete in the profession at large—especially since my single author, Evelyn Waugh, was wildly incorrect politically even by the loosest of the new standards. That and my distaste for abstraction—partly a reaction against the Thomism-lite that pervaded my undergraduate education—made me less and less 'revelant', as my students spelled it in the late 1960s. At any rate, with two decades left in the century, I thought that I'd pretty well exhausted Waugh.

I come from a family which acts on the mostly unexpressed principle that if something isn't working, do something else. I taught a course or two in popular culture that led me into Western American literature, a book or two, and election (by default) as the oldest person ever, though as junior as they come in experience in the field, to serve as president of the Western Literature Association. That got me little respect or attention from people who dealt out salary increases and other perks. I tried administration and was almost relieved "to return to my first loves, teaching and research," the academic equivalent of the politician's desire to spend more time with his family.

When all else fails, flee the vicinity, as my parents did Dust Bowl Kansas and my son post-dot-com Wall Street. A semester in Hungary gave me the imaginative space to learn to play with language, to discover that I could be not just an academic or a critic but a writer. In that identity, I was in a century and definitely of a century, and anyone who bothered to study my work could call me a twentieth century writer, however long I might live. But I was no longer, or not just, a twentieth century man.

And a good thing, because the century and I were running out of downs, as they say in Oklahoma. Unlike my European colleagues, I couldn't be forced to retire, and for years I couldn't imagine wanting to. But what was I going to call myself in the new millennium? Professionally, my situation was unprecedented. At the end of the previous century, people had a clear sense, enthusiastic or apprehensive, of *fin de siècle*, but there were no academic specialists in nineteenth century or Victorian literature because professors of literature were by God philologists. Criticism was left to the popular press or to more or less genteel cultural gurus like Edmund Gosse and Edward Garnett and to writer-critics like Henry James and Ford Madox Ford, none of them in the academy. So while the end of the 1890s and the subsequent death of Victoria in the first real year of the twentieth century were unsettling enough, they were unsettling to everyone in pretty much the same way.

One solution had a crazy kind of attraction. We could follow the example of the editors of the British magazine *The Nineteenth Century*, which in 1901 became *The Nineteenth Century and After*. Not until 1951 did the management reluctantly accept the fact that the nineteenth century was really over and the title change to *The Twentieth Century* before deciding not to finish the century and finally going belly-up in 1972. But that would put me in the same category as makers of the hurricane lamp or the 8-track tape, hopelessly out of date, useful and really welcome only in the oddest and most extreme circumstances.

Another course of action would have been to re-label myself as a specialist in modern literature. The problem was that the publication dates of the books in my course in the modern British novel increasingly failed to keep up with the calendar, and even the course in the American novels since 1945 tended to stall out in the mid 1970s.

Partly this is a matter of age. Robert M. Sapolsky, a neurobiologist, did an informal survey and found "that if you are more than thirty-five years old when a style of popular music is introduced there's a greater than ninety-five per cent chance that you will never choose to listen to it." That and other windows—like sushi or Twittering—close at a certain age. It's only sensible to recognize and accept that limitation, as when a gas station attendant remarked that a young Black man's pounding sound system must be annoying. I said that it was doing its job, just as Stan Kenton annoyed my father.

Evelyn Waugh, who was realistic about some things, rejoiced at turning sixty because no one could expect him to carry anything. He did not regard incuriosity about new developments, even in literature, as unhealthy. "There are," he wrote to the editor of an experimental magazine who asked him to contribute, "flibbertigibbets who in middle age attend international cultural congresses and busy themselves with the latest fashions. Few of them are notable for their literary production. A writer should have found his métier before he is 50. After that he reads only for pleasure; not for curiosity about what others are doing...In middle age a writer knows his capacities & limitations and he has a general conspectus of his future work."

As a writer, I could afford to agree with Waugh, but as a professor of literature, I had to feel a little sheepish about confessing that even when I read professionally, I read what I enjoyed rather than what I used to think I was obliged to. Thinking about books I reviewed in the 1990s, I realize that several of them were written by friends of long standing, another by the son of a friend. Others were about writers I've studied for most of my professional career. The most theoretical I asked for because it dealt with a subject I was writing about.

By this time, I had begun to realize that I might not want to teach forever, and more and more consciously I set about trying to transform myself into a man of letters, a writer independent of major research libraries. I began, as my ex-wife put it, to use contacts I had made in Europe in order to wander around talking to people and coming home to write about what I'd seen and heard. In Europe, I became known as a writer and critic and kept being invited to international conferences because, as Lewis Black says of the Super Bowl halftime lineup, "Why the fuck not?"

All this time the year 2000 was approaching. Technically, as purists finally got tired of pointing out, the end of the twentieth century came not at 11:59:59 plus one second on January 31, 1999, but at the same time next year. But 2000 was firmly implanted in the popular mind because of the millennial-looking three zeroes and by the fear that the Y2K problem would fry computers and end civilization as we know it.

At the end of 1999, I was in a motel room in Farmington, New Mexico, and I didn't wait up for the New Year countdown, even one supposedly momentous as this. But next morning I went to the window to see if the world was still there. It was. Now, to quote Steven Wright, "I'm still alive. Now what am I gonna do?"

What I did was go home and prepare a report to my department's executive committee on my plans for future scholarly and creative production to justify my tenure and professorship—an innovation I'd suggested years ago that helped get me fired from the administrative post. I handed it in, but before I met with the committee I headed west to New Mexico for a popular culture conference. About the time I reached Shamrock, Texas, I thought, "Wouldn't it be nice to just keep going!" I mentioned this to a friend at the conference. He wondered why I'd want to retire, since I had all my lectures written. "Yes," I said, "but I have to listen to them."

Back home again, I met with the committee to discuss my report. They praised it as a model for others to follow. That pleased me because I prided myself on being what a very serious colleague called "a good academic"—which doesn't necessarily mean being a pleasant colleague or malleable faculty member. In discussing my analysis of my career, I noted that student evaluations of my lecture courses were low—and that the numbers were justified. In contrast, those of my creative writing workshops were near the top of the department. Therefore, I said, wouldn't it make sense to let me concentrate on teaching what I'm good at?

The chair of the department—the worst I'd had in forty-five years, clearing a very high bar—said that wouldn't be possible. "Fine," I said, "I'd like to retire." (I should have held out for some perks because she was desperate to get rid of me.)

Again, I faced the question, "Now what am I gonna do?" As with many life-changing events—birth, marriage, death—some of the emotion was diverted into dealing with details. For one thing, I had to begin the process of clearing out the large office I'd occupied for more than three decades. I had to continue making arrangements to host an international conference and arranged to teach one last creative writing course, where I got the highest evaluations of my career.

But even while dealing with these details, I felt a sense of freedom because, as a professor emeritus, I had become so irrelevant in academic terms that I was no longer tied to a period. And before long, no longer to a university. I'd seen older colleagues attempt to maintain contact with the department, gradually fading like the Cheshire Cat, though less happily, and dying a lot faster than those who had left town. So I moved a thousand miles west and so far have managed to keep going.

What am I now that I've stopped being a Twentieth Century man? My business card identifies me as "Writer, Consultant." When people ask what kind and about what, I answer, "What have you got?"

I'm now beyond the Biblical three score and ten, beyond the twentieth century, beyond the need to consider the most restrictive standards of academic writing, though I seem unable to escape the genre entirely. I'm free, then, to move and write any way I want to—or can—in but not defined by the twenty-first century.

ERASURES

When I was a teenager, my mother somehow acquired a copy of an anthology of pieces, *The Bedside Esquire*, from the heyday of the magazine, and I probably read through all of it. I remembered only one story: about a man, the evidence of whose presence in the world was eroded as various people and documents vanish. Finally, rain washes away the ink of his signature until "Kovacs John," the last sign of his existence, disappears.

The notion that someone's existence could be totally negated struck me then and stayed with me over the years because the concept was unfamiliar and startling, though at the time, of course, I wasn't conscious of the implications. For one thing, I'd been thoroughly indoctrinated in church and parochial school with the concepts of the four last things: death, judgment, heaven, and hell. Those might not always have been consoling, but they did assign a dramatic destiny to human life and promised continuity of the self through all eternity. ("All" is redundant, but that's the language used in my catechism classes.)

More immediate and taken far more for granted was the web of my family connections. These extended, of course, among living relatives, some of whom we rarely or never saw and perhaps couldn't stand to be around because of feuds that the rest of us didn't know much about. But thanks to the family habit of storytelling, the web also reached into the past, in a few cases beyond the Civil War as far back as the English Renaissance to a Cambridge theologian and his offspring and even, though perhaps mythically, to an illegitimate offspring of John of Gaunt, Shakespeare's "time-honoured Lancaster." If you could have stories told about you, you would live on in the collective memory of the family.

Even more immediate was the cemetery across the road from our house, where, if nothing else, names and dates were carved in stone. That was about as permanent as my mind could encompass on a daily basis.

Perhaps I remembered Kovacs John because of the unusual name and order. I didn't realize for thirty years that, translated from Hungarian (with John as Janos) into English, the name would be John Smith, but in both languages the name is thoroughly generic. Nor did I realize how far down the social ladder he was, though I didn't imagine at the time that I had any status at all.

My name is a little less generic, but not by much—that's the reason I use the middle name in by-lines—and the older I get, the more poignant Kovacs John's story and fate seem to me. I don't think much about immortality—perhaps, like Count Greffi in *A Farewell to Arms*, I have outlived the possibility of becoming devout again—but occasionally I wonder if, more than how, I will be remembered.

Fortunately, I have a large and widespread family, so I can probably count on being remembered in oral tradition at least two generations down. And I have created a much wider graphic record than the unfortunate Mr. Kovacs in more than four decades as a scholar, poet, and essayist both in print and in electronic media. My work has appeared in a dozen countries besides the U.S., sometimes in alphabets I can't read. Ego surfing my full name on Google turns up between 9800 and 10,000 hits within the space of ten minutes (fluctuating like the Dow), many of them no doubt duplications, though even I don't have the patience to get to the end of the list.

Those entries could tell people that I existed and even, to an extent, something of what I had done. But it wouldn't say anything about who I was. And would any of it really keep my name in historical memory? Many of my publications, and arguably the most significant from a scholarly and therefore relatively impersonal perspective, deal with with the work of Evelyn Waugh, so the survival of those books and articles depends almost entirely on his place in the literary canon. That's if it endures at all. Most of my books and compilations about him are out of print—except for those from a small publisher who doesn't sell outside the U.S. and seems reluctant to fulfill any orders in the country. Even people whom one would think are professionally obligated to know some of the work aren't aware of it at best or refuse to acknowledge it at worst. The Brits lead in these categories, although they aren't the only contenders. But even scholars who admit to consulting my books relegate me to footnotes or lists of works consulted.

Publishers who haven't gone belly-up have remaindered or pulped books. A director of a university press which issued two of my books said, at our first meeting, "We couldn't do this without you." "Well," I said, "you seem to be doing fine after letting two of my books go out of print." Oh. Other presses are small, indeed miniscule.

The only books that seem to draw even occasional interest are *Mid-Lands*, my memoir-social history about my home town, Boonville, Missouri, and *Mid-Life Mojo: A Guide for the Newly Single Male*. On my rare visits home, people ask, "Are you the writer?" I try to answer with appropriate modesty. On the other hand, my son said to his mother that I should write something about the family. "Your father did," she said. "You have a copy." As for *Mojo*, I get perhaps one request a year for an on-line or radio interview. The most recent was for an interview on Sirius Satellite Radio's Catholic Channel—before they had seen the book. I didn't expect to hear from them again, and haven't. My most recent book, about Central European writing after Communism, may get a few reviews, but as cultural journalism it will have a short shelf-life.

Europeans seem more interested in my poetry than in my work in other genres. In Slovakia, I was asked about my position as a poet in the U.S. "Under the radar," I said truthfully. In Croatia, I was asked why I didn't write more poetry. "Because," I said, "I regard myself as primarily a writer of prose, and I don't think that something should be written as poetry if it can be said any other way." Both clauses of the response drew an uncomfortable silence and the second some foot-shuffling from the audience of poets.

While I was doing this work, I was not thinking of leaving a record of my existence. Granted, the scholarly work was designed to acquire status to help in getting an academic job and then tenure and promotion, but mostly I did it because my doctoral program had acculturated me to the belief that it was expected of what one of my contemporaries called "a good academic." Also, I discovered not only that I could do it without undue pain but that I enjoyed the process as much as the result. Over the years, the motives came to have decreasing importance as opportunities for other jobs narrowed and salary compression saw my stipend lag behind that of younger and less productive colleagues.

That realization gave me a new freedom to write stuff for the hell of it, like *Playing Cowboys*, in which I thanked university funding sources for rejecting my applications so that I could write the way I wanted to, less formal in style and less tied to the opinions of others. *Mid-Lands*, published the following month, was *Cowboys*' evil twin, completing a shift from a centrifugal to a centripetal process. *Mid-Lands* was not exactly introspective, but it began a process in which I tried to understand, if not myself, the contexts in which I have lived and developed.

Now, more than eight years into retirement, freed from the annual report of my activities to the department chair and dean, who seemed spectacularly uninterested, I enjoy the process of writing more than the result. Evelyn Waugh said somewhere that the trouble with amateur pornographers was that they were so eager to see the result that they ignored necessary craftsmanship. I don't seem in a hurry to see the result, since I submit for publication far less material than I write. However, since I doubt that I have the time to follow Horace's advice, filtered through Alexander Pope, to sit on my piece nine years, I'll have to turn loose of something soon, if I'm ever going to.

As for work already published, I should start giving away extra copies of books partly to spread my name in space if not necessarily in time and, more practically, to clear some space in bookshelves and in my garage. Of course, I'm not sure that every book would find a welcoming home. Even my children don't have room for or interest in the bibliographical work I've done. Some pious friends, if I have any left, might be shocked at my book of advice for middle-aged divorced men. But the books have to go, and it's better for me to distribute them than to burden my children.

Perhaps, as one referee said in rejecting the manuscript of a memoir about academic life in the second half of the twentieth century, I should keep it around for my children, though I can't be sure that any of them will read it. As I said, my son hasn't read the book about the family, and my daughter, told by colleagues that it was a big deal having a father who writes books, said, "Some fathers lay bricks. Some fathers write books." Fortunately, she married a man who values my work enough to collect even unpublished material so that he can pass it on to my grandchildren. That, along with family stories, may keep me, at least for a while, from being obliterated like Kovacs John.

But even if every copy of the my books and articles is burned or pulped or washed clean by the rain and if the electrons wink out into graphic black holes, I've realized that it won't matter to me. In the same vein, Evelyn Waugh replied to his brother Alec's suggestion about re-issuing their father Arthur's autobiography that either Alec was right and Arthur has ceased to exist or Evelyn was right and that, in the process of attaining eternal bliss, Arthur is indifferent to worldly things. In either case, I can assume a similar philosophical indifference.

In the meantime, there is the work itself. I've come to see that any effect it might have is far less important than the fact that I was able to do it and to keep doing it. To quote, a little pretentiously but not quite irrelevantly, Henry James's dying novelist in "The Middle Years": "We work in the dark. We do what we can. We give what we have. Our doubt is our passion. Our passion is our task. The rest is the madness of art." Perhaps my work has been all too sane, and in whatever time is left, it probably won't get any wilder, just franker and grumpier. Meanwhile, I have come to agree with W. H. Auden's view that "the underlying reason for writing is to bridge the gulf between one person and another." That isn't always accomplished, but as I grow older and drift away from scholarship and footnotes, it becomes a more and more important motive.

A Sequel or Epilogue

Until I googled the *Esquire* anthology and saw some familiar names and titles, "some I've reread in other venues and one I'd even taught"—these words were part of the first paragraph of the draft I sent to my son-in-law, who seems to be more receptive to my writing than the rest of my family put together, and in one of several annotations, he wrote "I'm very interested in this. I'm not as interested in where you found it (previous two sentences)."

No doubt he was right from an intelligent reader's standpoint, but he apparently doesn't know how a scholar's mind works in the process of verifying references. Anyway, even before I saw his comment I emailed my sister, who maintains the family home and some of its contents, to see if she could find *The Bedside Esquire*, which, in my pretty good visual memory, had a spine in silver with blue lettering. Meanwhile, I googled the title and found a table of contents. I had deduced from the name Kovacs that the author was Hungarian, and I've spent enough time in Hungary to locate three possibilities, Andreas Latzko, Lajos Zilahy, Sandor Hunyady, plus, I discovered, Felix Salten, author of *Bambi*, who was born in Budapest but grew up in Vienna. (I haven't the time or resources to try to discover how and why the editors of *Esquire* established the Hungarian connection, but it's an interesting question.) Two of the titles, "A Duel by Candlelight" and "The Five-Pengo Girl" didn't sound like anything that might be about a man erased from human history, but Zilahy's "But for This" looked promising.

My sister reported that she couldn't find the book and had no memory of it. Probably it got sold in a garage sale or donated somewhere. My first Google search indicated that Arizona State University had a copy, and that's only about twenty miles and a half hour each way from my house. Figure $12 in mileage costs, at least $5 in parking, and two or three dollars in photocopying. So I looked at amazon.com and found a copy for one cent, $3.99 postage and handling.

The copy that arrived within a week was an earlier edition with gold on the spine almost as faded as Kovacs' signature, but it had Zilahy's story, covering less than four pages. As I might have expected, the story was far more artful than I could have understood at the time. Stage by stage—the last time his name is spoken, the last time he was thought of, the burning of his birth records, the grave marker stolen by a ragged man to build a fire, the signature erased, letter by letter until even the curved strokes of the "v" are washed away—the omniscient author traces the inexorable but casual process by which "the life of the journeyman carpenter ceased and forever disappeared from this earth...But for this..."

I've always been a sucker for descriptions of a process—that's what saves for me much of John Steinbeck (who has three stories in the anthology)—which may be why I'm writing about the process of rediscovery and about the irony of the imaginary

Kovacs being preserved in art and standing for everyone whose recorded existence is threatened by time and natural decay.

My essay is an attempt to thwart or at least restrain that process, just as the physical book and all the rest of that printing and successive editions is a way of keeping the names of authors and editors on record. And this copy preserves the signature on the flyleaf—R. J. Lusk Jr., Milwaukee, Wisconsin November 24, 1943. At least I think it's Lusk—the signature is so fancy that I'm not sure about the capital L.

I googled the name and found a R. J. Lusk on FaceBook. There's a photo of a man, younger than any of my children, at the helm of what seems to be a large power-boat or small yacht. To find out more about him, however, I'd have to join FaceBook, and even my curiosity isn't sufficient to extend the process further or to further ensure the survival of my name in a place that public. So the Lusk who signed the book, Zilahy and the other contributors, and I will have to be content to rely on what records exist.

WHAT THE DISTANT SAY

People in the nineteenth century seemed fascinated by deathbeds, serving as spectators and critics of what might in postmodern terms be called the dying person's farewell performance. In Emily Dickinson's poem beginning "To know just how He suffered — would be dear—" the absent speaker practically lusts after details of the last moments, as in

> What was His furthest mind — Of Home — or God —
> Or what the Distant say —
> At news that He ceased Human Nature
> Such a Day —

The poem ends with the possibility of a heavenly union with God, and the possibility of heaven explains much of the spectator's fascination with dying moments.

But I've never even seen a discussion one way or the other about Gustav Flaubert's belief in the afterlife, and even in the supposedly scandalous *Madame Bovary* he merely suggests Emma's sexual writhings with a rocking carriage while presenting her death throes in great, and to modern audiences excruciating, detail.

Apparently we are as squeamish about death as the Victorians were about sex, preferring to concentrate on options rather than inevitabilities. But in both cases, the aversion may be due to a lack of opportunity to observe. For example, not many clips of death-beds make it onto YouTube, and the various CSI avatars deal quite clinically, if gruesomely, with the aftermath of death rather than the process of dying.

Direct observation is difficult for obvious reasons. In industrialized countries, most people on the point of dying are institutionalized in hospitals or nursing homes, and family members don't always have easy access to them. Furthermore, relatives and friends are increasingly scattered, often across great distances.

My experience may not be atypical. When my mother was dying of cancer, I drove some 1,800 miles to take my turn in the family relay vigil beside her hospital bed—and we could ignore visiting hours only because it was a small town and because my father and sister were very stubborn in very different ways. But only my father was with her when she died; my brother and sister and I were resting until each of us could take the assigned place on schedule.

One of the immediate tasks after Mom died was to notify relatives and friends, at least one of whom my parents had not seen for many years. My dad's sister flew in from Albuquerque, but she was the only member of the extended family to do so. Others might have been grateful for the sad news, but there was no way of contacting them, so the distant had no chance to say anything.

When my father died, I was just under 500 miles away at the other end of a phone call from my sister, and she, my brother, and I called our children in several states to assemble the immediate family for a funeral. The head of the Wichita branch of Dad's family was easy to locate, and he came to the funeral with at least one of his sons. So did Dad's surviving local friends, not many at his age. We didn't have to try to send the news to people from his past life because, if there were any, he never told us about them.

Dad probably didn't have anyone he wanted told, and I suspect that even people who want distant friends informed don't often tell anyone from their immediate circle who needs to be informed. One friend did tell his wife to let me know when he died, and she had seen me often enough over the years to know that there was a real bond. The widow of a friend who committed suicide called to ask me to inform other friends from that stage of our lives. Another replied to my email to her husband with information about her husband's death and some of the circumstances. I called a mutual friend to let him know, but he'd already seen the notice in the specialized journal devoted to their field.

Sometimes you know that a friend is terminally ill, but you know nothing about the people in his current life. It's less difficult to be supportive when the friend is physically close, for one can do practical things to make the process easier for both patient and visitor. But at a distance, support is harder to give. In two cases, my father's and a friend halfway across the country with whom I had kept in fairly close touch, I stopped telephoning because my calls seemed to depress them. I continued to write letters, which these days don't seem to require answers even from healthy people, and my siblings gave me bulletins about Dad's health.

But in the case of my friend, who was my only remaining contact in New York City, I had no way knowing if or when he had died until another friend from our days in graduate school saw the notice of the death in his undergraduate alumni magazine where our friend had taught. (Later, Google turned up the date of his death attached to a collection of his papers in a university archive.) By this time, the only person to whom I could pass on the news was my ex-wife.

But if that thus far surviving friend predeceases me, who is going to tell me about him? We don't have any remaining mutual contacts; we don't belong to the same professional associations; and I'm not sure that in his new residence he would be regarded as significant enough to merit an obituary in the local newspaper—which, though it has an on-line version, probably doesn't index its archives that fully.

Internet data bases are an uncertain source. The deaths of two other friends from graduate school show up in two items each on Google, but the entries refer to obituaries in campus newsletters. There are many other hits, but all deal with books and articles they published while living. Obviously I won't know if Google will list my death along with thousands of mentions of my books, but I don't expect my former colleagues to hear about my death except through the local newspaper, and I'd be astonished if they took much notice of my death.

But what about people I've maintained contacts with in a dozen or so countries over four continents? Will I hear about their deaths? Will they hear about mine? I've given my children the password to my email account, so if they don't lose it and if they can figure out how to send a message to "all," they won't have to sort through the 275 addresses currently in my contacts list to decide who might really want to know.

That assumes, of course, that people will want to know, as I do, about the death of a friend. The broader and more interesting issue is why I think it's important to know. It's not just a modern concern, as in Arthur Miller's line, "Attention must be paid." The same impulse runs through the tradition of pastoral elegy, in which the dead shepherd's/poet's sheep/poems or the keeper's bees must be informed as part of the ritual mourning, a way of coming to terms with the death of a master and the release to immortality of his works. This tradition runs from Ancient Greece, and probably well before, at least to W. H. Auden's "In Memory of William Butler Yeats," an ironic twist on the genre that overtly allows the poet's death to be kept from his poems.

I think that the survivors need to know because, like more formal elegists, we need to evaluate the ways in which that person helped to shape our lives, to readjust the pieces that make up our world, and to begin what Dickinson calls, in one of her most chilling lines, "Our faith to regulate." And, as the elegists insist, take heart from what that person has been and to go forward with, and as a result of, that knowledge with something that is anything but closure.

Robert Murray Davis wanted (as a teenager called Bob Davis before he realized how many Bob Davises there were) to be a newspaperman because he thought that was the way to become a writer. After a brief stint at a daily newspaper, he got sidetracked into graduate school and spent the next forty-five years teaching English at nine different universities in three countries until retirement from teaching, though not from writing and traveling. After he published a number of books on the English novelist Evelyn Waugh, visits to Europe turned his attention to writing about the American West and then, as he became aware that he could speak about his experience as well as about the work of other writers, to what is now called creative nonfiction. *Playing Cowboys: Low Culture and High Art in the Western* led to his presidency of the Western Literature Association. *Mid-Lands: A Family Album* explored life in post-war small-town mid-America and was followed other books combining autobiography and social history, most recently *The Ornamental Hermit: People and Places of the New West*.

In the 1980s he began to publish poetry both in the US and abroad, including the volumes *Outside the Lines* and *Live White Male*. He has been invited to read and lecture in a number of Central and Eastern European countries. These experiences, which someone described as wandering around and talking to people and coming home to write about it, led him into the field of cultural journalism, including writing about the literature of Post-Communist Slovenia, Slovakia, Hungary and Romania.

He now lives in the Phoenix area of the rogue state of Arizona and continues to review books on a variety of subjects, most often for *Southwestern American Literature*, *World Literature Today*, and *Evelyn Waugh Newsletter and Studies*. Currently he is editing Waugh's *Brideshead Revisited* for the Oxford University Press *Complete Works of Evelyn Waugh*. He hopes finally to sort out mounds of material for a book with the working title of "Unconforming Layers" about the Jemez Valley in New Mexico and its diverse inhabitants, and to go on wandering around and talking to people as long as he can.

www.ingramcontent.com/pod-product-compliance
Lightning Source LLC
Chambersburg PA
CBHW050857160426
43194CB00011B/2187